T0360579

Capital Shortage

The great majority of the population in colonial and postcolonial India lived in the countryside and were poor. Many were unable to find gainful work outside agriculture and remained dependent on a livelihood that provided only subsistence, and a precarious one. Seeking the roots of persistent poverty, Maanik Nath finds that the pervasive high cost and shortage of capital affected the peasant's ability to invest in land. The productivity of land, as a result, remained low and changed little. Bridging economic theory and historical evidence, *Capital Shortage* shows that climate, law, policy design, and interactions between these factors perpetuated a stubborn cycle of credit scarcity, low investment, and widespread deprivation over several decades. These findings can be tested against credit and development in preceding and succeeding periods as well as positioned in comparative global context.

Maanik Nath is Assistant Professor in Economic and Social History at Utrecht University.

Cambridge Studies in Economic History

Editorial Board

Cambridge Studies in Economic History comprises stimulating and accessible economic history which actively builds bridges to other disciplines. Books in the series will illuminate why the issues they address are important and interesting, place their findings in a comparative context, and relate their research to wider debates and controversies. The series will combine innovative and exciting new research by younger researchers with new approaches to major issues by senior scholars. It will publish distinguished work regardless of chronological period or geographical location

A complete list of titles in the series can be found at:
www.cambridge.org/economichistory

Capital Shortage

Credit and Indian Economic Development,
1920–1960

Maanik Nath

Utrecht University

Shaftesbury Road, Cambridge CB2 8EA, United Kingdom

One Liberty Plaza, 20th Floor, New York, NY 10006, USA

477 Williamstown Road, Port Melbourne, VIC 3207, Australia

314–321, 3rd Floor, Plot 3, Splendor Forum, Jasola District Centre, New Delhi – 110025, India

103 Penang Road, #05-06/07, Visioncrest Commercial, Singapore 238467

Cambridge University Press is part of Cambridge University Press & Assessment, a department of the University of Cambridge.

We share the University's mission to contribute to society through the pursuit of education, learning and research at the highest international levels of excellence.

www.cambridge.org
Information on this title: www.cambridge.org/9781009359078

DOI: 10.1017/9781009359023

First published 2023

A catalogue record for this publication is available from the British Library.

Library of Congress Cataloging-in-Publication Data
Names: Nath, Maanik, 1991- author.
Title: Capital shortage : credit and Indian economic development, 1920-1960 / Maanik Nath, Universiteit Utrecht, The Netherlands.
Description: Cambridge, United Kingdom ; New York, NY : Cambridge University Press, 2023. | Series: Cambridge studies in economic history | Includes bibliographical references and index.
Identifiers: LCCN 2022056425 (print) | LCCN 2022056426 (ebook) | ISBN 9781009359078 (hardback) | ISBN 9781009359047 (paperback) | ISBN 9781009359023 (epub)
Subjects: LCSH: Rural credit–India–History–20th century. | Credit–India–History–20th century. | Economic development–India–History–20th century. | India–Economic conditions–20th century.
Classification: LCC HG2051.I4 N358 2023 (print) | LCC HG2051.I4 (ebook) | DDC 332.70954–dc23/eng/20221201
LC record available at https://lccn.loc.gov/2022056425
LC ebook record available at https://lccn.loc.gov/2022056426

ISBN 978-1-009-35907-8 Hardback

Contents

Figures

Tables

Acknowledgments

The idea for this book originated while I was a doctoral student at the London School of Economics. I am grateful to my mentors during this time. I extend a special thank you to Tirthankar Roy. His guidance and patience as a supervisor helped me develop substantive parts of the book. Gerben Bakker's input greatly improved the quality of my work. I thank my doctoral examiners, Gareth Austin and David Washbrook, for illuminating discussions and extensive feedback on how to expand a preliminary version of the monograph.

Contributions from numerous scholars have helped refine the book. I am indebted to Anand Swamy and Bishnupriya Gupta for useful discussions over several years. I am grateful to Mukulika Banerjee, Howard Jones, Barbara Harriss-White, Taylor Sherman, Bas van Bavel, Jordan Claridge, Chris Colvin, and Karolina Hutkova for helpful conversations; to Vigyan Ratnoo, Jan Luiten van Zanden, Christiaan van Bochove, Kate Frederick, and Alka Raman for feedback on specific chapters; and to Maarten Prak for generous help with the final stages. Mauricio Canals-Cifuentes's help with designing maps greatly improved the quality of the book. I thank Michael Watson, the series editors, two expert readers, the team at Cambridge University Press, and copyeditors for help with refining major components of the book.

Finally, this book would not have been possible without Meher's counsel, my eternal source of encouragement.

1 Introduction

The 1957 motion picture *Mother India*, set in a rural village within newly independent India, follows the struggles of a poverty-stricken protagonist who had borrowed a loan of 500 rupees (about £40 then) from a local village moneylender. The moneylender, with the help of village elites, recovered the loan and additional interest by coercing the borrower to part with three-quarters of her harvested crop, leaving the protagonist in an unbreakable cycle of debt and poverty for the rest of the story.

Stories like these are common in popular depictions of the past. Credit exchange appears as an unequal struggle between the vulnerable borrower and the powerful lender. Money is essential to survival, and so are markets for credit. And yet, the credit market, perhaps more than any other, tends to be seen as a power game and a field of brutal exploitation.

Economic history and development economics attach a different meaning to credit. Credit was not just a source for survival but also a source for modernisation. Unfettered access to credit allowed people to tide over difficult times, consume enough when income dropped, and pay for this service when income returned to normal. Access also enabled individuals to start a business and existing business owners to grow and innovate. How do we reconcile both visions of credit – as an instrument of exploitation and as a symbol of distress against the view of credit as an instrument of economic development?

The book finds reconciliation between both visions through an analysis of rural credit markets in the Madras Presidency, a major province in colonial and early post-colonial India. It analyses historical sources documenting credit markets in the villages and districts of Madras over a period of four decades, investigating variations in the terms attached to credit, and the logic behind the application of these terms. This work tells us that lenders did lend but adjusted the terms to risks and the situation of the borrower. And that geography and enforcement problems shaped these risks and the economic situation of borrowers. In the end, these adjustments created many local variations in types of credit arrangements. Both harsh and lenient arrangements seem to co-exist.

Studying the logic behind lending arrangements explains why harsh terms exist and why lenient terms are not more pervasive. More specifically, the book asks: under what conditions do lenders give borrowers easy access to affordable loans? The history of credit markets in emerging market economies substantiates the importance of this question though is yet to provide a conclusive answer. Problems of selective access and high prices were common in credit markets across the Global South. Moneylenders, notaries and networks of family-run credit businesses commercialised capital markets and increased credit supply in Southeast Asia, Latin America and West Africa at different times in the nineteenth and early twentieth centuries. Loans were often expensive and easier to access for merchants and traders than they were for peasants.[1] The rationale behind lending arrangements in historical settings – or explaining *why* loans were supplied in the way they were – remains an underdeveloped field in the comparative history of emerging markets. A similar gap exists in the history of credit markets in South Asia.

Explaining the prices attached to credit in India has fostered an ongoing dual debate, separately among groups of economists and groups of historians. One side of the debate focuses on power imbalance and inequity, indicating that prices were high because poor borrowers did not have enough power to bargain for lower prices and better conditions from the richer moneylenders.[2] Often ignored in this approach is that

---

[1] The edited volume by Austin and Sugihara provides a series of cases studies documenting indigenous microcredit systems between the eighteenth century and early twentieth century. See Gareth Austin and Kaoru Sugihara, *Local Suppliers of Credit in the Third World, 1750–1960* (London: Macmillan, 1993). For regional studies of credit in Indonesia, Peru and West Africa, see Gareth Austin, "Factor Markets in Nieboer Conditions: Pre-colonial West Africa, c.1500–c.1900." *Continuity and Change* 24, no. 1 (2009): 23–53; David Henley and P. Boomgaard, *Credit and Debt in Indonesia, 860–1930: From Peonage to Pawnshop, from Kongsi to Cooperative*. A Modern Economic History of Southeast Asia (Leiden: KITLV Press, 2009); Juliette Levy, *The Making of a Market: Credit, Henequen, and Notaries in Yucatán, 1850–1900* (University Park: Pennsylvania State University Press, 2012); Luis Felipe Zegarra, "Information Asymmetries and Agricultural Credit: Evidence from the Pre-banking Era in Lima, 1825–1865." *Agricultural Finance Review* 79, no. 2 (2019): 217–33.

[2] For the economics of debt exploitation, see Amit Bhaduri, "A Study in Agricultural Backwardness under Semi-Feudalism." *The Economic Journal* 83, no. 329 (1973): 120–37; Amit Bhaduri, "On the Formation of Usurious Interest Rates in Backward Agriculture." *Cambridge Journal of Economics* 1, no. 4 (1977): 341–52. On the history of borrower exploitation in the provinces of colonial India, see Neeladri Bhattacharya, "Lenders and Debtors: Punjab Countryside, 1880–1940." *Studies in History* 1, no. 2 (August 1985): 305–42; Sugata Bose, *Credit, Markets, and the Agrarian Economy of Colonial India* (New York: Oxford University Press, 1994); David A. Washbrook, "The Commercialization of Agriculture in Colonial India: Production, Subsistence and Reproduction in the 'Dry South', c. 1870–1930." *Modern Asian Studies* 28, no. 1 (1994): 129–64; Neil Charlesworth, *Peasants and Imperial Rule: Agriculture and Agrarian*

policymakers tried addressing power imbalance. Successive regulatory attempts, in the colonial and post-colonial periods, to diminish the market power of moneylenders did not improve the borrower's position, suggesting that the underlying issue must lie outside of just power. Investigating the rationale behind the actions of lenders, the other side of the debate, the side that is currently filled with scholarship from economists, lays stress on risks and costs incurred by lenders to recover unpaid loans.[3] Since the 1970s, development economists have tested this approach in field experiments.[4] History of the lender's account is overlooked, an omission relevant to readers interested in both Indian history and modern-day development in rural India as types of lending arrangements in colonial times seem to have persisted to the present. Scholars and policymakers have recently cast a spotlight on the harsh lending terms imposed by microfinance institutions, showing that credit still poses the same kind of anxieties as it did a hundred years ago.

The book contributes to a broader discussion on financial inclusion and, thus, speaks to a connected global audience. Providing sufficient credit to poor borrowers is not necessarily an emerging market problem but a central concern in development economics and economic history of the world. Indeed, it is one of those topics in which the two disciplines

Society in the Bombay Presidency, 1850–1935 (Cambridge: Cambridge University Press, 1985); David Hardiman, *Feeding the Baniya: Peasants and Usurers in Western India* (Delhi: Oxford University Press, 1996).

[3] Anthony Bottomley, "Interest Rate Determination in Underdeveloped Rural Areas." *American Journal of Agricultural Economics* 57, no. 2 (1975): 279–91; Pranab K. Bardhan, "Interlocking Factor Markets and Agrarian Development: A Review of Issues." *Oxford Economic Papers* 32, no. 1 (1980): 82–98; Clive Bell, "Chapter 16: Credit Markets and Interlinked Transactions." In *Handbook of Development Economics*, edited by T. Paul Schultz and John Strauss, 763–830. Vol. 1 (Amsterdam: Elsevier B.V., 1988); Joseph E. Stiglitz, "Chapter 5: Economic Organization, Information, and Development." In *Handbook of Development Economics*, edited by T. Paul Schultz and John Strauss, 93–160. Vol. 1 (Amsterdam: Elsevier B.V., 1988); Timothy Besley, "How Do Market Failures Justify Interventions in Rural Credit Markets?" *The World Bank Research Observer* 9, no. 1 (1994): 27–47; Parikshit Ghosh and Debraj Ray, "Information and Enforcement in Informal Credit Markets." *Economica* 83, no. 329 (2016): 59–90.

[4] Subrata Ghatak, "Rural Interest Rates in the Indian Economy." *The Journal of Development Studies* 11, no. 3 (1975): 190–201; Pranab K. Bardhan and Ashok Rudra, "Terms and Conditions of Sharecropping Contracts: An Analysis of Village Survey Data in India." *The Journal of Development Studies* 16, no. 3 (1980): 287–302; Avishay Braverman and Joseph E. Stiglitz, "Sharecropping and the Interlinking of Agrarian Markets." *The American Economic Review* 72, no. 4 (1982): 695–715; Irfan Aleem, "Imperfect Information, Screening, and the Costs of Informal Lending: A Study of a Rural Credit Market in Pakistan." *The World Bank Economic Review* 4, no. 3 (1990): 329–49; Timothée Demont, "Microfinance Spillovers: A Model of Competition in Informal Credit Markets with an Application to Indian Villages." *European Economic Review* 89 (2016): 21–41.

interact most closely. A reading of both disciplines tells us that the poor had easier access to credit in some regions than others, even though the types of lenders were similar across regions. Banks were not always the major suppliers of credit and even when they were, they seldom catered to borrowers from all income groups and economic sectors. Notaries, intermediaries and cooperatives provided reasonably priced loans to large segments of the market before and alongside the spread of banks in Western Europe.[5] Indeed, credit from cooperatives facilitated transformative growth processes in parts of Europe as recently as the early twentieth century.[6] The book visits a part of the world where moneylenders and cooperatives did not supply enough affordable credit to stimulate growth. It finds that a tripartite set of risks, a set that includes region-specific ecology, the design and persistence of colonial institutions, and ineffectual market regulation, stifled lending, especially lending to the poor.

The book, in other words, designs a blueprint to investigate the (under) development of financial markets. In doing so, it contributes to institutional economic history, which foregrounds institutions like law, but has not paid sufficient attention to interactions between credit, debt law and informal arrangements. Familiar institutional typologies divides systems into 'formal' and 'informal'.[7] Typically, the distinction lies in

---

[5] For an overview of non-banking credit systems in pre-industrial France and Netherlands, see Larry Neal and Jeremy Atack, *The Origins and Development of Financial Markets and Institutions: From the Seventeenth Century to the Present* (Cambridge and New York: Cambridge University Press, 2009); Christiaan Van Bochove, Heidi Deneweth, and Jaco Zuijderduijn, "Real Estate and Mortgage Finance in England and the Low Countries, 1300–1800." *Continuity and Change* 30, no. 1 (2015): 9–38; Oscar Gelderblom, Joost Jonker, and Clemens Kool, "Direct Finance in the Dutch Golden Age." *The Economic History Review* 69, no. 4 (2016): 1178–98; Philip T. Hoffman, Gilles Postel-Vinay, and Jean-Laurent Rosenthal, *Dark Matter Credit: The Development of Peer-to-Peer Lending and Banking in France* (Princeton, NJ: Princeton Economic History of the Western World, 2019).

[6] Timothy W. Guinnane, "Cooperatives as Information Machines: German Rural Credit Cooperatives, 1883–1914." *The Journal of Economic History* 61, no. 2 (2001): 366–89; Timothy W. Guinnane, "A 'Friend and Advisor': External Auditing and Confidence in Germany's Credit Cooperatives, 1889–1914." *Business History Review* 77, no. 2 (2003): 235–64; Christopher L. Colvin, "Banking on a Religious Divide: Accounting for the Success of the Netherlands' Raiffeisen Cooperatives in the Crisis of the 1920s." *The Journal of Economic History* 77, no. 3 (2017): 866–919; Marvin Suesse and Nikolaus Wolf, "Rural Transformation, Inequality, and the Origins of Microfinance." *Journal of Development Economics* 143 (2020): 102429.

[7] For works on the rule of law and development, see Douglass C. North, *Institutions, Institutional Change, and Economic Performance* (Cambridge: Cambridge University Press, 1990); Daron Acemoglu and James A. Robinson, *Why Nations Fail: The Origins of Power, Prosperity, and Poverty* (London: Profile, 2012). For works on informal norms and trade, see Avner Greif, "Contract Enforceability and Economic Institutions in Early

regulation and scope of the rule of law. Economists and economic historians see independent courts and contract laws (the formal rules) as regulators of banks (the formal players).[8] Moneylenders are seen in a separate sphere as informal players in markets regulated by social norms.[9] Recent works on credit in colonial India have started to challenge these typologies, showing that moneylenders used mortgage contracts, and debt laws affected the supply of these mortgage loans in the nineteenth century.[10] The book shows greater dynamism in the coexistence and flexibility of institutional forms. Moneylenders were indeed affected by laws. They also vacillated between court-enforced and socially enforced contract types, blurring the boundaries between 'formal' and 'informal' systems. Lessons from this work, therefore, intersect institutional change and policy, showing how the design of laws and types of contract enforcement affected the affordability and inclusivity of non-banking credit.

Trade: The Maghribi Traders' Coalition." *The American Economic Review* 83, no. 3 (1993): 525–48; Robert H. Bates, "Social Dilemmas and Rational Individuals: An Assessment of the New Institutionalism." In *The New Institutional Economics and Third World Development*, edited by John Harriss, Janet Hunter, and Colin M. Lewis, 27–49 (London: Routledge, 1997).

[8] The relationship between courts and banking has a large scholarship. On the design of contract enforcement and its impact on banking operations, see Simeon Djankov, Rafael La Porta, Florencio Lopez-De-Silanes, and Andrei Shleifer, "Courts." *The Quarterly Journal of Economics* 118, no. 2 (2003): 453–517; Rafael La Porta, Florencio Lopez-de-Silanes, and Andrei Shleifer, "The Economic Consequences of Legal Origins." *Journal of Economic Literature* 46, no. 2 (2008): 285–332; Andrea Moro, Daniela Maresch, and Annalisa Ferrando, "Creditor Protection, Judicial Enforcement and Credit Access." *The European Journal of Finance* 24, no. 3 (2018): 250–81.

[9] Sagrario L. Floro and Pan A. Yotopoulos, *Informal Credit Markets and the New Institutional Economics: The Case of Philippine Agriculture* (Boulder: Westview Press, 1991); Andreas Madestam, "Informal Finance: A Theory of Moneylenders." *Journal of Development Economics* 107 (2014): 157–74; Dale W. Adams and Delbert A. Fitchett, *Informal Finance in Low-income Countries* (New York: Taylor & Francis Group, 1992). On the history of social enforcement and credit, see Gareth Austin and Kaoru Sugihara, "Local Suppliers of Credit in the Third World, 1750–1960: Introduction." In *Local Suppliers of Credit in the Third World, 1750–1960*, edited by Gareth Austin and Kaoru Sugihara, 1–25 (London: Macmillan, 1993); Ethan Bueno De Mesquita and Matthew Stephenson, "Legal Institutions and Informal Networks." *Journal of Theoretical Politics* 18, no. 1 (2006): 40–67.

[10] Rachel E. Kranton and Anand V. Swamy, "The Hazards of Piecemeal Reform: British Civil Courts and the Credit Market in Colonial India." *Journal of Development Economics* 58, no. 1 (1999): 1–24; Latika Chaudhary and Anand V. Swamy, "A Policy of Credit Disruption: The Punjab Land Alienation Act of 1900." *Economic History Review* 73, no. 1 (2020): 134–58; Latika Chaudhary and Anand V. Swamy, "Protecting the Borrower: An Experiment in Colonial India." *Explorations in Economic History* 65, no. C (2017): 36–54; Tirthankar Roy and Anand V. Swamy, *Law and the Economy in Colonial India* (Chicago: The University of Chicago Press, 2017).

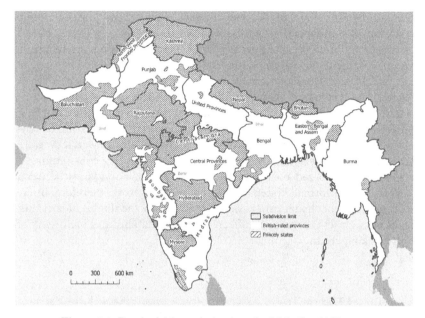

Figure 1.1 Provincial boundaries in colonial India, 1909
Source: Author.
Notes: Figure modelled on the map in the *Imperial Gazetteer of India Atlas*
(Oxford, 1909), 20.

Colonialism, Credit and Development in South India

The study of agricultural markets is central to understanding economic
development in colonial India. Two-thirds of the Indian population
relied on cultivation to make a living in 1900, a figure that did not change
much until the latter decades of the twentieth century.[11] Colonial India,
as drawn in Figure 1.1, spanned an enormous territory, with long coast-
lines in the east and west, as well as mountain ranges in the north and
south.[12] Rivers emanating from the mountains run through fertile valleys
in the north and, albeit to a smaller extent, in the south. The vast majority
of India's population cultivated on four landforms: coastal plains, dry
hinterland, fertile valleys and terraced hills. Colonial Madras was no

---

[11] Tirthankar Roy, *The Economic History of India, 1857–1947* (Oxford: Oxford University
Press, 2000), 104.
[12] India, during the colonial period, included regions governed directly by the British and
princely states governed by local rulers in alliance with the British Crown. This book
focuses on the Madras province of British-ruled India.

different. Madras spanned from the southern tip to the Deccan Plateau, which bridged south and central India. Laterally, the province ran from the western to the eastern coastline. Hill ranges ran across central areas in the north and south of the province. Three main rivers flowed from the west to the east, with its main tributaries also culminating downstream in the eastern deltas. The Madras province, geographically speaking, was a microcosm of the Indian sub-continent while its size, covering 48,500 square miles and housing 29 million people in 1950, justifies studies of the region as its own entity.[13] Agriculture employed millions but yielded low and unequal output in Madras, as it did with the rest of British-ruled India.

Growth and productivity stagnated in the agricultural sector throughout the colonial period and until 1960, in one account, the year when the Green Revolution began.[14] Agrarian India did experience growth in trade during the nineteenth century. Transport infrastructure improved, markets developed and cultivators shifted from payments in kind to transactions in cash.[15] Households transitioned from subsistence to cultivation for profit as cash crop acreage saw a steady increase. Despite a process of commercialisation and expansion in commodities traded, real incomes grew modestly and innovation was limited as production processes remained trapped in a low-yield regime. Output was volatile, with some years of mass famine.[16]

---

[13] Christopher Baker, *An Indian Rural Economy 1880–1955: The Tamilnad Countryside* (Oxford: Oxford University Press, 1984), 3.

[14] This view is presented in general accounts on Indian economic history and in national income estimates. For general accounts, see Dietmar Rothermund, *An Economic History of India: From Pre-colonial Times to 1991*. 2nd ed. (London: Routledge, 1993); B. R. Tomlinson, *The Economy of Modern India, 1860–1970* (Cambridge: Cambridge University Press, 1996); Roy, *Economic History of India*. For national income estimates, see A. Heston, "National Income." In *The Cambridge Economic History of India*, edited by Dharma Kumar and Meghnad Desai, 376–462 (Cambridge: Cambridge University Press, 1983); S. Sivasubramonian, *National Income of India in the Twentieth Century* (Oxford: Oxford University Press, 2000).

[15] John Hurd, "Railways and the Expansion of Markets in India, 1861–1921." *Explorations in Economic History* 12, no. 3 (1975): 263–88; Dan Bogart and Latika Chaudhary, "Engines of Growth: The Productivity Advance of Indian Railways, 1874–1912." *The Journal of Economic History* 73, no. 2 (2013): 339–70; Dave Donaldson, "Railroads of the Raj: Estimating the Impact of Transportation Infrastructure." *American Economic Review* 108, nos. 4–5: 899–934.

[16] Tomlinson, *The Economy of Modern India*, 48, estimates 16 million deaths as a result of famines between 1860 and 1900. Famines in 1876, 1896 and 1899 were prolonged and had a significant impact on most Indian provinces. The famine in 1943 was significant but had the largest impact on the Bengal Presidency. For general works on Indian famines, see Elizabeth Whitcombe, *Agrarian Conditions in Northern India* (Berkeley: University of California Press, 1972); David Hall-Matthews, *Peasants, Famine and the State in Colonial Western India* (New York: Palgrave Macmillan, 2005).

Credit supply offered little scope for investment-led growth in colonial and early post-colonial India. Commercial banks did not lend in the agricultural sector before 1960. Private moneylenders and cooperatives were the major suppliers of credit, the former being more predominant during the period. Missing commercial banks did not mean that credit suppliers were scarce. In Madras, moneylenders were present in every village, and each lender commonly provided loans to multiple borrowers. However, access to loans was selective, value of loans was small and prices of loans were often exorbitant. These conditions did not allow the majority of South Indians to invest in new production processes and often failed to provide needy borrowers maintenance in times of famine.

Two types of moneylenders provided credit in rural India. Indigenous bankers and traders from the cities provided credit to some cotton and wheat farmers in select districts within Bombay and Punjab.[17] In Madras, and across the majority of rural districts in colonial India, farmers with disposable income provided loans to other farmers. Lenders who were also farmers faced two concurrent challenges in bad years. When crops failed, they incurred losses in farming business from decline in quantity, and thus value, of produce, and incurred losses in credit business because borrowers could not meet their credit bills.

The colonial period was a turbulent time for commodity and credit markets in South India. Crop output was volatile, and development was continually interrupted by periods of negative output growth.[18] Debt defaults, as a result, were common and impossible to predict. Lenders found the precarity in earnings and defaults especially difficult to handle in the inter-war period. Commodity prices crashed during the Great Depression, ballooning the value of unpaid credit bills. Defaults compounded, fresh loans dried up and moneylenders were reluctant to renew old debts. This attracted the attention of policymakers. Soaring interest rates and high default rates in the context of stagnating living standards and rising inequality worried colonial officials and Indian nationalists.[19]

Colonial administrators and nationalists saw credit exchange as an exploitative arrangement. The government acted on a belief that investment remained low and peasants remained poor because market forces allowed moneylenders to extract rents from borrowers. Colonial officials feared peasant uprisings as a result of inequity and power imbalance.

---

[17] The presence of urban lenders in rural parts of Bombay and Punjab declined from the 1870s. The Epilogue provides a more detailed discussion of credit supply in these regions.

[18] Heston, "National Income"; Sivasubramonian, *National Income of India*.

[19] Kranton and Swamy, "The Hazards of Piecemeal Reform," provide a discussion of the policy motivations of colonial and nationalist administrators in the nineteenth century.

Adopting a different tone, nationalists argued that elite-favouring policies in the colonial regime affected the livelihoods of peasants. Key actors accused the colonial government of promoting regressive taxation laws and failing to regulate the power of rich moneylenders. The concerns, though motivated by different factors, encouraged the same policy response. Cutting across colonial and nationalist lines, policymakers promoted the protection of borrowers either as a method of preventing riots in the countryside or as a solution to inequality.

Provincial governments were responsible for regulating rural credit markets. As such, the provinces executed different policy responses at different times from the late nineteenth century. The Bombay Deccan was the first to regulate rural credit markets in 1879. The government in Punjab followed suit in 1900. Both governments regulated mortgage lending to limit the transfers of land from cultivators to urban money-lenders. Urban moneylenders scarcely lent in rural Madras so provincial policymakers did not believe that land alienation needed regulating.[20] Credit regulation in Madras, therefore, came later.

The government in Madras implemented a two-pronged approach to controlling the market power of moneylenders: one directly curtailing market power by regulating the prices charged by moneylenders and the other an indirect attempt to diminish market power by increasing com-petition in the market. On the direct approach, provincial officials enforced a price ceiling on loans from moneylenders in 1937. Moneylenders were legally bound to charge borrowers a fixed rate of interest that was significantly lower than the market average. On the indirect approach, the colonial government designed credit cooperatives to compete with moneylenders. The government introduced the first state-regulated cooperative in the Madras Presidency in 1904. The number of cooperatives saw a steady increase in the 1920s with particu-larly large, government-financed capital injections into the sector in the 1940s and 1950s. The government in early post-colonial Madras perse-vered with, and even strengthened, colonial-era interventions.

The timing of intervention is central to the book's structure. The book proceeds in two sections: one analysing the factors that explain lending patterns in the unregulated market and the other showing the impact of interventions on the supply of credit.

The first section analyses the ecological and institutional barriers to lending money and the ways these barriers affected lending patterns in

---

[20] I. J. Catanach, *Rural Credit in Western India, 1875–1930: Rural Credit and the Co-operative Movement in the Bombay Presidency* (Berkeley: University of California Press, 1970).

the unregulated market.[21] Farming was mostly rainfed and dependent on volatile rainfall patterns. Chances of crop failure were high, resulting in dual risks for borrowers and lenders. Poor borrowers that relied on seasonal income ran the risk of defaulting on loans and losing access to credit in subsequent years. Creditors risked losing earnings from capital, returning to more modest means than before. Climatic risk, in turn, affected enforcement structures in a regionally specific pattern. The design of contract laws was unsuited to recover loans from borrowers that did not wilfully default on loans, making courts an inefficient and expensive forum for dispute resolution. The book for the first time shows that lenders in rural India adapted pricing and enforcement strategies to risks and transaction costs. They allocated credit selectively in dry zones and more inclusively in irrigated regions. They relied on courts to recover loans when cost-efficient to do so otherwise resorting to informal contracts, compensating for the costs of enforcing contracts in the prices of loans.

The second section evaluates the design and consequences of credit intervention, showing that regulation was part of the problem of market failure. A political ideology prioritising equity over efficiency inspired the design of credit intervention in the colonial and early post-colonial period.[22] The book finds that tailoring the market to be fairer to the borrower was a superficial response to the underlying problem. After the government enforced the interest rate ceiling, moneylenders were no longer able to price loans adjusting for the risks of lending. Creditors

---

[21] The economic history of India tends to discuss geography and political institutions in separate discourses. On geography and economic development, see Tirthankar Roy, "Geography or Politics? Regional Inequality in Colonial India." *European Review of Economic History* 18, no. 3 (2014): 324–48; Sunil Amrith, *Unruly Waters: How Rains, Rivers, Coasts and Seas Have Shaped Asia's History* (New York: Basic Books, 2018); Tirthankar Roy, "Climate and the Economy in India." CAGE Working Paper Series, no. 445 (2019). On institutions and state in economic development in India, see David A. Washbrook, "Law, State and Agrarian Society in Colonial India." *Modern Asian Studies* 15, no. 3 (1981): 649–721; Abhijit Banerjee and Lakshmi Iyer, "History, Institutions, and Economic Performance: The Legacy of Colonial Land Tenure Systems in India." *American Economic Review* 95, no. 4 (2005): 1190–213; Akhil Gupta, *Red Tape: Bureaucracy, Structural Violence, and Poverty in India* (Durham, NC: Duke University Press, 2012).

[22] Welfare economics has long contended with Okun's Law or the trade-off between efficiency and equity. The Law explains the inverse relationship between income growth and equality. Arthur M. Okun, *Equality and Efficiency: The Big Tradeoff* (Washington, DC: Brookings Institution, 1975) shows that the 'leaky bucket' of redistribution diminishes the efficiency of resource allocation in a given economy. The book applies this trade-off in a different setting, focusing on market allocation and intervention, rather than redistribution. The book shows that the price ceiling (intervention) led to a contraction in supply, despite sustained demand, and a black market for loans at pre-ceiling prices (inefficient and inequitable outcome).

either stopped lending entirely or evaded the law. Credit supply contracted for the poor and remaining creditors went underground, supplying loans outside formal procedure and pricing loans as high or higher than prices in the unregulated market. Attempts to make the market more competitive did not solve the problem either. Prevailing political objectives led to a cooperative banking structure operating with low savings and weak regulation. The regulatory problem ultimately led to exclusion of poorer peasants from accessing credit and over-leveraged cooperative banks. Regulations to make the market more equitable, paradoxically, left borrowers more vulnerable to credit exclusion and high prices.[23]

The book has an enduring message, carrying lessons for credit and development in modern-day India.[24] The agricultural sector in South India continues to be fraught with challenges. Poverty levels are high and persistent, inequality levels are rising, and at the centre of these issues are the lack of credit access and harsh conditions attached to credit for low-income borrowers. The institutional setup and market structure changed after 1960. Credit suppliers multiplied with the entry of commercial banks and microfinance institutions in the agricultural sector. Problems of high default rates, selective access and high prices, however, did not disappear. Governments reacted in a similar pattern, acting on a belief that credit markets remained underdeveloped because they were informal and exploitative. *Capital Shortage* explains how this ideology was founded on a misdiagnosed problem. Risks and ineffective regulations persisted, continually constraining credit supply and restricting investment potential for the rural poor.

Sources

Studying rural credit markets comes with challenges because historical data is scarce. Markets operated within villages, yet contemporary commentators on credit tended to provide broad claims with aggregated data at the provincial level. Government reports and court judgements in colonial India, however, offer novel insights. Policymakers sought to inform policy interventions by compiling data at the district and

---

[23] The Epilogue suggests that climatic risks and the design of laws constrained capital markets across the major Indian provinces during the nineteenth and twentieth centuries.

[24] The Madras province splintered into five South Indian states after colonial rule ended: Tamil Nadu, Andhra Pradesh, Karnataka, Kerala and Odisha. When discussing credit markets in the period after division, the book refers to the entire region, drawing on examples from five South Indian states.

occasionally village level in official surveys. The number of credit reports compiled by the Madras government increased from the 1920s. That moneylenders often used contracts and approached courts leaves a trail of legal sources that are a valuable addition to official reports.

The book analyses two categories of government reports on credit: annual reports and isolated reports. In the annual category, yearly reports by the government departments responsible for recording land registrations and administration of cooperatives provide data and qualitative information on lending patterns in rural districts. In the isolated category, the first section of the book analyses village-level credit surveys from 1930 and 1935. The Banking Enquiry Committee, under the government's supervision, hired a team of investigators to survey credit in eighty villages during the late 1920s.[25] The *Report on Agricultural Indebtedness,* published in 1935, expands on the data provided by the Banking Enquiry Committee.[26] The report, through a larger number of investigators, surveyed 141 villages showing data on types of moneylenders, credit instruments used and purposes of borrowing. The second section of the book analyses a series of government-commissioned surveys in the 1940s and 1950s. Two of these surveys, in particular, offer village- and district-level data. One, published in 1946, estimated if credit laws in the late 1930s changed borrowing patterns in select regions. Another, commissioned by the Reserve Bank of India in 1951, surveyed villages across rural India between 1951 and 1954. The book situates data from government surveys against material from other micro-regional reports, including *District Gazetteers* and one-off official publications on climate and the agricultural sector.

Court records offer a novel set of sources that have yet to be fully studied in credit-related literature. Case files containing counsels' pleadings are inaccessible to the public. Apart from the laws themselves, the case records that are accessible contain summaries of pleadings and the court's final judgement. The book analyses case records from the Madras

---

[25] In the late 1920s, the federal government set up Provincial Banking Enquiry Committees across provinces and published a series of reports on each province in 1930. H. M. Hood chaired the Madras Banking Enquiry Committee. Hood spent the early 1920s as Collector (a term for tax collector during Company rule but evolved to mean Administrator of a district during Crown rule) of the Nellore district. Hood became part of the Legislative Council in the late 1920s and formed a team of policymakers to report on banking in the province. The 1930 report cost 59,000 rupees to compile.

[26] W. R. S. Sathyanathan composed the final report. Sathyanathan was a member of the Indian Civil Service and compiled the referenced report. The provincial legislature appointed Sathyanathan as a 'Special Officer' to report on rural credit in 1935.

High Court.[27] The third and fourth chapters examine select case judgements that consider the enforceability of credit contracts as well as the legality and impact of credit policies from the late 1930s and early 1940s.

Finally, the book supplements government reports and court records with material from contemporary studies, written by economists and policymakers directly involved in the committees that compiled government-commissioned surveys on rural credit in the 1930s and 1940s.[28] These articles and books provide further insights into the government's approach to rural credit.

The book now turns to the first substantive chapter, providing an overview of agriculture, commerce and governance in South India before and during colonial rule.

---

[27] There is no accessible resource for case judgements from lower courts. The book finds some judgements from district courts in contemporary accounts.

[28] The book makes special use of, and critically evaluates, data and qualitative material presented by five economists cum legislators in the provincial government: C. F. Strickland, P. J. Thomas, B. V. Narayanaswamy Naidu, K. G. Sivaswamy and M. L. Dantwala. Short biographies of these key actors are provided in subsequent chapters.

2 Agriculture, Commerce and Governance in the *Longue Durée*

For over a millennium, settlement, governance and development patterns differed by region and ecology in South India. Farmers settled permanently in areas with fertile soils near naturally irrigated deltas. From pre-colonial times and up to the nineteenth century, areas in the dry hinterland remained temporarily settled, and when land was cultivated in these regions, households were producing to subsist. Accordingly, governance was more entrenched in the irrigated areas than in the hinterland. The Chola regime, for example, empowered local leaders to collect taxes and invest in land improvement across coastal plains and fertile valleys. Territories in the hinterland were more fragmented. Local chiefs established militias to rule these regions, often guarding against threats from sultanate regimes in the north. Public spending in the hinterland areas was small. As a result, land saw rising yields and became valuable in regions near the western and eastern deltas. The quality of land in the dry, central part of South India, however, remained low. The differences in land quality, and earnings from land, between the deltas and the hinterland continued well into British rule.

The chapter provides historical context to the rest of the book, focusing on the growth divergence between the better-developed wet regions and the underdeveloped dry regions in peninsular India. Ecology mattered for economic growth because public investment in land improvement remained low in the most underdeveloped areas throughout history. Without sufficient facilities for irrigation and water access, farms were rainfed and farmers, especially those in the hinterland, were vulnerable to weather shocks. Yields were adequate enough to feed local residents in years with stable rainfall and low enough to threaten starvation in years with scarce rainfall. Naturally irrigated areas better protected farmers from seasonal uncertainty. The chapter shows that ecology-driven regionalisation in economic development persisted in the *longue durée*.

By looking at economic progress in the nineteenth and early twentieth centuries, the chapter also provides general lessons on the impact of colonialism on the agrarian economy of South India. Colonial rule introduced a scale effect, from railways and commodity trade, of which there was no parallel earlier. In miles of track laid and volume of goods transported, the region saw significant expansion in trade. That the economy stagnated under colonial rule, therefore, poses a puzzle.[1] As subsequent chapters of the book will show, the colonial regime did not invest in agriculture nor did it encourage private investment in land improvement. Despite growth in trade, supply-side disruptions from low productivity growth continued, and farmers remained vulnerable to harvest failure and famine. As a result, livelihoods for the average household in South India saw only marginal improvement in the nineteenth century and the first half of the twentieth century.

The chapter is divided into two sections. The first provides a summarised history of agrarian settlement, from Chola rule to 1800, across different ecologies in South India. The second explores the development of the agrarian economy in South India during the nineteenth century, evaluating proposed causes of economic stagnation.

The Agrarian Economy in Pre-colonial South India

The majority of cultivation in South India occupied three landscapes: fertile deltas near the coasts, mixed or garden areas partially inland from fertile deltas and the dry hinterland in the central parts. Two major rivers, the Cauvery and Godavari, ran from the west to the east coast. Other perennial rivers were concentrated near the south-east coast. Areas located near the east coast, and downstream the major rivers, contained the most fertile lands. The Cauvery delta in the south-east and the upland delta neighbouring the Godavari River in the north-east part of the region were major rice-producing areas. In colonial times, the Tanjore and Godavari districts were located in the rice-farmed valleys. Some areas partly inland from the deltas in the south-central parts of the province, the areas west of the Cauvery delta, had mixed land types. Within these areas, some localities were fertile while others were dry. The mixed areas, commonly referred to as the *Kongunad*, included the colonial districts of Madura and Trichinopoly, where contrasting soil types between neighbouring municipalities within the region allowed for the cultivation of both rice and millets. Canals and channels built in pre-

---

[1] Tirthankar Roy, *How British Rule Changed India's Economy: The Paradox of the Raj.* Palgrave Studies in Economic History (ebook, Palgrave Macmillan, 2019).

colonial times carried water from rivers to some inland districts. Soils in the *Kongunad* typically had more subsurface water supply than the entirely dry areas. Land in the central hinterland was dry, and soil types were not conducive to high-yield agriculture. This area formed the Ceded Districts during colonial rule and included the dry tracts in Bellary, Kurnool and Anantapur.[2] Wet and mixed areas had a different history of agrarian settlement than the dry hinterland.

The majority of South Indian territory was governed by two sweeping empires prior to British rule. The first was the Chola dynasty. The Chola empire survived three times longer than the British Crown in South India, governing vast parts of the peninsula from about the ninth century to the mid-thirteenth century. By the eleventh century, Chola kings ruled lands in the northern Malabar Coast in the west and the long Coromandel Coast in the east.[3] On the eastern side, the Cholas governed the majority of territory south of the Krishna River, including areas constituting present-day Tamil Nadu and Andhra Pradesh. They ruled over the most fertile lands, including the Cauvery delta and parts of the mixed *Kongunad* pastures. Chola rulers, however, did not control the entire peninsula. While Cholas controlled the majority of the eastern coastline, Chera rulers governed small kingdoms in the western parts of contemporary Tamil Nadu, including parts of *Kongunad*, and Pallava rulers controlled the western coastal territory in contemporary Kerala. During this period, the Hoysala and Kakatiyan dynasties took control of lands just north of Chola territory. Hoysala rulers oversaw a small empire extending from the dry uplands in contemporary central Karnataka, including the colonial districts of Bellary and Kurnool, to the western coastline, while Kakatiyan rulers governed over a marginally larger kingdom encompassing regions extending from contemporary south-western Andhra Pradesh to the south-Odisha coastline.

The second consolidated imperial power in South India was the Vijayanagara empire, ruling from the fourteenth to the sixteenth century. At its peak, Vijayanagara rulers governed an area that was larger than Chola rule, claiming territories previously governed by Chera, Pallava and Hoysala dynasties. Political and bureaucratic institutions were structured differently in each empire. The Vijayanagara empire was less centralised than Chola rule, containing fragmented, semi-autonomous kingdoms until its decline in the sixteenth century. Settlement and development patterns, however, followed similar trajectories across successive dynastic regimes.

---

[2] The region was termed the 'Ceded Districts' after the Nizam of Hyderabad conceded territory to the East India Company in 1800.

[3] Chola rulers also governed parts of Burma and Ceylon.

Historians studying inscriptions from ancient times suggest that early occupiers settled around the most fertile lands in South India. Deltas on either side of the Cauvery River, partially inland from the south-east coast, contained soils that retained moisture and are often cited as the desired location for early settlements. Over time, fertile areas became more densely populated. Once early settlers occupied the most fertile areas nearer the coasts, settlement spread inwards. As population density increased in the fertile areas, pastures inland from the deltas, those in the *Kongunad*, attracted more occupiers during Chola rule. Occupation spread south-west of the Cauvery delta. Chola rulers constructed wells and tanks in the *Kongunad* region, in areas surrounding colonial Trichinopoly, further attracting settlers to the 'mixed' region. The central, dry part of South India was temporarily occupied in the early modern period and earlier and became more densely populated only in the eighteenth and nineteenth centuries. Rice was grown in the deltas; a combination of millet, pulses and rice was grown in the mixed *Kongunad* areas; and dry millets were grown in the hinterland. Archaeological evidence shows that the naturally irrigated deltas, particularly those along the banks of the Cauvery and Godavari, nurtured rice cultivation in ancient times. Preceding the construction of artificial irrigation infrastructure, rice was cultivated in naturally irrigated fields during the Iron Age.[4]

How were settlements governed? During Chola times, well-settled parts of the region developed localised, hierarchical bureaucratic structures, with powers wielded according to caste and wealth.[5] Localities, or *nadus*, emerged as distinct administrative units in settled regions. *Nadus* literally translate to a portion of territory or a domicile and, in the context of pre-1700 South India, refer to a form of permanently settled neighbourhood. *Nadus* were small and densely populated when soil types were conducive to productive agriculture. Administrative proceedings in localities were conducted by groups of landowners, or *nattars*, as well as upper-caste religious titleholders. Historians debate the granular details, including the role of the king, *nattars*, and upper castes, and their respective relationship to the poorer peasants in localities within the wet and mixed regions. The traditional historiography views the Chola dynasty as a strong centralised state. Chola kings, in this interpretation,

---

[4] Eleanor Kingwell-Banham, "Dry, Rainfed or Irrigated? Reevaluating the Role and Development of Rice Agriculture in Iron Age-Early Historic South India Using Archaeobotanical Approaches." *Archaeological and Anthropological Sciences* 11, no. 12 (2019): 6485–500.

[5] Christopher Baker, *An Indian Rural Economy 1880–1955: The Tamilnad Countryside* (Oxford: Oxford University Press, 1984), 30–33.

appointed small cabinets and ruled vast territories with large armies.[6] Chiefs and *nattars* in the localities collected tax revenues on behalf of the king. A revised interpretation, championed by Burton Stein, paints a dichotomous, macro- and micro-political structure, one where the Chola dynasty governed as a 'segmentary state'.[7] Chiefs and *nattars* of local kingdoms were allied to kings, but *nadus* were fiscally autonomous. Local assemblies spent tax collections on the maintenance of temples, gifts to temple and administrative assemblies, and public works, including the maintenance of irrigation networks. Only small portions of tax revenues were allocated to the 'central state'. According to Stein, as settlements grew in size, larger assemblies, or *periyanadus*, formed to administer local governance. Groups of *nattars* cooperatively governed *periyanadus*, almost autonomously and independent of the interests of the central Chola royalty. Recent scholarship challenging Stein's distinction of local and central institutions in South India suggests that *periyanadus* were not separate from the central regime. Instead, their formation reflected increasing commercialisation.[8] The growth of local markets and integration with markets overseas motivated supra-local groups of landowners and merchants to establish associations, partly aiming to increase profits from cultivation in fertile areas. Washbrook consolidates these various assessments, suggesting that there were varied routes to 'citizenship' in South India, each conferred by entrenched local institutions.[9] In other words, governments built on, rather than redesigned, localised rules of engagement in Chola-era South India.

Less historically contested is that governance was entirely decentralised with law and order, trade, and tax powers devolved to local rulers during the Vijayanagara period. Chola rule crumbled in the fourteenth century, disintegrating into multiple kingdoms governed by ruling families. Geographically, the northern edge of the Deccan Plateau was the

---

[6] T. V. Mahalingam, *South Indian Polity.* 2nd ed. (Madras: Rathnam Press, 1967); Arjun Appadurai, "Kings, Sects and Temples in South India, 1350–1700 A.D." *The Indian Economic and Social History Review* 14, no. 1 (1977): 47–73; R. Champakalakshmi, *Trade, Ideology, and Urbanization: South India 300 BC to AD 1300* (Delhi and New York: Oxford University Press, 1996).

[7] Burton Stein, *Peasant State and Society in Medieval South India* (Delhi and Oxford: Oxford University Press, 1980). Stein adapted the segmentary state framework from Aidan Southall's studies on urban East Africa. See Aidan Southall, "The Segmentary State in Africa and Asia." *Comparative Studies in Society and History* 30, no. 1 (1988): 52–82.

[8] Noboru Karashima, *South Indian History and Society: Studies from Inscriptions A.D. 850–1800* (Delhi: Oxford University Press, 1984); Noboru Karashima and Y. Subbarayalu, "The Emergence of the Periyandu Assembly in South India during the Chola and Pandyan Periods." *International Journal of Asian Studies* 1, no. 1 (2004): 87–103.

[9] David A. Washbrook, "Forms of Citizenship in Pre-modern South India." *Citizenship Studies* 23, no. 3 (2019): 224–39.

dividing line between southern kingdoms and Mughal rulers. The decline of the Chola dynasty left a power vacuum in South India as areas immediately south of the Deccan region were no longer protected by a centralised military. Mughal rulers leading vast armed forces in the north had new opportunities to expand southwards. Threats from the north motivated fragmented kingdoms to consolidate military resources. The ruling family of the Vijayanagar region, an area that included the stretch between the banks of the Tungabhadra River in modern-day Hampi and barren lands in Bellary, established the Vijayanagara empire in the 1330s, seeking the allegiance of rulers across the peninsula. Vijayanagar, the town capital of the empire, was located in a vulnerable zone just south of lands ruled by the Deccan sultanates. Vijayanagara kings stationed military garrisons just south of the plateau to protect the fragmented political kingdoms in the peninsula. Ruling families paid tribute, including small armies, to the Vijayanagara rulers. The fiscal regime was more decentralised than the Chola dynasty. Rulers maintained control over tax collection and local expenditure in their kingdoms.[10]

The Battle of Talikota in 1565 marked the beginning of the end for the Vijayanagara dynasty. Sultanate rulers breached the Vijayanagara stronghold in the mid-sixteenth century. Following Talikota, ruling families either rebelled or refused to offer their tribute to the imperial ruler. The change in alliances brought about the disintegration of large South Indian kingdoms, offering expansionary opportunities not just to sultanates but also to territorial rulers, including kingdoms aligned with the Nayaka dynasty in the *Kongunad*, as well as European powers in coastal parts of the region.[11]

How did the South Indian economy develop during dynastic rule? Commerce thrived in the coastal areas and those pastures well suited for rice cultivation. Land markets developed and the value of fertile land increased during Chola rule. Good quality land was in high demand, and once localities were formed, occupiers claimed rights to land. However, few had access to owning property. Ownership was conferred and ratified by local assemblies and religious officials. Administrators granted *mirasi* rights, or rights to shares of communal lands, to upper castes and, in some cases, merchants that officiated in *nattars*. Inscriptions record *brahmadeyas*, or royal gifts of land plots, sometimes even small

---

[10] Karashima, *South Indian History and Society*; Burton Stein, *Vijayanagara* (Cambridge and New York: Oxford University Press, 1989).

[11] Velcheru Narayana Rao, David Dean Shulman, and Sanjay Subrahmanyam, *Symbols of Substance Court and State in Nāyaka Period Tamilnadu* (Delhi and New York: Oxford University Press, 1992).

localities, to upper-caste Brahmins as ritual officeholders in local temples. Shares to communal lands were frequently traded among the elites.[12] Proprietors were not always cultivators, and sharecropping tenancy contracts were common. Lower-caste peasants were tied to land as bonded and paid labour as well as tenants in the *nadus* near the eastern deltas. Rice cultivation in the deltas and parts of the mixed areas remained more labour and capital intensive than millet cultivation in the hinterland.

Commodity trade flourished on the coasts and in the deltas. The more settled areas of South India were trading in local and export markets. Evidence of settlements near the Cauvery delta in the fourth century BC, for example, established trading networks, transporting goods to parts of Asia and Europe. The economy, as a result, started to monetise. Chola and Vijayanagara rulers enforced land taxes, as well as taxes on artisanal production, and inscriptions record the payments of these in coin in the major trading hubs. Indeed, settlers in the Cholamandalam territorial division, the area including the Cauvery delta, did pay part of their tax obligations in money.[13] Stein recounts goldsmiths in the same region also paying local taxes in coin.[14] In the period after the Chola dynasty, tax farming became more entrenched and the militarised Vijayanagara regimes were more reliant on tax revenue than previous rulers. Coin payments gradually increased, partly reflecting rising payments for domestic bills, including military defences, gift-giving, temple maintenance and public works, as well as reflecting rising trade with overseas markets.

In the same period, domestic markets for agricultural produce expanded. Washbrook notes the transport of rice from the eastern deltas to the western coast and the trading of cattle, bred in the hills and sold to farmers in the deltas.[15] Commercial centres emerged in the wet and mixed areas. Routes for bullock trains were built, allowing for the movement of goods between populated settlements.[16] Hall finds the introduction of lower denomination coinage to match the requirements of tax collections from both rising domestic trade and trade with European posts under the Chola regime.[17] Much of this commercialisation, therefore, was occurring in the areas near both the most fertile soils (also the

[12] P. B. Mayer, "The Penetration of Capitalism in a South Indian District." *South Asia* 3, no. 2 (1980): 1–24.

[13] Kenneth R. Hall, "Coinage, Trade and Economy in Early South India and Its Southeast Asian Neighbours." *The Indian Economic and Social History Review* 36, no. 4 (1999): 431–59.

[14] Stein, *Vijayanagara*, 100.

[15] David A. Washbrook, "Merchants, Markets, and Commerce in Early Modern South India." *Journal of the Economic and Social History of the Orient* 53, no. 1–2 (2010): 266–89.

[16] Stein, *Vijayanagara*, 100.

[17] Hall, "Coinage, Trade and Economy in Early South India."

areas with the highest tax revenue per capita) and the ports. Regions in the vicinity of the Cauvery delta satisfied all conditions. Throughout the fifteenth and sixteenth centuries, productivity of paddy lands increased, offering new market opportunities for agriculturists and merchants. The port in Negapatam, modern-day Nagapattinam, just east of the Cauvery rice deltas, continually served as a major trading hub. The port was a centre for Chola traders and naval expeditioners between the ninth and fourteenth centuries, and the capital of Dutch and Portuguese settlements in the sixteenth and seventeenth centuries.[18]

How regionally concentrated was trade expansion in medieval South India? The historiography paints a vibrant picture of the naturally irrigated zones. Coastal plains, fertile valleys and mixed or 'garden' agricultural regions saw permanent settlement, property rights for upper castes and political administrators, the erection of local and supra-local state administrations, fiscal systems and growth in commercial activities from ancient to medieval times.

What about the dry hinterland? The driest, centrally located parts of the South Indian peninsula have been less researched than the well-irrigated deltas. This is logical, given source constraints. The reliance on inscriptions to interpret the history of pre-modern South India procures a focus on areas that were densely populated. Indeed, the number of inscriptions can in itself be a good measure of development patterns. Growing population per square mile; rising tax collection; and the construction of temples, monuments and irrigation channels encouraged durable documentation of settlements in the better-developed parts of the region. Scarce documentation of permanent agrarian settlement in the hinterland was reflective of the underdeveloped nature of the region.[19]

Subbarayalu's mapping of *nadus* offers the most granular measurement of regional development patterns in Southern India during the Chola period. The data shows that *nadus* increased in size disproportionately to distance from water sources. Localities near irrigated deltas were smaller, clearly demarcated by boundaries in the inscriptions and densely populated. Localities further away from water sources and good quality land were larger, not clearly demarcated by boundaries and sparsely populated. In other words, early settlers were deterred by the poor quality of land.[20]

---

[18] For more on the political economy of trade with European powers in fifteenth and sixteenth centuries, see Sanjay Subrahmanyam, *The Political Economy of Commerce: Southern India 1500–1650* (Cambridge: Cambridge University Press, 1989).

[19] Stein, *Vijayanagara*.

[20] Y. Subbarayalu, *Political Geography of the Chola Country* (Madras: State Department of Archaeology, Government of Tamilnadu, 1973), cited in Stein, *Peasant State and Society*, 92–95.

The central hinterland was the underdeveloped part of larger political realms well before colonial rule. The Vijayanagar town in itself was a military stronghold with dry lands. Non-military, agriculturist settlers in the hinterland consumed what they farmed. Markets were few and cultivators merely subsisted in good years. Millet cultivation was common. Some cattle were bred. Once the animals matured, pastoralists typically transported cattle to the rice-producing areas.[21] Studies of governance in localities suggest that settlements in the hinterland were more monocratic. *Nattars* were not prevalent in these regions. Assemblies of legislators were non-existent and temples were few. Brahmins established kinship networks and practised ceremonial duties in areas that were most densely populated. Singular chiefs ruled over small, dry settlements.[22]

The Chola dynasty claimed ownership over dry areas nearest the southern tip; Hoysalan and Kakatiyan rulers claimed control over the northern parts. Hoysalan rule extended from the centre to the north-west, while Kakatiyan rule extended from the centre to the north-east. In each of these three cases, the central parts were not developing at the same pace as the deltas or coasts. Each of the three dynasties maintained strong military garrisons in the dry interior, primarily to protect against the troops of sultanate rulers that attempted to expand southwards, through the hinterland. Independent chiefs controlled military troops and contributed these to the different dynasties. In the fifteenth century, many chiefs of hinterland localities pledged allegiance to the Vijayanagara rulers. When forts were built in the hinterland, rulers constructed them to house armies. Occupational structure developed alongside military hierarchies. The cooperation between landowners, religious leaders and merchants that developed in the fertile plains was non-existent in the dry hinterland. Chiefs wielded absolute power over territories on account of their control of local militias.[23]

Chiefs levied taxes on the few producers that settled, however, public spending was low. Rulers did not construct irrigation channels or transport networks in the hinterland. In the Chola period, irrigation infrastructure was built in two forms and in two regions. Chola rulers invested in the construction of channels and dams to divert water from the Cauvery river to deltas in the south-eastern delta. The most famous example of such constructions was the Grand Anicut, built early in Chola rule. While large

[21] Washbrook, "Merchants, Markets, and Commerce," 266–89.
[22] Subbarayalu, *Political Geography of the Chola Country*, cited in Stein, *Peasant State and Society*, 92–95.
[23] Stein, *Vijayanagara*.

projects were concentrated in the deltas, tanks were common forms of water storage in the mixed, south-central districts, areas surrounding the colonial districts of Madurai or Trichinopoly. Historians also note sizeable investments into the construction of small irrigation projects, and general improvement of cultivated lands, in the mixed areas during the fifteenth and sixteenth centuries.[24]

In short, from ancient times, well-irrigated sections remained densely populated and settlers accumulated wealth. Dry sections remained dangerously rainfed, sparsely settled or occupied by local militias and relentlessly poor. Low investment meant that land quality remained poor and markets underdeveloped in the dry areas. Recent evidence suggests that the non-marketisation of the dry hinterland persisted until the nineteenth century. Expansion in railway networks and increase in cash crop cultivation brought little reprieve to the region. The majority of hinterland peasants suffered through frequent famines.

On the eve of British control in South India, two sweeping empires had ended and an assortment of regimes ruled over the broken-up region. Haider Ali and Tipu Sultan ruled the north-west, Marathas and sultanate regimes governed the north-east, independent kingdoms and militias reigned in the hinterland, and European powers controlled ports and collected taxes in parts of both coasts. The East India Company, through military conquest, consolidated and governed the various kingdoms as one administrative unit from the early nineteenth century. The Indian Rebellion ended the East India Company's reign in 1857, bringing the majority of the South Indian peninsula under the authority of the Crown. The development trajectories of different regions within South India, however, did not change much. Land became more productive in the wet areas and in parts of mixed areas. In the driest tracts, farmers barely managed to subsist, a problem that persisted well into the twentieth century.

Colonialism, Commerce and Agriculture, 1800–1920

How did the Indian economy perform under colonial rule? National accounting estimates show a 'reversal of fortune', that Indians were richer under pre-colonial regimes than they were by the end of colonial rule. There is disagreement on the timing of this reversal. Scholars agree that the average Indian in 1600 was, in *real* terms, richer than the average Indian in 1900. Traditional historical contributions suggest that the reversal occurred during the early phases of British influence in India.

[24] Prasannan Parthasarathi, *The Transition to a Colonial Economy in South India: Industry and Commerce in the Eighteenth Century* (New York: Cambridge University Press, 2001), 53.

This interpretation, corroborating the California School's popularisation of the Great Divergence and spearheaded in the late 1990s by Parthasarathi, suggests that the eighteenth century marked a structural change in India's economy. Indian wages, according to Parthasarathi, were higher than those earned by British labour until the 1700s. In the transformative period, production of artisanal and labour-intensive manufactured goods declined while agricultural productivity, where once rising, began to stagnate.[25] Newer estimates of India's economy in the *longue durée* suggest a slower, more nuanced decline in India's economic performance. Incomes of Indian workers, as per amended estimates, declined from the seventeenth century.[26] The revised estimates disagree on Parthasarathi's timing of the 'divergence', suggesting that Indians were poorer than the British in the sixteenth century. Less disputed, however, is that India's 'fortunes' did reverse by the middle of colonial rule. Indeed, revised GDP estimates suggest that per capita income was 700 dollars in 1990 prices during Akbar's rule of Mughal India, falling to a low average annual earning of 500 dollars per capita in the early 1870s. Whereas the average worker in Mughal India earned close to 70 per cent of the average worker's income in Britain, this ratio fell to 15 per cent in 1870.[27]

GDP estimates show that the Indian economy performed poorly while ruled by the British Crown. Heston's estimates of price-adjusted GDP growth rates show a small yearly increase of 0.43 per cent between 1900 and 1946. Sivasubramonian's revised estimates suggest a more depressing story, with annual average (and price adjusted) per capita income growth rates of 0.22 per cent during the same period.[28] India's population size increased from a quarter of a billion to almost half a billion residents while estimates of sector-wise distribution of the labour force suggest that the number of adults employed in agriculture increased between 1881 and 1950.[29] By 1950, 76 per cent of India's labour force worked in the agricultural sector. Whereas manufacturing and services saw some

[25] Prasannan Parthasarathi, "Rethinking Wages and Competitiveness in the Eighteenth Century: Britain and South India." *Past & Present* 1998, no. 158 (1998): 79–109.

[26] Pim De Zwart and Jan Lucassen, "Poverty or Prosperity in Northern India? New Evidence on Real Wages, 1590s–1870s." *The Economic History Review* 73, no. 3 (2020): 644–67.

[27] Stephen Broadberry, Johann Custodis, and Bishnupriya Gupta, "India and the Great Divergence: An Anglo-Indian Comparison of GDP per Capita, 1600–1871." *Explorations in Economic History* 55 (2015): 58–75; Stephen Broadberry and Bishnupriya Gupta, "The Historical Roots of India's Service-led Development: A Sectoral Analysis of Anglo-Indian Productivity Differences, 1870–2000." *Explorations in Economic History* 47, no. 3 (2010): 264–78.

[28] S. Sivasubramonian, *National Income of India in the Twentieth Century* (Oxford: Oxford University Press, 2000), 273.

[29] Sivasubramonian, *National Income of India*, 13.

increase in net output, stagnation in the agricultural sector explains the low rates of GDP growth in colonial India.[30] How did the agricultural sector perform in Madras?

The Madras Presidency, drawn in Figure 2.1, extended from parts of the west coast to the entire south-east coast. The Company divided Madras into multiple districts and *taluks* or municipalities. The shift to Crown rule in 1857 created further administrative units, limiting the size of each district. In the post-colonial period, the province was divided and land was shared between five Indian states: Tamil Nadu, Andhra Pradesh and parts of Karnataka, Kerala and Odisha. Living standards of the average rural household across the region saw little improvement in the nineteenth and early- to mid-twentieth centuries. Real wages in Madras broadly stagnated or declined between 1873 and 1900.[31] Peter Mayer's estimation of living standards is equally cynical about wage patterns in the first half of the twentieth century. There was some increase in earnings between 1900 and 1920, however, growth was short-lived. According to Mayer's estimations, real wages declined substantially in parts of Madras between 1920 and 1970.[32] Anthropometric analyses offer similar results. Brennan et al. suggest that heights of South Indian emigrants to Fiji stagnated across the nineteenth and early twentieth centuries.[33] Famines devastated large parts of the region, particularly affecting dry terrains. The famine in 1876 led to widespread starvation in the driest tracts, the Ceded Districts of Bellary, Kurnool and Anantapur, in particular.[34]

The decline in living standards is surprising, considering the volume of trade grew exponentially in the same period. Transport networks and markets expanded across South Asia during the nineteenth century. Railway lines connected previously unconnected regions and reduced the costs of transporting people and goods between those regions previously connected by slower modes of transport, including bullock carts and palanquins. In kilometres of track, the area covered by railway lines increased by fifty times between 1850 and 1947. The cost of transporting

[30] Bishnupriya Gupta, "Falling behind and Catching Up: India's Transition from a Colonial Economy." *The Economic History Review* 72, no. 3 (2019): 803–27.

[31] Dharma Kumar, *Land and Caste in South India: Agricultural Labour in the Madras Presidency during the Nineteenth Century* (Cambridge: Cambridge University Press, 1965).

[32] Peter Mayer, "Trends of Real Income in Tiruchirapalli and the Upper Kaveri Delta, 1819–1980." *The Indian Economic and Social History Review* 43, no. 3 (2006): 349–64.

[33] Lance Brennan, John McDonald, and Ralph Shlomowitz. "Trends in the Economic Well-Being of South Indians under British Rule: The Anthropometric Evidence." *Explorations in Economic History* 31, no. 2 (1994): 225–60.

[34] Leela Sami, "Starvation, Disease and Death: Explaining Famine Mortality in Madras 1876–1878." *Social History of Medicine: The Journal of the Society for the Social History of Medicine* 24, no. 3 (2011): 700–19.

Figure 2.1 District boundaries in Madras, 1945
Source: Author.
Note: Figure modelled on the map in *Indian Agricultural Statistics* (Delhi, 1950), 103.

goods by rail, between markets substantially declined in the same period, affording substantial social savings to producers. Prices paid to transport one ton of goods for one kilometre by rail in the 1930s were 94 per cent lower than the same prices paid to carry goods by bullock cart in the early 1800s.[35] Markets expanded with the growth in railway construction.

[35] John Hurd, "Railways." In *The Cambridge Economic History of India*, edited by Dharma Kumar and Meghnad Desai, 2:878–904 (Cambridge: Cambridge University Press, 1983), 740.

Prices of grain, rice and cotton saw greater convergence across districts between 1860 and 1900.[36]

From the mid- to late-nineteenth century, new railway lines in South India connected farmers in the hinterland to markets in the deltas and export routes. The Madras Railway Company, established in 1845, built the first track, with carriages embarking from Madras city to Arcot in the mid-1850s. The goal of the company, and indeed the British Indian government, was to lay enough track to connect the centres of the major provinces. By the 1880s, a passenger could board a train in Madras city, and travel to Bombay and Calcutta with one connecting stop along the way. Internally, areas within the province also became better connected. Track laid by the Madras Railway Company offered direct connections between Madras city and Beypore near the western, Malabar coast. The hinterland was quickly integrated with the rest of the province. A single line connected Anantapur, Bellary and Kurnool in the driest parts of the hinterland to coastal Tanjore by the late nineteenth century.[37] Connections for the hinterland to the Deccan also increased. The Southern Mahratta Railway company constructed rail track between Bellary and southern parts of the Deccan in the 1870s and 1880s. Connections within the province and between provinces continued to increase after the Madras Railway Company merged with Southern Mahratta Railway Company in 1908. Rail lines also expanded in the southern parts of the province. The Great Southern of India Railway Company, established in 1858, linked parts of Tanjore to Trichinopoly, Salem and Coimbatore in the 1860s and 1870s.[38] Operating at a smaller level than the Madras Railway Company, Southern of India Railway continued to operate lines in the peninsular region until it was nationalised in the mid-1940s.

Between 1860 and 1891, the line of railway track operated by the Madras Railway Company and the Southern of India Railway increased from 137 miles to 1740 miles. Railway mileage open for the transport of goods and people increased by approximately eight times over the 1860s. The movement of goods expectedly increased at a similarly quick pace. Between 1871 and 1891, goods transported on rail lines operated by the aforementioned South Indian railway companies increased from 409,620 tons to 2.8 million tons.[39] In other words, the tonnage transported per

[36] Michelle McAlpin, "Railroads, Prices, and Peasant Rationality: India 1860–1900." *The Journal of Economic History* 34, no. 3 (1974): 664.

[37] David A. Washbrook, "The Commercialization of Agriculture in Colonial India: Production, Subsistence and Reproduction in the 'Dry South', c. 1870–1930." *Modern Asian Studies* 28, no. 1 (1994): 129–64, 129–130.

[38] *Madras Chamber of Commerce Centenary Handbook 1836–1936* (Madras, 1936).

[39] *Statistical Abstract Relating to British India* (London, 1870–1905).

railway mile within the Madras province alone increased by close to four times in the late nineteenth century. Railway connections to ports also increased commodity exports. The value of merchandise exports, in pound sterling, shipped out of Madras alone increased by about five times concurrently.[40] The expansion in railway networks provided peasants in Madras greater access to both regional and global markets.

Growth in transport connections between rural and urban areas led to increase in cultivated land in the nineteenth century. Millet, cotton and groundnut acreage increased from the 1850s. For prospective cotton farmers, the motivation was not just rail connectivity. Soaring cotton prices during the American Civil War encouraged an increase in cotton cultivation across the drier tracts.[41] Growing market demand overseas combined with declining costs of moving commodities from hinterland to coasts encouraged cultivators to seize the opportunity to profit from new export market opportunities. The stagnation in living standards, however, suggests that results from deepening market access were disappointing. Marketisation did not relieve destitution for the poorest.

Nationalists writing during colonial rule offered one explanation, that the commercialisation process encouraged crop substitution which, when combined with population growth, led to a decline in living standards. R. C. Dutt, among others in a group of Indian nationalist politicians demanding stronger protectionist policies, argued that cash crop acreage substituted food grain cultivation from the mid-nineteenth century.[42] At the same time, population size increased rapidly. The supply shortage of food production combined with rising demand, in the nationalists' opinion, led to widespread starvation. Supply shortages created an additional problem of increasing grain prices, which in the context of stagnating nominal wages put additional pressures on the rural poor. Some historians provide interpretations that corroborate this narrative. David Arnold suggests that increasing cash crop cultivation led to grain riots in the early twentieth century. The integration of local agriculture with export markets altered the supply chain of grain production. Grain was no longer sold in bazaars but stockpiled in warehouses and then exported, creating supply disruptions in the face of burgeoning demand. By hoarding grain, traders benefitted from price spikes, leaving peasants in the countryside with food supply shortages. Running through this narrative is the assumption that marketisation, a transformative process

[40] *Statistical Abstract Relating to British India.*
[41] Washbrook, "The Commercialization of Agriculture," 129–130.
[42] Michelle McAlpin, "Railroads, Cultivation Patterns, and Foodgrain Availability: India 1860–1900." *The Indian Economic and Social History Review* 12, no. 1 (1975): 43–60, 53.

in the nineteenth century caused by the expansion of transport networks, led to food shortages and peasant unrest. The grain riots across the province in 1918, according to Arnold, were motivated by 'popular resentment against the expanding grain trade'.[43] Historians believe peasants were rioting in the early twentieth century to protest the lack of protection against market forces, especially those that affected the prices of food. At first sight, the increase in railway mileage and expansion of domestic markets seemed to have marginalised the poor. Stopping the analysis here, however, would give us only a superficial explanation for persistent poverty in the region.

Historians writing in the 1970s and 1980s disputed some of the suggestions made by nineteenth-century nationalists. Though cash crop cultivation increased, it accounted for a small share of total agricultural output. In 1885, of the 22.5 million acres cultivated, rice, millets and pulses cultivation operated 19.6 million acres while acreage under cotton and oil seeds, the principal cash crops in the region, amounted to 2.7 million acres.[44] By the turn of the twentieth century, cotton area continued to contribute a small portion of total agricultural land, just 5 per cent of total area in the province.[45] This trend continued into the 1930s, as the next chapter will show. Crucially, evidence suggests that though cotton acreage did increase after 1860, it did not substitute rice or cereal cultivation. Cotton acreage increased and grain acreage did not decline throughout colonial rule. McAlpin's assessment of transported commodities suggests that though rail lines carried cash crops and some grains, the majority of grain was consumed in local markets. In the same period, population numbers declined in the dry tracts of Bellary and Kurnool, the areas most affected by nineteenth-century famines. In other words, neither crop substitutions nor demographic explosions created grain supply shortages in Madras.[46]

A possible addendum to the nationalists' hypothesis is that commercialisation left poor peasants exposed to market fluctuations. Those peasants cultivating cotton, in particular, were negatively affected because of rising grain prices. Peasants owning small parcels of land and growing a single cotton crop each year struggled to purchase grain as prices soared. The price of cotton increased for most of the period but at a slower rate than the price of grain. Earnings from cultivating cotton

[43] David Arnold, "Looting, Grain Riots and Government Policy in South India 1918." *Past & Present*, no. 84 (1979): 145.
[44] *Statistical Abstract Relating to British India* (London, 1896), 54.
[45] McAlpin, "Railroads, Prices and Peasant Rationality," 681.
[46] McAlpin, "Railroads, Prices and Peasant Rationality," 681.

declined relative to prices paid for food consumption. The outcome was declining real wages for one group of peasants.[47] However, the number of cotton cultivators remained a small portion of the total agricultural population. Additionally, the rise in cotton production throughout the period is then counter-intuitive. If cotton cultivators could not afford to purchase food, then why would the number of farmers acquiring land to cultivate cotton rise? Why did the countryside see food shortages, and rising grain prices caused by supply disruptions, despite rising production of both food and cash crops? Questions of stagnating growth, declining living standards and causes of widespread famines remain unanswered. Another explanation needs to be found to explain why market penetration did not leave farmers better off.

One suggestion is that improperly defined property rights channelled the benefits of marketisation to the rich while keeping the poor perpetually destitute. Spatial regimes changed with British rule. Colonial officers established territorial boundaries with hierarchical forms of governance, adding more bureaucratic layers than pre-colonial rule and embedding uniformity across previously different kingdoms, empires and dynasties. Spaces moved away from being organised communally towards ones organised legally and politically. Collective administrations governing *nadus* and *periyanadus* declined or dissolved. Courts were established by the East India Company to oversee trade and criminal disputes. Contract laws were designed and enforced from the late nineteenth century. The British conceptualised India as a region with villages, municipalities, districts and major provinces, consolidating previously fragmented political units.[48] Boundaries were drawn to demarcate these units in the nineteenth century. Branches of government expanded. High-ranking colonial officers secured appointments in the provincial administration, while low-ranking officers worked in district government positions. The British bestowed district administrators with powers to collect land taxes. District officials recorded the size of land plots, providing titles to the owners of each plot. However, the land market did not function without encumbrance. The colonial government reverted to pre-colonial forms of property rights in some regions, granting elites ownership over large estates. Estates were at times as large as several hundred villages. The government also occasionally granted land rights to upper castes and temple officials. Land endowments distorted investment incentives and perpetuated rural inequality. Land proprietors paid taxes to the colonial regime, yet rarely cultivated lands themselves. Elites divided their estates into plots and leased them out to permanent tenants. Rents were higher than tax obligations, incentivising rentiers to profit from exploitative lease contracts instead of investing on improving the productivity of the lands being rented.[49] Land gifting also restricted occupational mobility. The wealthy inherited land, while the poor remained landless and relied on wage earnings. The bargaining power of labourers and tenants remained low, while the rents accumulated by the rich steadily increased.[50] Growth and productivity rates stagnated, while tenants who made profits from marketisation had no choice but to allocate surplus to rising land rents.

Property rights and elite capture, however, do not entirely explain regional growth patterns in the Indian peninsula. As the fourth chapter in the book will show, land grants to elites made up a small portion of total acreage in colonial Madras.[51] From the 1820s, land titles and the right to sell land were held by cultivators. Property rights were transparent as farmers had proprietorship over the majority of the estates in the province. As a result, the land market flourished. Growing trade increased the value of land from the 1850s. Land markets saw growth in the number and value of transactions at the same time that transport networks and commodity markets penetrated the countryside. Small- and medium-sized estates proliferated.[52] Previously landless labourers acquired uncropped lands to grow cotton in the dry districts. The number of new titles issued for lands in the lowest revenue class within the Bellary district almost doubled between 1890 and 1930. The majority of these new owners were labourers hoping to benefit from new cash crop cultivation. As expected, the value of cash-credit transactions increased at a similarly fast rate during the same period.[53] The change from subsistence-focused production to marketisation of commodities and rise in cash crop cultivation expectedly saw a rise in demand for cash loans across Madras from the mid-nineteenth century. Increases in the number and value of land sales and credit transfers should translate to higher growth rates – an assumption, however, that does not hold for

[49] Tirthankar Roy and Anand V. Swamy, *Law and the Economy in Colonial India* (Chicago: The University of Chicago Press, 2017).
[50] Ravi Ahuja, "Labour Relations in an Early Colonial Context: Madras, c. 1750–1800." *Modern Asian Studies* 36, no. 4 (2002): 793–826.
[51] Tsukasa Mizushima, "From Mirasidar to Pattadar: South India in the Late Nineteenth Century." *The Indian Economic and Social History Review* 39, nos. 2–3 (2002): 259–84.
[52] Washbrook, "The Commercialization of Agriculture."
[53] Bruce Robert, "Economic Change and Agrarian Organization in 'Dry' South India 1890–1940: A Reinterpretation." *Modern Asian Studies* 17, no. 1 (1983): 59–78; Washbrook, "The Commercialization of Agriculture."

South India. We return to the original problem. Why do we still observe stagnant output and productivity growth rates despite property rights protection and burgeoning demand for factor inputs?

The explanations so far discussed ignore one crucial supply-side factor – the quality of land that was cultivated to produce crops. Ecology and the constraints region-specific climate patterns placed on the efficiency of land offer an underlying explanation for the contradiction between rising trade and declining growth. Land quality changed little, and poor-quality land was unable to endure weather shocks without substantial loss in crop output. Drought, in particular, repeatedly damaged crop growth in Madras.

Indeed, cropped area followed climate patterns in the first half of the twentieth century. Total land area did not change. About the same quantity of land was available for sowing after 1900. Over the following decades, as shown in Figure 2.2, the area cropped, that is the sowed area that grew plants each year, incurred repeated negative shocks. Take the 1918 season, for instance. Low precipitation caused significant plant damage. Cropped area across Madras declined by 7 per cent relative to the previous year. Mid-way through the season, surveyors forecasted this land damage to cause food output to decline by approximately 25 per cent.[54] A substantial shock to the livelihoods of farmers. Expectedly, crop damage had a lagged effect on commodity prices. Prices increased after the harvest, a particularly noticeable hike in early 1919.

Markets offered new and profitable opportunities but ecology created deep supply constraints. As suggested by McAlpin, 'clearly, the market structure and the transport system could not alleviate severe food shortages caused by repeated crop failures'.[55] Baker records the emergence of a conflict between rising demand and the scarcity of 'productive resources' in the colonial period, an especially ferocious conflict in the areas most vulnerable to crop failure.[56] The problem was more severe in some areas. Soils in the wet districts were nitrogen and phosphate deficient and did not drain easily. As the book will later suggest, low fertiliser use and frequent waterlogging constrained yield growth in rice fields. Despite these issues, wet zones were not prone to the same level of risk as the dry districts. Growth rates were low but famine was not a danger for peasants in wet areas. Dry lands, in contrast, continued to be both nutrient and water deficient throughout colonial rule, problems that continually threatened widespread starvation. Population grew faster

---

[54] *Season and Crop Report of the Madras Presidency* (Madras, 1919), 23. Decline in cropped area led to compounded decline in crop output.

[55] McAlpin, "Railroads, Prices and Peasant Rationality", 681.

[56] Baker, "*An Indian Rural Economy*", 136.

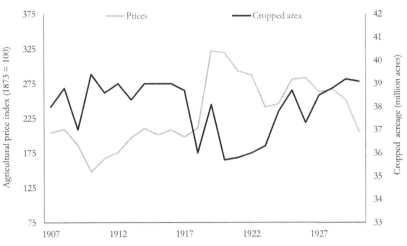

Figure 2.2 Fluctuations in cropped area and agricultural prices, 1907–30
Sources: "Season and Crop Report," 1907–30; Michelle McAlpin, "Price Movements and Fluctuations in Economic Activity (1860–1947)." In *The Cambridge Economic History of India*, edited by Dharma Kumar and Meghnad Desai, 2:878–904 (Cambridge: Cambridge University Press, 1983).
Notes: Direct measures of crop output were inconsistently and unreliably collected by colonial officials in Madras. The amount of land cropped was systematically collected each year between 1904 and 1940, partly because this measure affected changes in the design and assessment of land taxes. Surveyors reported the amount of sowed land with plant growth after the sowing season and before the harvest. Changes in cropped land followed seasonal patterns. Cropped area increased in good seasons and decreased in bad ones. Prices follow McAlpin's agricultural price index.

than output in the nineteenth and early twentieth centuries. Food grain production per capita declined steadily throughout the colonial period.

That land quality matters is evident in the fact that peasants in irrigated areas were less vulnerable to famine. Drought affected crop output across the province. Yet, the problem was more severe in unirrigated areas. Droughts, such as the one in 1918, quickly turned into famine in districts such as Anantapur and Bellary.[57] The government established famine camps and extended tax remissions to farmers in regions badly affected by the 1918 crisis, though crop failure of that magnitude had already caused significant harm.

Living standards were higher in the deltas than in the dry regions. Parthasarathi's analysis of grain wages paid to landless labourers suggests

[57] *Season and Crop Report*, 1–2.

that wages in Madras' rice deltas were higher than wages in Britain throughout the eighteenth century.[58] The dry tracts were much poorer in the same period. Further, seasonal grain and cash wages in the driest tracts saw substantial declines in the nineteenth century. The better-developed mixed districts of Salem and Tinnevelly had higher living standards, but real wages in these districts also saw declines during company and crown rule. The Tanjore delta saw a marginal rise in real wages paid to labourers during the late nineteenth century, but a decline in living standards in the early- to mid-twentieth century.[59] Irrigated regions were also more monetised than the drier tracts. Kumar records the payments of grain wages to labourers across the Ceded Districts, while cash was more widely accepted in the deltas in the early nineteenth century. By the eve of the twentieth century, monetisation penetrated the drier regions, due to rise in both the acreage under cash crops and trade of commodities in markets owing to the spread of railway networks. In this period, living standards stagnated and farmers with access to better quality land were less vulnerable to crises than farmers with access to dry lands.

The trend of low output growth was not unique to Madras and was an India-wide phenomenon during the colonial period. Using Heston's estimates of net domestic product at constant prices by sector, Figure 2.3 constructs annual rates of change in agricultural output between the 1880s and the end of colonial rule. The graph shows that output growth, adjusted for inflation at 1947 prices, showed little sustained growth throughout the period. Output increased at a rate between 0.7 and 1.4, where data points below 1 on the graph indicate negative growth rates between years $n + 1$ and n. The agricultural sector saw negative output growth rates in thirty out of the sixty-one years in focus. The high amplitude of fluctuations in annual growth rates do reduce after 1925, however, we do not see uninterrupted periods of positive growth during colonial rule. Each quinquennium contained at least two years of negative growth between 1925 and 1947. When annual output growth was positive, rates of growth were not substantial enough to induce improvements in living standards. Sivasubramonian's estimates, adjusted for inflation, show a similar, if not more gloomy picture, for growth rates in the early twentieth century. From his calculations, the agricultural sector saw negative annual growth rates in twenty-five out of forty-six years between 1900 and 1946. When positive, output growth was too small to have any significant effects on living standards. The average rural Indian household remained poor

---

[58] Parthasarathi, "Rethinking Wages."   [59] Mayer, "Trends of Real Income."

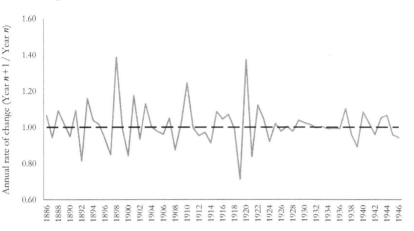

Figure 2.3 Annual change in agricultural output at constant prices in colonial India, 1885–1946

Source: Heston, *National Income*.

Notes: Output measured as net domestic product. Numbers originally presented in million rupees and inflation-adjusted to 1947 commodity prices. The author calculates the rate of change by dividing net domestic product in year *n* + *1* by the same measure in year *n*. Change below 1 indicates negative output growth between years *n* and *n* + *1*.

throughout the period, often barely able to subsist. Population size almost doubled, but grain production per capita declined by 30 per cent between 1901 and 1946.[60] Cash crop acreage increased and did not substitute grain production in the nineteenth century. Food crops remained the major source of agrarian output across South Asia.[61]

Property rights protection did little to help the tracts most vulnerable to the risk of harvest failure. The areas with non-transparent property rights were often located in fertile or mixed areas, ones that saw more growth than the dry districts. Land was transferable and frequently exchanged in dry areas from the late nineteenth century.[62] An institutional framework, if applied in isolation from the physical environment, offers little explanation for why parts of Madras were better off than

---

[60] A. Heston, "National Income." In *The Cambridge Economic History of India*, edited by Dharma Kumar and Meghnad Desai, 376–462 (Cambridge: Cambridge University Press, 1983), 410.

[61] McAlpin, "Railroads, Cultivation Patterns," 43–60.

[62] Robert, "Economic Change and Agrarian Organization"; Washbrook, "The Commercialization of Agriculture."

others. Food shortages were acute in areas with poor land quality. Other areas managed better. Laws and the design of rights to land did matter. However, they mattered in conjunction with ecology and the risks posed by volatile rainfall. As subsequent chapters of the book will show, climatic risks had region-specific consequences for the functioning of courts, the negotiability of contracted instruments and the informality of intra-village enforcement networks.

An approach that focuses entirely on market forces ignores the underlying issue – low land yields left peasants especially vulnerable to price fluctuations. Without the capacity to diversify production or adopt productivity-enhancing production techniques, small farmers could not budget for or recover easily from price shocks. The colonial government made matters worse but not by facilitating trade and commerce. Regressive land taxes affected peasants in bad years. A flat tax on low-yield land exacerbated the poverty cycle for peasants, a problem that was particularly acute for those peasants farming in the dry regions. Poor peasants were left with compounding tax bills in years where crops failed, further restricting their earning potential. Political officials and the judiciary combined regressive tax policies with laws to protect peasants from market forces, an approach that stunted growth rates while also failing to properly address inequities caused by the free market. In this context, what was needed was public investment in improving land, the lack of which stagnated yields.

In the absence of crop insurance and public investment, capital markets were vulnerable to ecological risk and institutions not suited to mitigate the risks faced by the providers of credit. The outcome was an illiquid credit market, one that saw growth in the supply of small, short-term and expensive loans and constraints on the supply of large, cheap and long-term loans, ones suited to land improvement. Before constructing the institutional narrative, that is identifying the impact of region-specific institutions on credit supply, in Chapters 4 and 5, the next chapter of the book will first compare risks faced by farmers in different ecological zones.

In summary, living standard estimates of the average agriculturist during colonial rule corroborate two patterns. One is that income per capita in most regions stagnated or declined over the course of the colonial and early post-colonial period. The other is that ecology continually mattered. Peasants in fertile regions had higher living standards than peasants in dry tracts. Access to cheap credit, to fuel private investment in land improvement, was needed to manage ecological risk better. In this context, the book provides an explanation for why credit remained supply-constrained and expensive.

Conclusion

South India remained an agrarian economy well into the twentieth century. Some regions within the Madras Presidency were better suited to agriculture than others. From the ninth century, naturally irrigated areas saw higher land yields than dry areas, commercialisation and capital accumulation. Imperial rulers established tradable property rights for groups of landowners, invested in infrastructure to store water, as well as constructed and maintained temples. The colonial government built new forms of irrigation or refurbished old tanks and wells in the already well-irrigated tracts near the province's perennial rivers. Areas that were dry and rainfed 1,000 years ago remained underdeveloped by the twentieth century. Kingdoms in the hinterland were avoided by early settlers and became hubs for military garrisons in the medieval period. Rulers built forts and housed large armies in the dry regions to fend off opportunistic advances by rulers in the north. Any farming in the hinterland was largely subsistence focused before British rule.

During British rule, public investment remained low and policy choices inadequate to address the vulnerabilities of poor farmers exposed to a high risk of crop failure. Commercialisation and the rise of cash crop cultivation in the nineteenth century brought some reprieve but not enough to mitigate the risks of harvest failure in the driest regions. Acreage under cotton and millet cultivation increased simultaneously. As the next chapter corroborates, without adequate access to water and sufficient protection from seasonal instability, peasants farming small plots in the hinterland subsisted in good years and starved in bad ones.

Why, despite rising trade and commerce, did peasants not have enough capital to invest in land improvement? The rest of the book will focus on explaining why private investment was both needed and lacking in Madras. Structural transformation, one brought about by an expansion in cheaply supplied capital, was essential to alter the trajectory for dry, rainfed regions. The rise in cash crop cultivation and escalating land values did increase the demand for cheap credit. Credit supply did not match this burgeoning demand.

3   Climate and Credit[*]

Moneylenders faced a central problem in providing credit to peasants in colonial Madras: borrowers regularly defaulted on loans. High default rates, in turn, affected the rural money market in a specific pattern. Urban bankers did not lend in the countryside. Farmers themselves provided credit to other rural households in the province. High default rates in one year constrained credit supply in the next. The problem seems to have been more severe in some regions than others. Credit markets were more constrained in central areas of the province than near the coasts.

What explains regional variation in credit supply? According to contemporary studies in the late colonial and early post-colonial period, as well as mainstream historical accounts, rich moneylenders monopolised the supply of credit. The non-competitive structure of credit markets allowed the rich to over-price loans and keep the poor in a state of permanent debt bondage. This approach typically considers the proportion of indebtedness as a measure of the problem. Markets were less competitive and cultivators borrowed more, relative to their income, in some regions than others.[1] This chapter shows that the size of indebtedness and market structure did not indicate market constraints. Instead, the chapter suggests environmental factors as the source of regional variations in credit supply. Lenders adopted different strategies to hedge default risk in wet and dry districts, and, therefore, a general account of

[*] Parts of Chapters 3 and 4 are published in an article in the *Economic History Review*, Maanik Nath, "Credit Risk in Colonial India." *The Economic History Review* 75 (2022): 396–420. This is an open access article distributed under the terms of the Creative Commons CC BY license, which permits unrestricted use, distribution, and reproduction in any medium, provided the original work is properly cited. © 2021 The Authors. The *Economic History Review* published by John Wiley & Sons Ltd on behalf of Economic History Society.
[1] Government reports typically associated the size of debt with the level of poverty. The *Tanjore District Gazette* in 1915, for example, was perplexed that cultivators in a well-off municipality were as indebted as cultivators in a poorer municipality.

credit markets based entirely on the lender's power cannot work. That account should factor in strategies to deal with risk.

The reference to geography and regionality is important. The majority of cultivation in Madras was rainfed, however, wet districts benefitted from proximity to irrigated river deltas. Private investment was low and public investment was not high enough in the dry districts, leading to little increase in acreage with access to irrigation infrastructure.[2] The problem persisted throughout the period. The dry corridor in central Madras had an abundance of low-quality red soil and remained poorly irrigated in the colonial and early post-colonial period. Increases in irrigated area during this period largely responded to canal and dam construction. When dams were built, the government designed them poorly and constructed them near fertile areas, leaving the dry districts continually water-scarce. The wet districts were not without a share of problems. Rainfall was volatile and unpredictable across the province. Data from meteorological stations suggests that droughts were common in the central corridor while waterlogging was common in the deltas. However, the risks of crop failure were higher in the dry districts than in the wet. This presents a greater set of challenges for money markets in the dry districts than those in the wet districts.

How did geographical variations impact credit supply? Client selectivity was one way for creditors to manage risk. Rich cultivators, through crop-diversification, were better-equipped to manage the risks of crop failure than the poor cultivators in the dry districts. This problem was less severe in the wet districts. Smallholders in wet districts faced a lower risk of harvest failure than the poor in dry districts. In the dry districts, creditors provided loans to the rich while the poor were excluded from participating in the credit market. In the wet districts, however, money markets were more liquid and cultivators across income categories borrowed from moneylenders. Fragmented credit markets accentuated the problem. Money rarely travelled from villages in wet districts to villages in dry districts.

The chapter's findings corroborate the contributions of development economists, which suggest that creditors selectively choose borrowers to manage the risk of lending.[3] The chapter goes further, places geography at the centre of lending barriers and suggests credit access as an avenue

---

[2] Private investment was particularly low and funded just 1.7 per cent of the irrigation construction in India. Public money financed the majority of irrigation works. See Latika Chaudhary, Bishnupriya Gupta, Tirthankar Roy, and Anand V. Swamy, *A New Economic History of Colonial India*. 1st ed. (London: Routledge, 2016) 105.

[3] Joseph E. Stiglitz and Andrew Weiss, "Credit Rationing in Markets with Imperfect Information." *The American Economic Review* 71, no. 3 (1981): 393–410, show that

connecting the environment to regional and household inequality in South India.

The chapter proceeds in three sections. The first describes agricultural features in the province and introduces the key areas of distinction between wet and dry districts. The second discusses features of the credit market in wet and dry districts. The third presents the mechanisms through which environmental factors impacted the supply of credit.

Climate and Cropping Patterns, 1920–1950

As discussed in the previous chapter, Madras contained three ecological zones with distinct climate patterns and natural landscapes: wet (irrigated), dry (rainfed and semi-arid) and mixed zones. The districts highlighted in Figure 3.1 represent each of the three zones. Ecology determined cropping patterns in each district, and regional cropping patterns persisted throughout the colonial and early post-colonial period.

Cropping patterns did not differ much between wet districts. Deltas near rivers on the west and eastern coast were blessed with alluvial soil. Rusty-red lateritic soil was commonplace in low-lying areas partially inland from deltas. Both soil types were more conducive to surface water retention than other black and red soil varieties, allowing farmers to grow rice in the deltas.[4] Tanjore, East Godavari and South Kanara were primarily rice-producing districts. Crop types did not vary much within these districts either. In nine out of eleven municipalities in Tanjore, rice occupied over 85 per cent of cultivated acreage in 1930.[5]

Farmers grew dryland millets, pulses and cotton in the dry districts, though millets were more commonly found than the other crops in these areas. Figure 3.1 shows a central corridor in the hinterland, one that included the districts furthest away from perennial rivers in the eastern and western parts of the province. Land in the central corridor was a mix of red and black soil types. Red loam, or a mix between sand and clay, was the most common soil type across the central part of the province. The soil was porous and could not cultivate crops other than millets.[6] The Cuddapah district, for example, was primarily millet-farmed with some cultivation of pulses. The northern part of the central corridor, including the Bellary district as well as districts neighbouring Bellary,

credit rationing is a commonly used method for banks to mitigate lending risk. When prices are not a good indicator of risk, client selectivity is evidence of risk management.
[4] *Techno-Economic Survey of Madras: Economic Report* (Madras, 1961), 69–75.
[5] *A Statistical Atlas of the Madras Presidency* (Madras, 1936), 749–82.
[6] *Techno-Economic Survey,* 69–75.

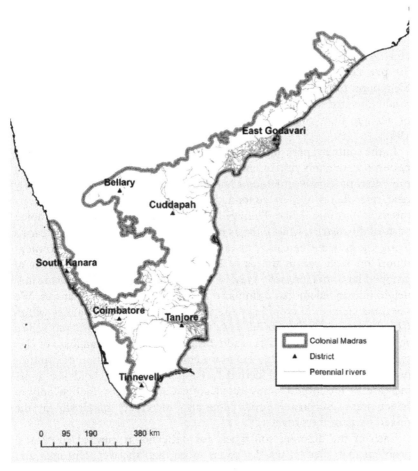

Figure 3.1 Perennial rivers in colonial Madras
Source: *Statistical Atlas*.
Notes: Each district contained between six and nine municipalities. District points were placed in the largest municipality. The author selected these districts to reflect a mix of irrigated and dry agricultural regions.

such as Kurnool and Anantapur, had a larger amount of black soil than other areas in the province, enabling some cotton cultivation in these areas.[7] Though cultivation of cash crops did see expansion from the mid-

---

[7] *India Crop Calendar* (New Delhi, 1954), 5–8.

nineteenth century, it accounted for a minority of total production by 1930. Cotton was the most widely cropped of the cash crops and was primarily grown in the drier hinterland. Yet, in seven out of eight municipalities in the Bellary district, millet cultivation occupied more than 50 per cent of total acreage. Cotton was most prominent in the Siruguppa municipality in Bellary, still only occupying 37 per cent of total cultivated acreage.[8] Dry millets continued to occupy a larger share of acreage than cotton in the dry corridor, well into the 1940s and 1950s.[9]

In the southern parts of the province, closer to the peninsula, cropping patterns were a mix of rice, millets and pulses. Each district contained a mix of crops. Some settlements had access to irrigated land, particularly near river deltas. Others contained dry soil types, not suited to water-intensive farming. Take Tinnevelly, for instance. Rice fields occupied parts of the district, while farmers in other municipalities sought to earn a living by growing cereals, pulses and sugarcane. From a government report on land use in the early 1930s, approximately 50 per cent of cropped land in Tinnevelly grew rice. Districts such as Coimbatore and neighbouring Salem had a similar mix of irrigated and dry features. We see some changes in cropping patterns across a few municipalities within Coimbatore and Salem in the early twentieth century. Sandy red soil in some parts had a looser surface and drained more easily than loam or clay textures, creating a suitable environment for the cultivation of groundnuts in the late colonial period.[10] Cash crop acreage did see some increase as groundnuts substituted cotton and millets, though only in select areas. Sugarcane production also increased marginally in the mixed parts of the province.[11]

Each of the different soil types was deficient in mineral content, a problem that affected the dry zones more than the wet. Nitrogen and

---

[8] *Statistical Atlas*, 323–60.

[9] The persistence of millets as dominant crops in the hinterland is corroborated in previous studies of the dry districts. See David A. Washbrook, "The Commercialization of Agriculture in Colonial India: Production, Subsistence and Reproduction in the 'Dry South', c. 1870–1930." *Modern Asian Studies* 28, no. 1 (1994): 129–64.

[10] *India Crop Calendar*, 5–8.

[11] G. N. Rao and D. Rajasekhar, "Commodity Production and the Changing Agrarian Scenario in Andhra: A Study in Interregional Variations, c. 1910–c. 1947." In *The South Indian Economy: Agrarian Change, Industrial Structure and State Policy c. 1914–1947*, edited by Sabyasachi Bhattacharya, Sumit Guha, Raman Mahadevan, Sakti Padhi, D. Rajasekhar, and G. N. Rao, 1–50 (Delhi: Oxford University Press, 1991), 15; K. C. Nair and A. C. Dhas, "Agricultural Change in Tamil Nadu: 1918–1955." In *The South Indian Economy: Agrarian Change, Industrial Structure and State Policy c. 1914–1947*, edited by Sabyasachi Bhattacharya, Sumit Guha, Raman Mahadevan, Sakti Padhi, D. Rajasekhar, and G. N. Rao (Delhi: Oxford University Press), 128.

phosphoric acid levels were low, leading to issues in water absorption.[12] To solve severe nutrient deficiencies, wet and dry cultivation needed a steady supply of both cattle manure and artificial fertilisers.[13] However, manure use did not change much and cultivators in Madras rarely used artificial fertilisers in the colonial and early post-colonial period.[14] The government reported some increase in manure and fertiliser use in the wet zones in the early- to mid-twentieth century.[15] Fertiliser use was lower in the dry than in the wet areas. Cash crop acreage, over-cultivation and high temperatures continued to erode nutrients in the hinterland soil.[16]

Productivity growth in the agricultural sector stagnated during the colonial and early post-colonial period. When crop output grew, this growth was usually driven by an increase in acreage cropped.[17] Baker's estimation of land yields corroborates this pattern. Yields per acre for the major crops saw some growth in the early twentieth century and then declined annually between the 1920s and the late 1940s.[18] Levels of productivity showed more regional variation, differing by crop type. Rice cultivation outperformed millet and cotton in monetary terms.[19] Per acre, rice crops fetched higher earnings than cotton and millet crops.[20] Sugarcane cultivation accrued the highest growth in yields. However, sugarcane was cultivated in a small area of the central province and the high yields, therefore, benefitted a marginal share of the rural population.[21]

Rice farming in the deltas was more labour and capital intensive than cereal cultivation in the dry districts. Delta municipalities reported an average population per cropped acre of between one and three. In contrast, there was, on average, less than one person per cultivated acre in hinterland municipalities in 1930.[22] Population per cropped acre within municipalities in the East Godavari district ranged from 1.65 to

[12] *Techno-Economic Survey*, 69–75.

[13] For a discussion on the use of organic fertilizers in indigo farms in Bengal, see Prakash Kumar, *Indigo Plantations and Science in Colonial India* (Cambridge: Cambridge University Press, 2012). According to, Srabani Sen, "Scientific Enquiry in Agriculture in Colonial India: A Historical Perspective." *Indian Journal of History of Science* 45 no. 2 (2010): 199–239, natural fertiliser did not provide enough nitrogen to deficient soils and imports of artificial fertiliser was low in the colonial period.

[14] Christopher Baker, *An Indian Rural Economy 1880–1955: The Tamilnad Countryside* (Oxford: Oxford University Press, 1984), 513–14.

[15] Haruka Yanagisawa, "Elements of Upward Mobility for Agricultural Labourers in Tamil Districts, 1865–1925." In *Local Agrarian Societies in Colonial India: Japanese Perspectives*, edited by Kaoru Sugihara, Haruka Yanagisawa, and Peter Robb, 199–238 (Surrey: Curzon Press, 1996), 205–8.

[16] Baker, *An Indian Rural Economy*, 513. [17] *Techno-Economic Survey*, 81–82.

[18] Baker, *An Indian Rural Economy*, 508. [19] *Techno-Economic Survey*, 80.

[20] *Agricultural Statistics of India* (Delhi, 1951).

[21] Nair and Dhas, "Agricultural Change in Tamil Nadu," 130–32. [22] *Statistical Atlas.*

2.43. In contrast, the same measure of population density in Bellary municipalities ranged from 0.28 to 0.65.[23] Rice cultivators regularly invested in purchasing livestock and running ploughs. In areas with cereal cultivation, on the other hand, working and breeding cattle, as well as ploughs per capita, were much lower. The quality of cattle was also higher in the wet zones than in the dry zones. Working cattle in Tanjore, for example, were better-fed than the working cattle in the hinterland.[24] Some areas in the hinterland reported large numbers of livestock, however, farmers in the hinterland did not commonly use working cattle in the cultivation process. Breeders reared livestock and hosted weekly cattle markets in some central municipalities, the Palmaner municipality in the Chittoor district for example. Cattle were either bred in these municipalities or brought to them by breeders in neighbouring regions to sell to the farmers primarily based in the deltas. Data also shows that carts per capita were higher in the rice-growing municipalities than in the dry municipalities.[25]

Land under rice cultivation was more valuable than other land types. The government collected more than 2 rupees per person in land revenue from landholders in delta districts. The corresponding figure for the hinterland was below 1 rupee in 1930.[26] From a survey in 1930, the average value per acre of land in the Shiyali municipality in the Tanjore district was around 800 rupees as compared to an average value of approximately 60 rupees in the Adoni municipality in the Bellary district. Other indicators of economic development in Adoni and Shiyali highlight regional disparity in development outcomes. In Adoni, millets and cotton occupied 52 and 23 per cent of cultivated acreage, there were 0.4 people and 0.02 ploughs per acre, and the municipality collected 0.64 rupees per acre in land revenue. In Shiyali, rice occupied 95 per cent of cultivated acreage, there were 1.2 people and 0.1 ploughs per acre, and the municipality collected 3.5 rupees per acre in land revenue.[27] The chapter will return to comparisons of Adoni and Shiyali municipalities when discussing regional variations in credit supply.

Land value increased proportionally to water access. Inequality in water access between the richer wet and poorer dry districts widened during British rule.[28] The government constructed dams, canals and

---

[23] *Statistical Atlas*, 125–70, 323–60.

[24] In this context, working cattle refers to bullocks and buffaloes while breeding stock refers to cows, young bulls, she-buffaloes and young buffaloes. Yanagisawa, "Elements of Upward Mobility," 208.

[25] *Statistical Atlas*.   [26] *Statistical Atlas*.   [27] *Statistical Atlas*, 323–60, 749–82.

[28] Prasannan Parthasarathi, "Water and Agriculture in Nineteenth-Century Tamilnad." *Modern Asian Studies* 51, no. 2 (03, 2017): 485–510, 487.

channels near the river deltas, while replacing tanks, that were poorly maintained in the pre-colonial period, with wells in the south-central districts.[29] In the process, water access increased substantially in the wet districts, partially in the mixed districts and insignificantly in the driest districts. Financial constraints, modernisation agendas and political conflicts explain the distribution of irrigation infrastructure in Madras.

The colonial government struggled to raise enough capital to invest in irrigation projects. When serious discussion around irrigation began in the mid-nineteenth century, the government first tried to encourage private British firms to invest in the construction of large irrigation projects in Madras.[30] This attempt failed as the government could not convince firms that they would see sufficiently high returns from investments in rural India. The government undertook the responsibility to invest in irrigation projects but raised little funding in London capital markets. The government relied on local revenue collection to finance irrigation projects. It extended large projects, including canals and dams, in higher revenue-earning areas, the districts near river deltas in particular.[31] The Upper Anicut, constructed in the nineteenth century, and the Mettur Dam, constructed in the 1930s, were examples of the dams and channels that distributed water from the Coleroon and Cauvery rivers to the deltas in Tanjore. The Cauvery-Mettur project, initiated by the colonial government in 1934, included the construction of a 70-mile canal, which carried water from the Cauvery River to the plains, an artificial reservoir of 59 square miles to hold channelled water and a dam to prevent flooding. *The New York Times* praised the government in Madras for constructing the 'largest masonry dam in the world' and for extending '301,000 acres of new irrigation to the existing 1,000,000 acres of delta land'.[32] The project irrigated rice cultivation primarily in the western parts of the Tanjore and South Arcot districts.

The regional allocation of smaller infrastructure projects, including tanks and wells, further highlights the government's desire to modernise

---

[29] Yanagisawa, "Elements of Upward Mobility," 202; David Mosse, "Colonial and Contemporary Ideologies of 'Community Management': The Case of Tank Irrigation Development in South India." *Modern Asian Studies* 33 (1999): 306–8; Parthasarathi, "Water and Agriculture," 504–8; Aditya Ramesh, "The Value of Tanks: Maintenance, Ecology and the Colonial Economy in Nineteenth-century South India." *Water History* 10, no. 4 (2018): 267–89, 268–69; Velayutham Saravanan, *Water and the Environmental History of Modern India* (London: Bloomsbury Academic, 2020), 37.

[30] Aditya Ramesh, "Indian Rivers, 'Productive Works', and the Emergence of Large Dams in Nineteenth-Century Madras." *The Historical Journal* 64, no. 2 (2020): 1–29, 5–8.

[31] Ramesh, "Indian Rivers"; Saravanan, *Water and the Environmental History*, 38.

[32] "Big Irrigation Job under way in India." *The New York Times*, 30 June 1930.

productive areas.[33] The government built new wells and replaced old tanks in the mixed areas, with targeted investments in Coimbatore and Salem during the nineteenth century. By 1900, there were 502 wells in the Coimbatore district, almost one-quarter of total wells in all the Tamilnad districts.[34] The focus on the mixed districts continued in the 1950s, a decade during which the post-colonial government invested in extending canals from the Cauvery and Noyyal rivers to the Coimbatore and Erode districts.[35] Irrigation projects, both large and small, in the driest districts, such as Bellary, remained limited throughout the period.[36]

Political conflicts over water resources added an additional barrier to the extension of canals and dams. In the colonial period, the Cauvery River ran through the Mysore Princely State and the Madras Presidency. Governments of both provinces signed treaties in 1892 and 1924 on the sharing of water from the river. Governments legally challenged the construction of canals if they deemed the canal to violate the treaties' terms by diverting shared water away from either province.[37] Courts had the power to halt the construction of disputed canals.

Data from official agricultural reports shows that irrigation infrastructure was concentrated in few regions. According to an official survey, 50 out of 241 municipalities reported a ratio of irrigated to cultivated land above 50 per cent. In 80 per cent of municipalities, the majority of cultivated land was unirrigated in 1930.[38] This trend did not change during the colonial and early post-colonial period. The average ratio of irrigated to cropped land increased marginally for the majority of the province. When irrigation investment increased, it did so in naturally irrigated areas, such as the deltas in the Tanjore district. Following the construction of the Mettur Dam, as illustrated in Table 3.1, the ratio of irrigated land to net cultivated land increased in the Tanjore district between 1931 and 1951. Similarly, government reports suggest that land was fertile and well irrigated, due to proximity to river deltas and high investment in the regions near the western coast. Land in the western districts was conducive to rice cultivation as well as the cultivation of non-food crops such as coconut and rubber. Dismissing the possibility of

---

[33] Ramesh, "The Value of Tanks"; Ramesh, "Indian Rivers."
[34] Parthasarathi, "Water and Agriculture," 497.
[35] Saravanan, *Water and the Environmental History*, 148.
[36] Parthasarathi, "Water and Agriculture," 497.
[37] Velayutham Saravanan, "Technological Transformation and Water Conflicts in the Bhavani River Basin of Tamil Nadu, 1930–1970." *Environment and History* 7, no. 3 (2001): 289–334; *Report of the Cauvery Water Disputes Tribunal Volume II: Agreements of 1892 and 1924* (New Delhi, 2007).
[38] *Statistical Atlas.*

Table 3.1 *Ratio of irrigated area to cropped area, 1921–1951*

Region	1921	1931	1941	1951
Madras	0.27	0.26	0.27	0.31
Tanjore	0.74	0.74	0.80	0.85
Cuddapah	0.21	0.21	0.21	0.23
Bellary	0.02	0.02	0.02	0.03

Source: *Census of India*, 103–5.
Notes: Calculations made by the author.

drought in the South Kanara district, the government reported, 'Famine is unknown and the district produces more food grain than is required.'[39]

Rainfall was volatile and agricultural output growth was sensitive to fluctuations in rainfall. The British-ruled government invested in meteorology from the late nineteenth century. Frequent droughts and famines persuaded government officials to record weather patterns across colonial India.[40] By 1930, most municipalities had their own meteorology stations, recording daily rainfall patterns. Analysing average annual rainfall over a sixty-year period, Figure 3.2 illustrates regional variation in climate patterns across municipalities. Delta areas received significantly higher annual rainfall than the hinterland. Data from eleven meteorological stations in Tanjore shows that the district received about 45 inches of rainfall in an average year. In contrast, an average year in the Cuddapah district received 27 inches of rainfall. As an example of dry and poorly developed district in colonial Madras, Bellary received an average annual rainfall of 23 inches.[41] In a bad year, the driest municipality in Bellary recorded as low as 5–6 inches of rainfall in a twelve-month period. In contrast, the driest municipality in Tanjore received 18–20 inches in a bad year. On the dry central corridor, the Census reported in 1951 that,

The main area liable to periodical famines in Madras State comprises the whole of Anantapur district the eastern taluks of Bellary district and the western taluks of Kurnool district adjoining Bellary district. Inadequate and ill-distributed rainfall in both the monsoons and consequent failure of crops are of frequent occurrence in this area.[42]

---

[39] *Statistical Atlas*, 13.
[40] Sunil Amrith, "Risk and the South Asian Monsoon." *Climatic Change* 151, no. 1 (2018): 17–28, 19.
[41] *Statistical Atlas*, 323–60, 407–42, 749–82.
[42] *Census of India Vol. III: Madras and Coorg*. Part I (Madras, 1951), 8. Hereafter source referred to as *Census of India*.

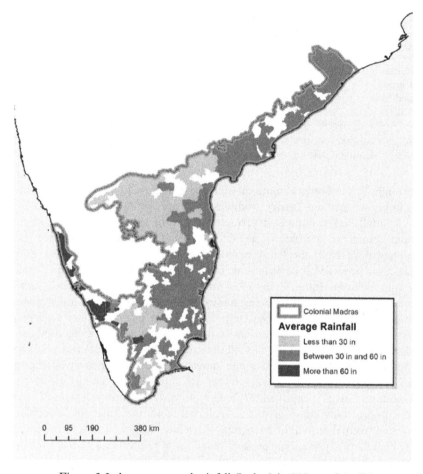

Figure 3.2 Average annual rainfall (inches) in 208 municipalities, 1870–1930

Source: *Statistical Atlas.*

Notes: The British government set up meteorological stations in most municipalities from the late nineteenth century. In most cases, the source calculates average annual rainfall from 1870 to 1930. In a minority of cases, meteorological stations were established later and the source calculates the average from the start of the station to 1930. In a handful of municipalities, the meteorological stations were only fifteen years old by 1930. For example, a meteorological station was created in the Pamarru municipality in the Kistna district in 1915. The data for this municipality is based on a fifteen-year average. The author uses data from the nearest meteorological station when municipalities did not have one of their own.

Rainfall was seasonal and concentrated in short spells. Colonial India received two seasonal monsoons. The south-west or summer monsoon ran from approximately June to September, and the north-east or winter monsoon ran from approximately October to December. As such, cultivation in rural Madras was also seasonal. Rice farmers generally farmed in one cycle, sowing in June, transplanting in October and harvesting in December. In good years, some millet farmers managed to harvest two sets of crops during the year. Crops were sown in June for harvest in October and sown in September for harvest in January. Crops sown before and harvested after the south-west monsoon were referred to as the *kharif* crop. Crops sown before and harvested after the north-east monsoon were referred to as the *rabi* crop. Outside the monsoon, the temperature was too hot and rain too scarce to nurture crop growth.

Farming in the majority of colonial Madras relied heavily on the north-east monsoon.[43] The delta districts, in the north of the province, in particular, got a 'fairly distributed rainfall from both monsoons'.[44] However, for the majority of central districts, annual yields were unpredictable and relied on rainfall patterns in a concentrated three-month period, between September and November each year. For many farmers in the driest parts of Bellary, few inches of rainfall spread over three months was the only water supply in bad years. In these circumstances, failure or delay in the monsoon led to crop failure. Smallholders and tenants in dry zones were constantly vulnerable to famine.

Colonial administrators spent little public money on improving land yields in the driest parts of the province despite being aware of the challenges faced by poor farmers in these regions. Describing the status of cultivators in Bellary, one government-employed district surveyor commented in 1915 that the ability for the average farmer to live above subsistence level in Bellary depended, 'on the rains of June and July'. One failed monsoon threatened the livelihoods of farmers and in the event of two successive monsoons failing, the surveyor claimed, 'cattle die in thousands', and the farmer, 'hardly emerges from one famine before he is submerged under another'.[45] As long as land was vulnerable to seasonal shocks, supply-side disruptions in crop production remained. In bad years, the government set up famine camps and provided food

---

[43] *Census of India*, 95. Areas on the western coast benefitted from the south-west monsoon. However, the majority of cultivation in the province took place on the eastern section.

[44] *Techno-Economic Survey*, 72.

[45] *Madras District Gazetteers: Bellary*. Part I (Madras, 1915), 101. Hereafter, source referred to as *District Gazetteers: Bellary*.

entitlements to the poor in vulnerable districts. Welfare initiatives, how-ever, were small-scale and did not stop mass starvation in years of harvest failure.

Provincial policymakers took a more interventionist stance in the production process when food shortages were widespread in the late 1930s and early 1940s. The government reported that food shortages occurred because population growth had outstripped millet and rice production and the war disrupted food imports. To investigate possible solutions to food shortage, the government increased funding into agri-cultural science research in the late 1930s and launched the Grow More Food campaign in the early 1940s. Through state-sponsored research on improving inputs into production, the government hoped to improve yields of the major food crops. The provincial government tried to increase the use of new seed varieties, manure and artificial fertiliser. In rare cases, the government issued small loans to farmers, conditional on the purchase of fertiliser. However, output and productivity growth remained low. The uptake of new seed types and artificial fertilisers was low, especially among smallholders. When new seeds were deployed, they were deployed by few large landholders. Yields for the major crops, therefore, remained unchanged. Farmers across the province faced soil erosion. Farmers in dry regions remained much worse off as they relied on seasonally low and volatile rainfall. Millet yields on irrigated farms declined by 30 per cent and millet yields on rainfed farms halved between the early 1930s and mid-1940s.[46] Research initiatives were carried for-ward by the state government in the 1950s, though had little impact on incomes earned by peasants.

In short, rainfed cultivation in tropical climate created a fragile agri-culture industry in colonial and post-colonial Madras. Evidence on yields, land prices and population density suggests that farmers in the wet districts were better off than those in the hinterland, and this regional disparity persisted throughout the colonial period. Attempts were made to manage water access in the naturally irrigated parts of the region, continually ignoring the dry areas. Water scarcity, poor soil quality and insufficient irrigation facilities led to a high likelihood of crop failure in a large part of the province. Public investment did little to solve the problem. Private investment in land improvement could have seen high returns for farmers and positive development outcomes, especially in dry areas. However, as we will see in the rest of the chapter, credit supply was stunted and selective, especially in the dry areas.

---

[46] Baker, *An Indian Rural Economy*, 505–15.

Credit Supply in Rural Madras

Credit was a required input in South India. Savings were too low to fund private investment in rural areas.[47] Farmers, especially smallholders and tenants in the dry regions, relied on credit to carry out production. Interviews of district government officials, narrated in famine reports, recorded that smallholders needed credit to either build new wells and tanks or improve dilapidated ones. Peasants also needed credit to purchase or rent land, cattle and ploughs.[48] Credit, however, was in short supply in the famine-prone regions. Lack of water access and poor-quality inputs, combined with low levels of private investment, suggest that supply did not match demand for credit in the dry regions. In a survey of credit markets across select villages in the late 1920s, loans were classified according to purpose of borrowing. Debts accrued to purchase land, improve the quality of land and construct on land amounted to a small sum of 2 rupees per occupied acre in Bellary. In contrast, debtors borrowed 50 rupees per occupied acre to service these expenses in the three villages surveyed in Tanjore.[49] Investments to improve land yields were hindered by supply constraints in dry regions, while credit demand was more easily serviced in the wet districts.

When the demand for credit was met, it was met by moneylenders. Commercial banks and regulated forms of finance did not supply credit in rural areas. Corporate, joint-stock and indigenous banks operated in cities but not in villages. Cooperative banks provided some credit but only captured a small share of the rural market. The colonial government tried to expand credit supply by providing welfare loans, termed *takkavi* loans, from the late nineteenth century. The government's initiative was unsuccessful. Narrow coverage and small loans limited the scope of the project. An official report estimated that moneylenders captured 93 per cent, cooperatives six per cent and government welfare loans 1 per cent of total market share in 1935.[50]

Different types of moneylenders operated in colonial India. From the mid-nineteenth century, urban traders and merchant bankers operated

---

[47] Raymond W. Goldsmith, *The Financial Development of India, 1860–1977* (New Haven, CT and London: Yale University Press, 1983).
[48] *Report of the Famine Code Revision Committee.* Vols. I, II (Madras, 1938).
[49] *Madras Provincial Banking Enquiry Committee Report.* Vols. I–V (Madras, 1930), 60–70. The source classifies borrowing by purpose. Debts accrued to finance the purchase of land, improvements to land and construction on land amounted to 51,714 rupees in five villages in Bellary and 103,200 rupees in three villages in Tanjore. The recorded occupied area was 21,916 acres in Bellary and 2,046 acres in Tanjore.
[50] W. R. S. Sathyanathan, *Report on Agricultural Indebtedness* (Madras, 1935) 40.

rural lending businesses, providing credit to some farmers growing cash crops in Bombay and Punjab.[51] In most districts, however, farmers themselves controlled the supply of credit. Rural households with disposable income provided loans to other households in the same village. Colonial officials referred to the merchant bankers as 'professional moneylenders' and farmer cum creditors as 'agriculturist moneylenders'. They differed by their primary occupation. Whereas moneylending was the primary occupation of professional moneylenders, agriculturist lenders primarily cultivated land and provided credit if they had money to lend. The Provincial Banking Enquiry Committee commented in 1930 that 'the major part' of rural moneylending in Madras was 'from one *ryot* [peasant farmer] to another' and that professional moneylending was rare in the rural districts.[52]

Professional moneylenders existed, however, were reluctant to lend to farmers in Madras. The *Nattukottai Chettiars* had vast credit operations, running banking houses across the province. They provided credit to export businesses and urban industries in South India, as well as rubber plantations in Burma and Malaya. Similarly, banking businesses run by the *Kallidaikurchi Brahmins* were headquartered in urban centres around the southern districts of Tinnevelly, Ramnad and Madura, though scarcely lent to farmers in South India. They also provided large sums of credit to plantations in Malaya instead.[53]

As shown in Table 3.2, agriculturist moneylenders dominated the supply of credit in villages. A government report in 1935 classified village moneylenders according to their profession. The survey finds that lenders cum cultivators were more common in rural credit markets than merchant banking houses. Over three-quarters of moneylenders were agriculturists in 114 out of 141 surveyed villages in 1935. The only exception to this rule was the Nellore district where, in the two villages surveyed, 58 professional moneylenders competed with 29 agriculturist moneylenders.

Agriculturist moneylenders had some benefits over professional moneylenders. Information costs were low when lenders and borrowers belonged to the same profession and the same village. Lenders did not

---

[51] Gujarati and Marwari lending businesses entered the rural market in some cotton- and wheat-growing areas of Bombay and Punjab from around 1860. According to Guha, indigenous banking houses in Bombay, such as the Marwari traders, operated credit businesses with branches in the cities and agents deploying money in rural areas Darling, writing in the 1930s, further sub-categorised professional moneylenders in Punjab by sub-castes of trading communities, including the Bania, Arora and Khatri lenders. Malcolm Darling, *The Punjab Peasant in Prosperity and Debt*. 4th ed. (Bombay: Oxford University Press, 1947); Sumit Guha, "Commodity and Credit in Upland Maharashtra, 1800–1950." *Economic and Political Weekly* 22, no. 52 (1987): A126–40.

[52] *Provincial Banking Enquiry*, 220.   [53] *Provincial Banking Enquiry*, 30.

Table 3.2 *Moneylenders in 141 villages, 1935*

Village Type	Villages (1)	Agriculturist Lenders (2)	Total Lenders (3)	Ratio (2) to (3)	Ratio (2) to (1)
Mostly Wet	73	1,184	1,357	0.87	16.22
Mostly Dry	66	1,245	1,436	0.87	18.86

Source: *Report on Agricultural Indebtedness.*
Notes: Data extracted from a survey of 141 villages in Madras. Village data aggregated to district level in the source. The government surveyed between 1 and 16 villages in each of the 25 districts. The source does not provide names of the villages. The distinction between 'Mostly Wet' and 'Mostly Dry' is made by the author. Mostly Wet villages are in the districts where the majority of cultivated acreage produced rice. The opposite is the case in the Mostly Dry villages. Mostly Wet districts include Ganjam, East and West Godavari, Kistna, Nellore, Chingleput, South Arcot, Tanjore, Ramnad, Tinnevelly, Malabar and South Kanara. Mostly Dry districts include Guntur, Vizagapatam, Chittoor, Salem, Coimbatore, Trichinopoly, Madura, Kurnool, Bellary, Anantapur, and Cuddapah. Total Lenders measures the number of agriculturists and professional moneylenders in the villages. Calculations made by author.

have to travel far to monitor the peasants they were lending to. As such, borrowers could not wilfully default on loans. One official in the Ganjam district crudely summarised the information advantages posed by the agriculturist moneylender, suggesting that the lender could 'catch hold of his client in the right time to recover his money'.[54]

Counting the number of moneylenders in villages would suggest that rural credit markets were competitive in colonial Madras. Large land-owners did lend money, as did smaller landowners and tenants with disposable income. Government-employed village surveyors were surprised to find in the late 1920s that, 'there are moneylenders everywhere', a feature of village credit markets that continued into the 1930s.[55] As illustrated in Table 3.2, 2,429 agriculturist moneylenders operated in 141 surveyed villages in 1935. There was some variation between districts. There were fewer lenders per village in wet districts when compared to villages in dry districts. This figure was driven by select villages. For example, there were about four moneylenders per village, across five surveyed villages, in South Kanara and only two lenders per village in the eight villages in Tanjore. Market structure differed in other wet districts. There were seventeen agriculturist moneylenders in the one village

---

[54] Reported by the Sub-deputy Registrar of the Ganjam district to the Provincial Banking Enquiry Committee in 1929. *Provincial Banking Enquiry*, 1088.
[55] *Provincial Banking Enquiry*, 220.

surveyed in the East Godavari district and approximately fifty-two lenders per village in eight villages in the Tinnevelly district. In the dry districts, markets in Bellary were more concentrated than others. There were approximately four lenders per village in the two surveyed villages in Bellary. In the majority of other dry districts, there were between twenty and thirty lenders per village.[56] The number of moneylenders per village, however, does not imply that money was easily accessible.

Financial linkages between urban and rural areas were weak. In few cases, moneylenders accessed loans from indigenous banking houses, borrowing from merchant bankers at a lower price than the prices charged on loans to rural peasants. Indeed, when this system operated in Madras, evidence suggests that village moneylenders borrowed, 'at 8 to 12 per cent' from urban bankers and credited this money to poor peasants at higher prices.[57] Evidence also suggests that petty traders in villages, such as shopkeepers, at times borrowed from indigenous banking houses in cities and circulated these loans to farmers. Shopkeepers borrowed at a lower cost from bankers than cultivators did on the rural credit market. In practice, however, rural lenders rarely borrowed from urban credit businesses. Money did not flow easily from city bankers to peasants. The farmers cum moneylenders in Madras relied almost entirely on their disposable income to lend to peasants. As the Provincial Banking Enquiry Committee reported in the late 1920s, 'the ryot moneylender does his business almost entirely on his own capital'.[58]

Disposable income was the requirement to lend but was easily constrained in rural Madras. Wealthy landowners with savings allocated a part of this disposable income to moneylending. Less wealthy farmers allocated profits made in year n to the credit market in year $n + 1$.[59] Creditors may have also been borrowers in the same year or borrowers in one year and creditors in the next. Borrowers and lenders were not necessarily distinct agents in the credit market. Indeed, the colonial government reported that a cultivator cum moneylender 'may borrow for his own needs during the cultivating season'.[60] This feature created a distinctive risk structure. Crop failures simultaneously bankrupted borrowers and constrained the supply of money. Cultivators without profit in year n both defaulted on loans and restricted the availability of credit in year $n + 1$. Professional moneylenders could diversify their lending

[56] *Report on Agricultural Indebtedness.*   [57] *Provincial Banking Enquiry*, 219.
[58] *Provincial Banking Enquiry*, 220.
[59] P. G. K. Panikar, *Rural Savings in India* (Bombay: Somaiya Publications, 1970), shows that this trend persisted in the early post-colonial period.
[60] *Provincial Banking Enquiry*, 220.

portfolio. When borrowers and lenders were both agriculturists, there was much greater likelihood of contagion, and an inability for lenders to absorb risks easily. Crop failure impacted all parties, and losses passed on from party to party more quickly. In other words, fragility in the agricultural sector reinforced credit and investment constraints in localised village credit markets. Farmers recycled money within villages, but this led to liquidity constraints following harvest failure.

The credit market operated seasonally in South India. Money was easier to borrow in some months than others. Monsoons were biannual, with cycles of cultivation operating around the timing of rainfall. The demand for credit was high in the autumn, while the demand for repayment was expected at the end of the harvest when commodities were to be traded.[61] Moneylenders in rural villages commonly provided loans on a short-term basis of four to six months.[62] Lenders provided loans in monthly instalments, matching changing input requirements during the production cycle. Cultivators borrowed in one month to cover the costs of fertiliser while borrowing in another to finance the renting of cattle.[63] Lenders charged monthly rather than annual interest rates. With the credit market operating on such short-term arrangements, credit supply changed seasonally.[64] The market was liquid after good harvests and noticeably constrained after bad seasons.

The government considered crop insurance initiatives to help farmers manage the risks posed by climate volatility, however, did not install an insurance scheme in the colonial and early post-colonial period. In the decade between 1938 and 1948, the monsoon failed three times. The provincial government marked cycles in 1938–39, 1945–46 and 1947–48 as 'bad years' with a more serious famine in the winter of 1945.[65] The contention with the possibility of insuring crops was always the extraordinary indemnity costs, given the frequency of failed harvests.[66]

It is unsurprising then that default rates were high in colonial Madras. According to the Banking Enquiry's survey of seventy-six villages in the

---

[61] Tirthankar Roy, "The Monsoon and the Market for Money in Late-colonial India." *Enterprise & Society* 17, no. 2 (2016): 324–57, 15–20.
[62] C. F. Strickland, "Cooperation and the Rural Problem of India." *The Quarterly Journal of Economics* 43, no. 3 (1929): 500–31, 510.
[63] *Provincial Banking Enquiry*, 86–88.   [64] *Provincial Banking Enquiry*, 221.
[65] *A Scheme of Crop Insurance for the Province of Madras* (Madras, 1949), 9.
[66] For barriers to designing crop insurance schemes in colonial and contemporary India, see V. M. Dandekar, "Crop Insurance in India." *Economic and Political Weekly* 11, no. 26 (1976): A61–80; Pramod Kumar Mishra, *Agricultural Risk, Insurance and Income: A Study of the Impact and Design of India's Comprehensive Crop Insurance Scheme* (Aldershot: Avebury, 1996); Reshmy Nair, "Crop Insurance in India: Changes and Challenges." *Economic and Political Weekly* 45, no. 6 (2010): 19–22.

late 1920s, creditors provided 37 per cent of total loans for the repayment of prior debts. As illustrated in Table 3.2, 2.2 million rupees out of the total 5.9 million rupees credited to borrowers went towards servicing previously defaulted debts in all the villages surveyed. The problem was not unique to the year this data was collected. The Banking Enquiry reported on credit markets in the 1928–29 season, prior to the commodity price crash in the early 1930s.[67] Prices declined from the previous year but not enough to cause structural changes in default rates.[68] Moreover, high default rates was a systematic concern in the rural credit market due to the frequency of crop failure. Naidu and Vaidyanathan, writing in a period of rising commodity prices in the late 1930s, stated that 'the root cause of the indebtedness of the Indian peasant is the insufficiency of his income which is the result of uneconomic holdings, lack of attention to improved methods of cultivation, manuring, irrigation or the introduction of seasonal crops … and the frequent failure of crops due to bad seasons'.[69]

If, as noted by Naidu and Vaidyanathan, seasonal uncertainty and the weak fundamentals of the agricultural system were the root cause of high default rates, then results from the Banking Enquiry's survey of default rates in 1929 present a regional puzzle. As shown in Table 3.3, default rates were higher in villages located in wet districts when compared with those in dry districts. A larger percentage of loans in the wet villages went towards servicing previous defaults than in the dry villages. The villages recorded in the Bellary district were located in the Adoni municipality. The area contained, 'a light black soil' and was 'at the mercy of deficient monsoons'.[70] Yet, each of the three villages in this region reported ratios of debt servicing to new loans of under 20 per cent in 1929. In contrast, the Gollapallam village in the Coconada municipality in the East Godavari district recorded that 90 per cent of new loans went towards debt servicing. The municipality was optimally located and contained fertile soils by the Godavari River delta. The Tanjore district did show

[67] The impact of the Depression on the credit market is discussed in Chapter 4.

[68] Michelle McAlpin, "Price Movements and Fluctuations in Economic Activity (1860–1947)." In *The Cambridge Economic History of India*, edited by Dharma Kumar and Meghnad Desai, 2: 878–904 (Cambridge: Cambridge University Press, 1983).

[69] Bijayeti Venkata Narayanaswami Naidu and P. Vaidyanathan, *The Madras Agriculturists' Relief Act: A Study* (Annamalainagar: Annamalai University, 1939), 2; B. V. Narayanaswamy Naidu was a barrister and economist. Following his call to the Bar in 1929, Naidu was appointed Professor of Economics at Annamalai University in 1930. In 1939, the university promoted Naidu to Vice Chancellor. In the 1937 election, Naidu won enough votes to secure a place in the Madras Legislative Assembly. The book will return to Naidu's views on credit in subsequent chapters.

[70] *District Gazetteers: Bellary*, 84–92.

Table 3.3 *Default rates in seventy-six villages, 1929*

Village Type	Villages	Total Borrowing (rupees)	Prior Debts (rupees)	Default Servicing (per cent)
Mostly Wet	33	2,987,151	1,199,589	40
Mostly Dry	43	2,885,445	975,327	34
Total	76	5,843,836	2,157,918	37

Source: *Provincial Banking Enquiry*, 56–75.
Notes: Data extracted from a survey of seventy-six villages in 1929. The grouping of Mostly Wet and Mostly Dry villages was conducted in the same format as Table 3.2. Prior Debts refer to the amount borrowed to repay defaulted loans. Default Servicing measures the percentage of loans, relative to total lending in the village, provided to repay defaulted loans. Ratios calculated by the author.

lower default rates on average. However, one village reported prior debt servicing rates above 40 per cent, which was higher than the rates in Bellary. A particularly puzzling finding as the village surveyed in Tanjore was located in the Shiyali municipality, a fertile location near the Cauvery River.

Why were default rates lower in dry villages than in wet villages? One suggestion focuses on the purpose of borrowing, that peasants in wet regions borrowed for consumption purposes and did not invest expensive debt in productive, income-generating businesses. The view that peasants borrowed recklessly was popular among colonial administrators across rural India. Writing on credit in 1920s Punjab, Malcolm Darling believed that borrowers spent high-priced credit on expensive ceremonies after which the small-scale nature of their farming businesses forced them to default on loans.[71] In Darling's view, lenders could exploit borrowers because peasants were illiterate and unthrifty. Other colonial administrators echoed Darling's findings on rural India's non-enterprising culture, suggesting that thrift, wayward spending and, in some cases, indolence among peasants explain high default rates, low

[71] Darling, *The Punjab Peasant in Prosperity and Debt*. Malcolm Lyall Darling, educated at Kings College Cambridge, joined the Indian Civil Service in 1904. Darling spent most of his civil service tenure working on rural finance policies in the Punjab province. Darling held influential positions as the Registrar of Cooperatives between 1927 and 1930, as well as Chairman of the Punjab Land Revenue Board between 1938 and his retirement in 1940. Darling's book differed from other colonial accounts as it argued that indebtedness in itself was not bad for the rural economy. Peasants, according to Darling, need to borrow to be prosperous. This book is widely cited by contemporary scholars working on the topic.

Table 3.4 *Credit composition in seventy-six villages, 1929*

Village Type	Villages	Fresh Lending (rupees)	Ceremonies (per cent)	Working Capital (per cent)
Mostly Wet	33	1,787,562	15	45
Mostly Dry	43	1,910,118	16	57
Tanjore	3	206,500	16	28
Bellary	6	354,802	24	36

Source: *Provincial Banking Enquiry*, 56–75.
Notes: The distinction of Mostly Wet and Mostly Dry follows the same format as Table 3.2. The Banking Enquiry Committee estimated the total value of loans provided in each village. This was categorised by purpose of borrowing. Fresh Lending is the total lending minus the lending for the repayment of prior debts. Ceremonies is the ratio of lending for marriage and ceremonial expenditure to total lending. Tax Payments is the ratio of lending for the payment of old land tax bills to total lending. Working capital includes borrowing for cultivation expenses, trade expenses and expenses for land improvements. The table excludes credit for large capital expenses including land purchase, construction and education.

investment and weak rural development. In an interview with the *Times of India*, Francis Skrine suggested that 'thrift, however, is not a characteristic of the Dacca peasant, any more than it is of his brethren elsewhere, and all his surplus and sometimes a great deal more, is absorbed, as a general rule, by his fatal passion for costly ceremonials'.[72] The interview was published in 1893, in an article provocatively titled, 'India's "Dumb Millions"'.

In practice, data from the Provincial Banking Enquiry shows that the majority of peasants in Madras borrowed not to consume but to invest in agricultural production. As recorded in Table 3.4, lending for ceremonial expenses, as a ratio of total fresh lending, accounted for 15 per cent in wet villages and 16 per cent in dry villages. The majority of credit provided went towards servicing working capital expenses and large capital investments, including land purchase and education. Borrowing patterns in Tanjore and Bellary corroborate this assessment. The ratio of consumption to total credit, in this case the ratio of ceremonial to total lending, was 16 per cent in Tanjore and 24 per cent in Bellary. Working capital credit exceeded consumption credit in both regions. More puzzling, consumption debt was higher, but default rates were lower, in

[72] India's "Dumb Millions." *The Times of India*, 23 January 1893. Francis Henry Skrine joined the Indian Civil Service in 1868. Skrine joined commissions to support famine relief in Bihar and Madras in the 1870s. Skrine spent the 1890s in the customs revenue department in Calcutta prior to retiring in 1897.

Bellary than in Tanjore. Credit for large capital investments was higher in Tanjore than in Bellary. Credit for the purchase of land accounted for 34 per cent of total lending in the three villages surveyed in Tanjore.[73]

Perhaps the cause of high default rates was credit prices. It is plausible to suggest that interest rates were higher in the wet villages than the dry villages. Borrowers were defaulting on loans due to their inability to repay expensive credit in the wet villages. However, it is also plausible to suggest the opposite, that if rice-growing regions were likely to have a more stable season than dry ones, this should reflect in lower price of credit. As a result, one would expect loans in wet regions to have been cheaper than loans in dry regions owing to the lower likelihood of crop failure.

In practice, the evidence shows that neither assumption held true. There was little district-level variation in the price of credit. Lenders provided loans seasonally and charged interest on these loans at monthly intervals.[74] According to the Banking Enquiry, annualised interest rates varied between 12 and 24 per cent, and this variation existed across most districts. Indeed, the report suggests that interest rates varied between 9 and 24 per cent in villages within the wet Tanjore district and between 12 and 24 per cent in the villages within the dry Bellary district. A survey of the Bellary district noted that money rates varied 'from 1 to 2.5 per cent *per mensem*'.[75] In the Tanjore District Gazetteer, the surveyor reported that interest rates 'never seem to fall below ten and in some cases rises as high as 24 per cent'.[76] According to the District Gazetteer of the Godavari district, a primarily rice-growing region, 'the rates of interest on loans are much as the same as usual, 12–24 per cent being common'.[77] Moreover, it does not seem likely that interest rates on loans in wet districts were more likely to congregate at the lower end of the range. According to the Tanjore district surveyor, interest rates varied, 'by the security offered and the amount borrowed'.[78] Rates varied by type of loan, however, there is no evidence to suggest that the range of interest rates differed greatly by geographical region. The relationship between size of loan, security attached to loans and prices of loans is discussed in the next chapter.

In short, this section shows that farmers supplied most of the credit in the agricultural sector and the market operated seasonally. Agricultural fundamentals affected the borrower's ability to repay and the lender's

---

[73] *Provincial Banking Enquiry*, 56–75.
[74] Strickland, "Cooperation and the Rural Problem"; Roy, "The Monsoon."
[75] *District Gazetteers: Bellary*, 101.
[76] *Madras District Gazetteers: Tanjore*. Part I (Madras, 1915), 112.
[77] *Madras District Gazetteers: Godavari*. Part I (Madras, 1915), 91.
[78] *District Gazetteers: Tanjore*, 112.

disposable income to lend. Default rates were higher in the wet regions than the dry, and this problem was not driven by lending composition or interest rate variations. The next section shows that lending strategies explain regional differences in both default rates and the volume of credit supplied. Creditors adopted safer lending strategies in dry districts and more risky strategies in wet districts. As a result, default rates were subdued in the dry but high in the wet areas.

Geography and Selective Lending

Farms in the wet districts were not entirely protected from climate uncertainty. Areas near the coast were prone to significant seasonal and annual volatility in rainfall. Rice farming was water-intensive, and rice regions were vulnerable to lower-than-required rains in some years, as well as waterlogging in those years with a strong north-east monsoon. Annual rainfall patterns reported in meteorological stations across the province provide an estimate of the rainfall range, arrived at by calculating the difference between maximum and minimum annual rainfall in a sixty-year period.[79] Meteorological stations around the coast reported significantly higher rainfall volatility than stations in the hinterland. The Shiyali municipality in Tanjore reported a maximum rainfall of 103.26 inches in 1913 and a minimum rainfall of 24.43 inches in 1892. In its maximum year, the annual rainfall in Shiyali exceeded its sixty-year average by 43.58 inches, double the amount of annual rainfall in the minimum year. In contrast, the Adoni municipality in the dry Bellary district reported a maximum rainfall of 53.31 inches in 1916 and a minimum annual rainfall of 11.25 inches in 1876. Using range as an estimate of unpredictability, rainfall in the Shiyali municipality was 47 per cent more volatile than rainfall in the Adoni municipality.

Variations in geographical features within the Tanjore district suggest that crop failure was a problem on the deltas and in the regions marginally inland from the deltas. The Cauvery River ran from the Coorg province in western Madras, now the Karnataka state, down to Ramnad and Tanjore in eastern Madras, now the Tamil Nadu state. The river drained in the Tanjore delta where it met the Bay of Bengal. The river had eight tributaries, the eastern of which was the Coleroon River which flowed out of the intersection between the Tanjore delta and the coast. Waterlogging and salinity were problems in the delta region. The eastern delta had, on

---

[79] The period runs from 1870 to 1930. However, this is contingent on the meteorological station remaining in operation during that period. The time period shortens in cases where the government set up the station later than others.

average, a 30 per cent higher annual rainfall than the rest of the basin.[80] Poor soil drainage meant that higher-than-average rainfall led to flooding and crop failure. In 1918, Harrison, an agricultural chemist reported to the provincial government that 'certain portions of the Delta (Tanjore) are badly drained and are tending to become saline'.[81] In the same period, the District Gazetteer reported that 'in almost every year there have been breaches in the river banks, and losses of crops of a more or less serious nature'.[82] In one such example, excess rainfall from the north-east monsoon in the winter of 1900 led to flooding and damaged rice crops in the Shiyali municipality, located in the Tanjore district.[83]

Water management projects did not solve the problem. The colonial and post-colonial government considered large hydraulic projects, such as canals and dams, as solutions to the flooding problem. The building of the Cauvery-Mettur Dam in the 1930s was an example of this in the colonial period. The government commissioned the construction of the reservoir upstream of the Tanjore delta. However, the dam overflowed in years with excess rainfall, leading to flooding and subsidence in the downstream Tanjore delta.[84] The outcome of the Mettur Dam construction in 1930s was a continued reliance on unstable rainfall in the downstream Tanjore deltas.

The unpredictable pattern of rainfall led to volatility in rice output during the period. The late 1940s and early 1950s are good examples of the large annual variation in output. A good year in 1953–1954 followed a stretch of volatile rainfall between 1949 and 1953. Much of the variation in total crop production was driven by annual changes in rice output. Low yields in the late 1940s prompted the provincial government to commission 'soil and irrigation research' to understand the causes of 'alkalinity, salinity or other defects or deficiencies' in rice-producing areas.[85] The good year between 1953 and 1954 saw an increase of 1.7 million tons of food production from the previous year. According to a government report, rice contributed to 76 per cent of this increase. Further explaining the increase in food production in the mid-1950s, the report claimed that 'seasonal factors' explain 50 per cent of the annual changes.[86] Major and minor irrigation accounted for 9 and 11.5 per cent, respectively, while fertiliser and manures drove 14.7 per cent of

[80] S. Vedula, "Optimal Irrigation Planning in River Basin Development: The Case of the Upper Cauvery River Basin." *Sadhana* 8, no. 2 (1985): 223–52, 225.

[81] *A Soil Survey of the Tanjore Delta*. Vol. III (Madras, 1921).

[82] *District Gazetteers: Tanjore*, 153.   [83] *District Gazetteers: Tanjore*, 153.

[84] Vedula, "Optimal Irrigation Planning," 225.

[85] *Agriculture and Fisheries in the Madras State* (Madras, 1954), 8.

[86] *Techno-Economic Survey*, 80.

the output increase.[87] This substantiates the persistent importance of stable rainfall in crop production. Crop failure was likely in water-scarce areas with volatile rainfall. Dam construction had limited impact on this outcome.

Crop durability differed by region, offering borrowers different capacities for loan repayments in wet and dry districts. Rice cultivation, though more valuable, had higher water and labour requirements than dry crops. In contrast, cotton and millets were 'rain-prudent crops, growing under varied conditions of rainfall and sustained by the deep moisture-holding capacity of black soil'.[88] The versatility of the millet crop allowed some landholders the flexibility to grow both cotton and cereal crops.[89] Though richer, Tanjore reported a lower amount of double-cropping than the less-developed, drier South Arcot, Salem and Coimbatore.[90] Areas inland from the delta benefitted from crop rotations. Cultivators in the drier Tanjore municipalities grew millets and groundnut in years with limited rainfall and rice varieties with lower water requirements in good years.[91] One crop acted as insurance for the other in the dry areas. Indeed, from a survey of villages in the Kistna district, the Provincial Banking Enquiry found that cultivators growing 'five crops together on one bit of land' was common.[92] Creditors in these regions were in a position to recover loans even if one crop failed.[93] On the disadvantages of single-cropping, the Banking Enquiry observed, 'the *ryot* may borrow from two places from the same crop and pay neither'.[94] Single-cropping cultivators in rice-producing regions, therefore, had less of an insurance on droughts and waterlogging than double-cropping cultivators in dry districts.

Additionally, credit requirements were low in the dry districts and high in the wet districts. The Provincial Banking Enquiry estimated that the average debt per acre across the province was 58 rupees in 1930. Surveys of cultivation costs suggest that 58 rupees is a reliable figure of the average working capital required per acre in a single rice-growing season. The average cost of cultivation per acre varied between 45.99 and 85.14

[87] *Techno-Economic Survey*, 80.
[88] Sandip Hazareesingh, "Cotton, Climate and Colonialism in Dharwar, Western India, 1840–1880." *Journal of Historical Geography* 38, no. 1 (2012): 1–17, 9.
[89] Hazareesingh, "Cotton, Climate and Colonialism," suggests that cotton tended to mature later than millets in the nineteenth century.
[90] *Techno-Economic Survey*, 94–95.   [91] *District Gazetteers: Tanjore*, 100.
[92] *Provincial Banking Enquiry*, 14.
[93] This practice was more plausible in black soil areas. Areas with red clay soil allowed for little flexibility in crop cultivation. Here, the cultivator was dependent on growing millet all year round.
[94] *Provincial Banking Enquiry*, 220.

Table 3.5 *Cost of rice cultivation per acre in select estates, 1926 (in 1930 prices)*

Plots	Minimum (rupees)	Maximum (rupees)	Average (rupees)
9	45.99	55.47	50.93

Sources: *Provincial Banking Enquiry*, 168; McAlpin, "Price Movements."
Notes: Data collected by the Lalgudi Sivagnanam Co-operative Agricultural Society between 1925 and 1926. The cooperative examined the expenses per acre incurred by nine small landholdings during two cultivation cycles. The table shows the data from the costs estimated in the first crop. Costs in the second crop show similar figures. Minimum indicates the landholding with the lowest reported expenses. Maximum shows the landholding with the largest. Average is the mean of all nine observations. The author adjusts costs to 1930 prices, using McAlpin's price index, for easier comparison with Table 3.6.

rupees in 1930 prices. Surveys of cultivation costs in rice-producing districts, presented in Tables 3.5 and 3.6, show that the average cost of rice cultivation was between 48 and 68 rupees per acre. As such, the Provincial Banking Enquiry's estimate of 58 rupees is a strong proxy of the average borrowed per acre in the deltas. The cultivation of millet and cotton in the dry districts yielded a lower set of expenses per acre than 58 rupees. According to Rao and Rajasekhar, sorghum and cotton cultivation in Bellary cost the cultivator, on average, 9 and 12 rupees per acre, between a quarter and a fifth of the expenses incurred by rice cultivators in Tanjore.[95] Rao and Rajasekhar's estimates seem to overstate costs. In other estimates, the minimum cost of cultivating dry millets in late 1920s Bellary was as low as 5 rupees per acre, less than one-tenth the cost of cultivating rice in Tanjore.[96] These estimates do not take into account the credit borrowed to finance capital requirements or land purchases. Costs of cattle and ploughs were expectedly higher. As a point of comparison, a pair of cattle used for ploughing in cotton fields in the Bellary district cost between 200 and 400 rupees while the cost of a pair of untamed bulls was approximately 100–120 rupees in the 'southern districts' in 1939.[97] The government estimated the pan-India average

[95] Rao and Rajasekhar, "Commodity Production," 17.
[96] Washbrook, "The Commercialization of Agriculture," 146. The estimated costs do not include the seasonal wages paid to farm labourers.
[97] Washbrook, "The Commercialization of Agriculture," 138; Bahadur Rao and B. V. Narayanaswamy Naidu, *Report of the Economist for Enquiry into Rural Indebtedness* (Madras, 1945), 47. The cost of cattle was higher in 1939, relative to the early 1930s, owing to upward swing in prices post-Depression. The difference in cost also reflected variation in the quality of the cattle. The same is true of the cost of living index in the 1940s. Prices of commodities soared during the early 1940s.

Table 3.6 *Cost of rice cultivation per acre in select districts, 1939 and 1947 (in 1930 prices)*

District	1939 (rupees)	1947 (rupees)
East Godavari	62.16	57.21
Nellore	62.16	42.29
South Arcot	85.14	77.61
Tanjore	51.35	55.22

Sources: *Indian Agricultural Statistics*, 174; McAlpin, "Price Movements."
Notes: Table refers to irrigated land and excludes data for unirrigated rice cultivation. The source contains incomplete information on unirrigated paddy areas. Rice requires a minimum level of irrigation to be cultivated, thus eliminating any possibility for bias in the data. The author adjusts the costs presented in the source to 1930 prices using McAlpin's agricultural price index. Commodity price inflation was high in the 1940s, which would show bias in the data if unadjusted.

annual cost of living at 230 rupees in 1945, approximately 177 rupees in 1930 prices.[98]

The size of borrowing increased with the size of landholding. Yet, size of borrowing did not increase linearly relative to size of landownership. In other words, there was a declining marginal increase in additional borrowing with each additional acre owned. According to a survey of 564 families in 1935, debt per capita among large landowners was over four times higher than debt per capita among smallholders. However, the debt per acre accrued by large landowners was 38 per cent lower than the debt per acre accumulated among smallholders.[99] The Provincial Banking Enquiry's estimate of 58 rupees per acre exceeded the average borrowed by tenants in richer deltas and smallholders in the dry interior. However, the figure is lower than the average borrowed by smallholders in the rich deltas and large landholders in the hinterland. Farm labourers borrowed less than the average smallholder. According to one report in 1935, one moneylender provided loans of 25 rupees, half the recorded debt per acre, to farm labourers.[100]

Landholding size was generally small in colonial India. By the 1920s, the average landholder owned around 6 acres.[101] Madras was not much different. Government reports compiled by the provincial administration in Madras typically classified small holdings as plots sized under 5 acres,

---

[98] Rao and Naidu, *Report of the Economist*, 47; Prices adjusted using McAlpin, "Price Movements."
[99] *Report on Agricultural Indebtedness*, 42.   [100] *Report on Agricultural Indebtedness*, 16.
[101] Strickland, "Cooperation and the Rural Problem," 504.

small to medium holdings as plots sized between 5 and 15 acres, medium to large holdings as plots sized between 15 and 25 acres, and large holdings as plots sized above 25 acres.

The average size of landholding was larger in dry districts than wet regions. Between 1870 and 1920, there was a rise in the number of small holdings of less than 5 acres and a consolidation of previously frag-mented large holdings of more than 25 acres in Bellary. The number of medium-sized farms did not see much change in the dry areas. As such, the average size of land plots remained higher in the dry districts than in the wet. The average landholding in seven municipalities in the dry Anantapur, Bellary and Kurnool districts was 12.12 acres in 1930. In contrast, the average size of landholding in five municipalities in the East Godavari, Ganjam, Ramnad and Tanjore districts was 3.7 acres.[102] The average landholding size in the Adoni municipality in Bellary was 10.79 acres in comparison to an average size of 4.88 acres in the Shiyali municipality in Tanjore.[103] Large land plots did not mean land rental was common in dry areas.[104] In Bellary, tenancy was rare while labourers were commonly temporary workers that worked seasonally and emi-grated in bad years. Indeed, the 1951 Census recorded large movements of labour from famine-prone areas to rice deltas in the year following crop failure.[105] In contrast, tenancy was common and permanent in Tanjore. The delta reported a large number of tenants and cultivating owners while also reporting a low number of temporary labourers.[106] Tenants accessed the credit market, at times borrowing from landlords on sharecropping arrangements.[107] Labour was more permanent, creat-ing a more conducive structure for investment.

Farmers in dry districts, through higher average landholdings, exploited risk-bearing economies of scale more than cultivators in wet districts. The lack of improvements in technology, including irrigation, seeds and fertiliser, meant that scale provided average landholders insur-ance against environmental fluctuations. In 1929, as shown in Table 3.7, the average landholder in the Adoni municipality in Bellary earned just over half the revenue of the average landholder in the Shiyali municipality in Tanjore.[108] However, landholders in Bellary borrowed significantly

---

[102] *Statistical Atlas*, 17–62, 125–70, 749–82, 783–816.
[103] *Statistical Atlas*, 323–60, 749–82.
[104] Land tenure systems, and laws surrounding ownership and tenancy, are discussed in Chapters 4 and 5.
[105] *Census of India*, 14–22.   [106] *Census of India*, 14–22.
[107] *District Gazetteers: Tanjore*, 108–11.
[108] This analysis assumes that the cultivator in Bellary did not crop-diversify. As discussed, cultivators in dry regions diversified more than cultivators in wet regions. This

Table 3.7 *Annual revenue per average landholder, 1929*

Municipality	Land Size (acres)	Crop	Annual Yield (tons per acre)	Output (tons)	Price (rupees per ton)	Annual Revenue (rupees)
Adoni	10.79	Sorghum	0.25	2.7	75	203
Shiyali	4.88	Rice	0.48	2.3	171	393

Sources: Provincial Banking Enquiry, 9–12; *Statistical Atlas,* 323–60, 749–82; *Agricultural Statistics of India,* 105–6.

Notes: The author choses one municipality in Bellary (Adoni) and one in Tanjore (Shiyali). Average land size was taken from the *Statistical Atlas*. Yields are for 1937 and taken from the *Agricultural Statistics of India*. This should not bias the results for 1930 as yields remained stagnant throughout the period. Output was calculated by multiplying yields with land size. Price of each crop was obtained from the *Provincial Banking Enquiry*. Surveyors in the Banking Enquiry Committee analysed prices from two markets in each district across the province in the year 1928–29. Agriculture in that year was not exposed to unpredictable price shocks and therefore reflects an average price from a successful harvest. The source provides prices per maund. The author scales up prices to per-ton estimates for easier analysis. Annual Revenue was calculated by multiplying prices with output. The table assumes that cultivators did not diversify crops.

less than landholders in Tanjore. As previously noted, the costs of cultivation were low in Bellary. From a survey of select villages in each district, the average debt per acre in Bellary was 17 rupees in 1929 and 21 rupees in 1935. In contrast, the average debt per acre in Tanjore was 116 rupees in 1929 and 86 rupees in 1935.[109] In other words, average landholders in Bellary were more likely to repay loans than average holders in Tanjore, as they benefitted from scale. Lower risk-bearing economies of scale in Tanjore led to higher default rates in comparison to dry regions.

Creditors selectively allocated credit to the large landholders in the dry districts, whereas lending was less risk-averse in the wet districts. As the borrower's default risk reduced inversely to scale of landownership, excluding poor borrowers was one way for lenders to manage the risk of lending in the dry districts. Inequality in landownership was higher in the dry districts, compared to the wet regions. In Bellary, for example, where land was either owned by poor peasants in several scattered

diversification could increase the annual revenue earned by the average landholder in Bellary.

[109] The Provincial Banking Enquiry Committee Report and Report on Agricultural Indebtedness arrived at these figures by dividing the total lending by number of acres in each village surveyed.

holdings under 5 acres or owned by holders of consolidated 20-acre estates, creditors had an uncomplicated method to manage default risk.[110] Lenders excluded smallholders in dry areas because, without the benefit of diversification, these borrowers cultivated single crops on poor-quality land.[111] Large landowners in the dry areas benefitted from scale and diversification, therefore, were less likely to default on seasonal loans. Lending in wet districts, in contrast, was more inclusive. Poor peasants accessed credit more easily in Tanjore than in Bellary. As presented in Table 3.8, the credit market was smaller and more concentrated in Bellary, when compared to Tanjore. The volume of money credited in Bellary villages was approximately two-thirds the size of total lending in Tanjore villages. Fewer households borrowed in the former. As shown, 40 per cent of households borrowed in Bellary. In contrast, 80 per cent of households borrowed in Tanjore. Fewer households borrowed, but the average credit per borrower in Bellary was almost three times larger than the average in Tanjore.

Data on the number and value of mortgages registered during the inter-war period support the finding that credit supply was smaller and more selective in Bellary than in Tanjore. Between 1921 and 1934, the value of mortgage loans per acre in Bellary varied between 0.6 and 1 rupee, much smaller than the range of 2.4 and 3.6 rupees per acre in Tanjore. As for number of borrowers, there were between one and two mortgagors per 1,000 acres in Bellary, in contrast to the range of five and eight mortgagors per 1,000 acres in Tanjore.[112] The debt per borrower, however, was high in Bellary as the average mortgagor borrowed between 410 and 503 rupees.[113] In Tanjore, the average size of mortgage borrowing was between 416 and 488 rupees.[114] The average mortgagor borrowed more than twice the annual revenue of a 10-acre farm in Bellary and only marginally higher than the annual revenue of a 4-acre farm in Tanjore.

Other wet and dry districts showed similar trends in the number and size of mortgages during the 1920s and early 1930s. The value of mortgages per acre was between two and three times higher in the wet districts than the same figure in the dry areas.[115] Lenders credited mortgagors

---

[110] Washbrook, "The Commercialization of Agriculture," 132–34.

[111] *Provincial Banking Enquiry*, 15–17.

[112] *Report on the Administration of the Registration Department* (Madras, 1921–34); *Statistical Atlas*, 323–60, 749–82.

[113] Average loan size estimated by dividing total value by total number of mortgage registrations.

[114] The average size of borrowing was higher in Bellary than in Tanjore in nine of the fourteen surveyed years.

[115] Classification of districts as 'wet' and 'dry' conducted in the same format as Table 3.2.

Table 3.8 *Borrower characteristics in 141 villages, 1935*

Village Type	Lending per Village (rupees)	Borrowers per Household	Borrowers per Lender	Debt per Borrower (rupees)
All Villages	109,339	0.8	27	206
Tanjore	59,595	0.8	96	332
Bellary	39,365	0.4	11	812

Source: Report on Agricultural Indebtedness.
Notes: Data was taken from a credit survey of 141 villages across the province. Between 1 and 16 villages were surveyed in each district. Lending per Village was measured by dividing the total value of lending (including all surveyed villages in the district) by the number of villages surveyed. Borrowers per Household were measured by dividing the number of borrowers by the total number of households in the villages. Borrowers per Lender was measured by dividing the number of borrowers by the number of moneylenders (agriculturist and professional included). Debt per Borrower was measured by dividing the total lending by the number of borrowers. Calculations made by the author.

between 3 and 4 rupees per acre in the wet areas, and between 1 and 2 rupees per acre in the dry districts. The average size of mortgage loans, however, was systematically higher in the drier tracts. An average mortgagor in dry districts borrowed between 384 and 471 rupees, whereas the typical mortgage transaction in wet districts averaged between 316 and 393 rupees.[116] In 1927, for example, mortgagees provided loans worth 3.7 rupees per acre in wet districts and 1.8 rupees per acre in dry districts. In the same year, the average mortgagor borrowed 344 rupees in wet districts and 412 rupees in dry areas.

The combination of few borrowers and high average loan sizes was a typical feature of credit markets in districts neighbouring Bellary. Take Anantapur for instance – a district approximately 60 miles and a short train journey away from Bellary. The district had marginally more rainfall than Bellary each year. Soil quality in most of the district was suitable for the cultivation of millet and pulses.[117] Cash crop cultivation was low. When the soil allowed, peasants were able to grow cotton in some municipalities. Earnings from agriculture were precarious in the district. Droughts were frequent. Starvation was pervasive in bad years. Credit markets in Anantapur operated as they did in the neighbouring districts. Agriculturists provided the majority of loans. Borrowers used most loans

[116] *Report on the Administration of the Registration Department* (1921–34).
[117] *Statistical Atlas,* 361–406.

for productive purposes. Consumption loans were few. Interest rates on the majority of cash loans varied between 9 and 18 per cent, the price range charged by most rural lenders across the province.[118] As was the case in Bellary, the value of mortgages per acre in the Anantapur district was far lower than the value of loans in wet districts. Mortgagors accrued debts worth 0.5 rupees per acre in 1929.[119] In the same year, however, the average debt per borrower was much higher than the provincial average, amounting to 639 rupees per borrower in the Banking Enquiry's survey of select villages in the district. Explaining why debts accrued per borrower were high, the surveyor commented that the borrowers, 'were proprietors of whole or part of the land they cultivated and therefore naturally commanded higher credit'.[120] The likelihood of crop failure affected the peasant's ability to access credit in Anantapur.

In short, ecological risk affected peasants in dry regions more than it affected peasants in wet districts. However, risk affected rich peasants in dry districts less than poor peasants in wet districts. Low growth and stagnant inequality, particularly in the dry districts, was a problem. However, climate volatility and poor land quality was the root of this problem. The constrained money market, with further constraints after bad harvests, restricted investment potential for poor peasants, especially in the dry districts. The chapter, in other words, finds a two-pronged problem of credit allocation in South India. One was the constraints on the disposable income available to lend. The other, and more important, was the challenges in accessing credit when borrowers were vulnerable to climate shocks. As subsequent chapters show, colonial and post-colonial governments disrupted the money market further, in an attempt to alleviate poverty by further reducing access to credit for the rural poor. In light of evidence presented in this chapter, the colonial government's policy response to further reduce the volume of credit borrowed is puzzling.

Money did not often travel from villages in wet districts to villages in dry districts, restricting the volume of credit accessible to peasants in dry districts. Writing on rural Indian money markets in 1929, L. C. Jain notes, 'In rural areas the general level of the rates of interest does not show notable fluctuations ... It is well known that excess of money in one rural centre in India does not flow, as it should, to an area where it may be in defect.'[121] In other words, farmers with disposable income in one

---

[118] *Provincial Banking Enquiry*, 1045–46.
[119] *Report on the Administration of the Registration Department* (Madras, 1929); *Statistical Atlas*, 361–406.
[120] *Provincial Banking Enquiry*, 1046.
[121] L. C. Jain, *Indigenous Banking in India* (London: Macmillan, 1929), 99.

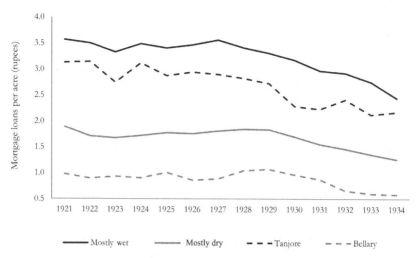

Figure 3.3 Value of mortgage loans per acre, 1921–34.
Sources: *Report on the Administration of the Registration Department; Statistical Atlas.*
Notes: The Registration Department recorded the number and value of
mortgages registered in each district across the province. The distinction between
wet and dry districts was drawn in the same format as Table 3.2. The value of
mortgages was divided by the number of acres in each district. Acreage obtained
at the municipality level from the *Statistical Atlas*. The author added up the
municipalities to calculate the total acreage in each district. Throughout the
period, the Registration Department recorded mortgage registrations in the
Negapatam municipality, located in the Tanjore district, separate from the
district data. The figure excludes acreage and mortgage data for the Negapatam
municipality in the Tanjore series but includes it as part of the 'Mostly Wet'
series. The graph excludes the South Arcot district as mortgage data was not
reported for several years.

village did not lend in other villages where money was scarce. If the risk
of crop failure deterred lenders from lending to peasants in the same
village, it would likely be a deterrence for lenders from other villages.
Nevertheless, as we will see later in the book, expansion in the supply of
credit in dry villages would not necessarily solve the problem of selective
allocation. Credit was allocated by the risk profile of the borrower and so
the volume supplied, in its absolute form, was not at the root of the issue.

Could lenders use formal procedures to better manage the risks of
lending? The finding, as reported in Figure 3.3, that lenders infrequently
secured loans with mortgage contracts in high-risk areas is, *prima facie*,
counter-intuitive. Mortgage contracts, and their enforcement in courts,

can offer lenders a viable option to recover defaulted loans easily. We should see a high volume of, and less selective, mortgage lending in riskier markets. The next chapter turns to an analysis of contract enforcement systems to explain why credit contracts were uncommonly used in high-risk regions.

Conclusion

Credit supply was seasonal and volatile in Madras. External borrowing was limited as commercial and indigenous banks did not lend in the villages. Cultivators with disposable income were the only source of credit. Markets were illiquid and credit scarce because change in the volume of credit supplied in each village was correlated with the profitability of agriculture. Supply expanded after good years and declined after bad years. The frequency of bad years simultaneously increased default rates and stunted the supply of credit in villages.

Creditors faced different levels of risk depending on the region in which they were lending. Peasants in the drier parts of Madras struggled to access credit. Smallholders in wet districts were better able to manage climate volatility than smallholders in dry districts. Scale offered a distinct advantage to the farmers in dry districts. Costs per acre of cultivation were lower in the dry districts and reduced inversely to land size. Furthermore, larger landholders were able to insure against climatic risk by diversifying and rotating cropping patterns. The chapter shows that large landholders in dry districts were more likely to repay loans than the smallholders in both wet and dry districts. Moneylenders, as a result, managed risk by selectively choosing their clients. Farmers across income categories borrowed in the wet districts, however, lenders provided credit only to the richer cultivators in the dry districts.

The chapter shows that geography played an important role in the relationship between credit access and inequality. The poor had access to credit in the irrigated areas. Peasants in the dry areas had limited potential to invest owing to limited credit access, perpetuating poverty in these areas over time. Investment rates were low in the dry areas and high in the wet areas, resulting in persistent regional inequality. Policies to artificially irrigate the wet areas, and lack of policy initiatives to irrigate the dry areas, seem to have exacerbated the problem in the colonial period.

Climate volatility also complicated enforcement systems in the unregulated credit market. The next chapter turns to a study of land rights, courts and costs of enforcing credit contracts to explain why formal procedure did not help lenders manage default risk.

4   Courts and Credit

How did moneylenders enforce the repayment of loans in colonial Madras? Informal, private negotiation was one method. Enforcing contracts was another. Mortgages and promissory notes were two typically used contracts in rural credit markets. Courts emerged and spread in the nineteenth century, while laws enforced at different points in the nineteenth and early twentieth centuries regulated the types of contracts used. Land and tax laws, implemented in the early nineteenth century and amended in the early twentieth century, regulated the use of mortgage instruments. Land laws defined the proprietary rights of landowners and tenants. These rights differed depending on the region and type of land tax arrangement. Nineteenth-century contract laws regulated the use of promissory notes. The 1872 India Contract Act and 1881 Negotiable Instruments Act included guidelines on the use of promissory notes in credit transactions.

Economic historians tell us that poorly designed laws and rising court cases made judicial proceedings expensive in colonial India.[1] Economic theory tells us that creditors price the costs of enforcement into interest rates on loan transactions.[2] In doing so, creditors transfer dispute costs to the borrower. This chapter expands on both assessments, demonstrating that creditors in 1930s Madras adjusted prices when enforcing region-specific contracts in courts.

Contract law, and the costs of enforcing contracts, played an important role in the decisions made by rural creditors. Writing in 1954, Frank

---

[1] On land laws and mortgages, see Tirthankar Roy and Anand V. Swamy, *Law and the Economy in Colonial India* (Chicago: The University of Chicago Press, 2017). On contract laws and negotiated instruments, see Marina Martin, "An Economic History of Hundi, 1858–1978," PhD thesis, London School of Economics and Political Science (2012).

[2] Anthony Bottomley, "Interest Rate Determination in Underdeveloped Rural Areas." *American Journal of Agricultural Economics* 57, no. 2 (1975): 279–91; Timothy Besley, "How Do Market Failures Justify Interventions in Rural Credit Markets?" *The World Bank Research Observer* 9, no. 1 (1994): 27–47.

Moore suggested that expensive court proceedings contributed to the high overhead costs borne by private moneylenders in rural India.[3] Indeed, indigenous bankers cited enforcement costs as a sufficient reason to not lend in the Madras countryside but in the Burmese plantations instead. In an interview with the Provincial Banking Enquiry Committee, one Chettiar banker claimed, 'I know in Southern India cases have taken ten years and sometimes even centuries to be finally decided.'[4] The agriculturist moneylenders were not as deterred by the enforcement cost problem. Creditors had personal relationships with borrowers and could enforce repayments more easily than urban credit businesses. When creditors failed to obtain repayments with informal arbitration, contract laws allowed creditors to enforce repayments through courts while charging the borrower higher interest rates to account for court and legal fees. In this context, the chapter shows that enforcing promissory notes generated a lower set of expenses than enforcing mortgages.

Creditors used contracts depending on the type of client and size of loans. The chapter finds that the relationship between loan size and the cost of enforcing the contract determined whether creditors used mortgages or promissory notes in rural Madras. The size of loans, a combination of the principal and interest, needed to be high enough to satisfy the cost of enforcing contracts in courts. Large loans to rich landowners satisfied court enforcement more easily than small loans to poor peasants. As a result, loans to the poor were, at least on first issue, unsecured and enforced informally. Only when the size of loans compounded, high enough to satisfy the costs of contract enforcement, did creditors attach contracts to loans. On initial default, creditors extended the primary loans with the added protection of a promissory note. On additional default, creditors upgraded the promissory note to a mortgage instrument. Informal enforcement was the cheapest form. Enforcing promissory notes was more expensive while executing land transfers generated the highest costs.

Creditors enforced repayment on loans to the poor through a three-stage 'loan upgrading' process, where each stage generated a higher level of enforcement costs. As visualised in Tables 4.1 and 4.2, when defaults inflated small loans to a size high enough to allow it, creditors upgraded unsecured loans to contracted ones. Lenders transmitted the costs of

[3] Frank J. Moore, "Money-Lenders and Co-Operators in India." *Economic Development and Cultural Change* 2, no. 2 (1954): 139–59, 140–41.
[4] Cited in Christopher Baker, *An Indian Rural Economy 1880–1955: The Tamilnad Countryside* (Oxford: Oxford University Press, 1984), 283.

Table 4.1 *Loan size and credit instrument*

Borrower Category	Principal Size	Credit Instrument	Interest Rates
Rich	High	Mortgage	Low
Poor	Low	Unsecured	High

Table 4.2 *Multi-layered enforcement*

Credit Instrument	Enforcement Type	Enforcement Cost	Price Increase
Unsecured	Informal	Low	Stagnant
Promissory Note	Courts	Rising	Mild
Mortgage	Courts	High	High

enforcing these contracts to higher interest rates. Expensive contract enforcement highlights the inverse relationship between transaction costs and equity in rural credit. Indian courts offered expensive judicial protection to moneylenders. Borrowers compensated moneylenders for high enforcement costs.

The chapter analyses land laws and contract laws as well as new material from administration reports, judicial reports and credit surveys in the early 1930s. The price crash makes the early 1930s a useful period to study enforcement in rural credit. Enforcement problems were most acute when repayment rates were low. Indeed, default rates were high in the early 1930s. Unable to recover loans informally, creditors provided loan extensions with attached contracts and ultimately relied on courts to enforce repayment. The need for formal enforcement entrenched the multi-layered lending structure during this period. The early 1930s presents an additional benefit of the market being unregulated. As discussed in the next chapter, this distinctive loan and enforcement structure in Madras explains why credit intervention in the late 1930s failed to have the desired impact.

The chapter is divided into four sections. The first outlines the evolution of courts and judicial proceedings in colonial India. The second and third analyse the market for mortgage and contracted credit in late 1920s and early 1930s Madras. The final section provides an analytical framework to explain the transmission of enforcement costs to the prices of credit in the multi-layered loan format.

Courts in Colonial South India

The East India Company established courts to resolve civil and criminal disputes across provinces in the late eighteenth and early nineteenth centuries. *Panchayats* or local village administrations were forums for civil disputes in the period prior to the expansion of Company rule.[5] Company officials abolished *Panchayats* and replaced them with a centralised court structure in the eighteenth century. The Company organised Royal Courts in 1727 under Royal Charter from the King. Warren Hastings transplanted the court model, establishing a three-tier court structure in the Company-controlled Indian provinces. Hastings was originally a military leader, playing a vital leadership role in the Company's acquisition of Bengal from Mughal rulers. Hastings led forces that accompanied regiments led by Robert Clive and Hector Munro in the famous Battle of Plassey in 1757 and Battle of Buxar in 1764. The Company appointed Hastings the first Governor of the Bengal Presidency, a position that extended to all Company-controlled provinces in the 1770s. In this administrative position, Hastings established district and provincial Company courts in 1772.[6] District courts were the primary forum for rural disputes. Provincial courts heard appeals from district courts. The 'federal' *Sadar Adalat* heard final appeal proceedings under Company Rule.[7] Provincial administrators hired British judges to administer company proceedings in the courts. The Company created two *Sadar Adalats*, separated according to civil and criminal proceedings. Judges in the *Sadar Dewani Adalat* settled civil cases, while those in *Sadar Nizamat Adalats* resolved criminal disputes. The Company transplanted this structure to Madras in 1802.

Some company officials in early nineteenth-century Madras believed that the replacement of indigenous administrative procedures with colonial legal institutions was not an entirely successful initiative. Spearheading this criticism was Thomas Munro. Munro played an important role in the conquest of Madras. Under Munro's leadership, the company army gained vast territory in the battles against Tipu Sultan and the Nizam of Hyderabad in the late eighteenth century. Following victorious battles, the company promoted Munro to leadership positions. The company ultimately appointed Munro as Governor of Madras in

---

[5] *Panchayat* literally translates to 'assembly' and describes a form of village administration where a group of administrators solve disputes and implement local reforms within villages across rural India.

[6] Orby Mootham, *The East India Company's Sadar Courts 1801–1834* (Bombay: N. M. Tripathi, 1983), 3–5.

[7] *Sadar Adalat* translates to 'Main Court' and was the top provincial court until 1857.

1819. In this position, Munro attempted to devolve some judicial power to pre-colonial indigenous administrations. The organisation of company courts, according to Munro, was 'too great a departure from native institutions to work with success'.[8] As Governor, Munro enforced two policy changes to courts.

The first was changes in rules relating to the selection of judges in *Sadar Adalats*. Provincial governors and members of the provincial council were also judges in *Sadar Adalats* in the late eighteenth century. In 1807, Company officials altered the composition of court benches to include a chief judge and two puisne judges. The Chief Judge was a member of the governing council, while the others were not required to be members of the provincial government. The selection criteria of judges underwent significant changes under Munro's Governorship.[9] Munro recognised the importance of judicial experience in the selection criteria for the appointment of judges. Though the Chief Judge was a legislator, Munro enforced a minimum qualification barrier for puisne judges to ensure *Sadar Adalats* were administered by those who have prior experience in lower provincial courts.[10] The Company selected judges in lower courts from the civil service. Despite having judicial experience, these judges were civil servants by training. In 1825, Munro increased the number of puisne judges in the Madras *Sadar Adalats* to three in order to avoid delays in judgements.

The second judicial policy change in the early nineteenth century dealt with the official role of the *Panchayat*. During his tenure as Governor of Madras, Munro believed that successful control required the merging of British forms of administration with indigenous Indian institutions.[11] He criticised the abolishment of indigenous forms of justice administration. Munro believed that the introduction of pre-colonial forms of village administration would legitimise Company rule through decentralised power centres. According to his memoirs,

Munro strongly advocated the revival of the native institution called 'panchayat' – a court of arbitration composed of five or more persons – and the transfer of the duty of superintending the police from the Judge to the Collector, who, moving frequently about his district, and mixing with the people, had better means of effectively supervising the police than were available to a stationary judicial

[8] Alexander J. Arbuthnot, *Major-General Sir Thomas Munro, Governor of Madras: A Memoir* (London: Kegen Paul, Trench, 1889), 109.
[9] Mootham, *The East India Company's Sadar Courts*, 104–7.
[10] Mootham, *The East India Company's Sadar Courts*, 104–7.
[11] Arbuthnot, *Major-General Sir Thomas Munro*, 109.

officer. The union, for similar reasons, of the offices of Collector and Magistrate, and the utilization of the village officials to deal with petty offences and with petty suits, were also included in his proposals.[12]

Following the transfer of powers to the Crown in 1857, colonial officials attempted to further integrate combinations of western and indigenous institutional structures. *Sadar Adalats* were abolished and High Courts were established across provinces. Dual justice structures under the *Sadar Adalat* system were streamlined to single appellate courts. Village *panchayats* were revived through various reforms in the nineteenth and early twentieth centuries. The 1871 Mayo Resolution and Lord Rippon's resolution in 1882 legitimised village administrations and devolved local policymaking to *panchayats*. The 1907 Royal Commission increased the power of *panchayats* to deal with petty civil disputes, including credit defaults.

The decentralisation of judicial power to *panchayats* has prompted some debate on whether its revival marks a continuity or discontinuity of indigenous legal organisation. One argument is that the newly revived *panchayat* marked a continuity in legal traditions as it was governed by a newly formed group of legal agents with a vested interest in maintaining the transition to colonial forms of justice.[13] Another interpretation argues in favour of a discontinuity in legal structures. Abraham emphasises the creation of a court hierarchy, the appointment of court registrars to ensure the functioning of court procedure, appointments of trained attorneys, the issuing of summons and recording case trials. However, Abraham also suggests that this transition was weakened by the recruitment of local judges, magistrates, court officials and staff. Customs of caste and religion seemed to have influenced the directives issued by judges.[14]

Despite its revival, the official role of the *panchayat* was limited by the end of the colonial rule. By the 1950s, 'the chief work of the panchayat' was the provision of some public goods through the construction of roads and wells and the administration of civil disputes, including credit defaults that were too small to be considered in courts.[15] Credit defaults were more commonly heard in district courts with the High Court as the main forum of appeal. Rural credit disputes were initiated in small cause

---

[12] Arbuthnot, *Major-General Sir Thomas Munro*, 109.
[13] Marc Galanter, "The Aborted Restoration of 'Indigenous' Law in India." *Comparative Studies in Society and History* 14, no. 1 (1972): 53–70.
[14] Santhosh Abraham, "Colonial Law in Early British Malabar: Transparent Colonial State and Formality of Practices." *South Asia Research* 31, no. 3 (2011): 249–64.
[15] *All-India Rural Credit Survey*, Vol. II (Bombay, 1957), 76.

courts prior to entering a hierarchy of appellate courts, including lower and higher district courts with a final forum of appeal at the provincial high court.[16] Colonial governments supplemented this transition in the court structure with changes in the rules for judge selection. The 1861 High Court Act and the 1935 Government of India Act specified minimum qualification experience for judges to qualify in Indian courts. British barristers qualified as high court judges only with prior judicial experience in colonial India.[17]

Enforcement in rural credit markets followed changes in the structure of courts. By 1850, rural credit disputes were governed by courts, rather than customary law and village administration. Contracts substituted social capital as method of risk mitigation. Lenders reported first-time defaulters in civil courts. Indeed, a recent study shows that moneylenders in the Bombay Deccan were less incentivised to show leniency to defaulters following the transition to courts.[18] Writing in 1954, Moore believed that 'the traditional relationship between creditor and debtor in the Indian village was upset by the introduction of the British legal system'. According to Moore, 'customary limitations on interest gave way to enforceable contracts legalizing unlimited compounding interest'.[19]

Were contracts easily enforceable in courts? Did they come at a cost to the moneylender? Moneylenders in Madras used different versions of contract. Mortgages functioned separately from loans that were contracted but not secured by immovable property. Subsequent sections in this chapter discuss variations in the design, use and cost of credit contracts.

Land Tax, Property Rights and the Mortgage Market

Land tax was the largest source of revenue for the East India Company and later the British crown-ruled government. In agreement with rich landlords in Bengal, the East India Company ratified the Permanent Settlement agreement in 1793. According to the agreement, large estates

---

[16] Cases from high courts could appeal to the Privy Council in London, the Federal Court after its inception in 1934 and the Supreme Court post-independence. However, there were strict conditions on the admittance of disputes in the Privy Council. Cases above a certain value could qualify. Credit disputes rarely qualified for appeal in a court higher than the provincial high court.

[17] Part IX, chapter 2, Government of India Act 1935.

[18] See Rachel E. Kranton and Anand V. Swamy, "The Hazards of Piecemeal Reform: British Civil Courts and the Credit Market in Colonial India." *Journal of Development Economics* 58, no. 1 (1999): 1–24. The authors argue that the presence of courts increased competition in the credit market, but punishments on defaulters were more severe than the preceding period where lenders relied on informal enforcement mechanisms.

[19] Moore, "Moneylenders and Co-operators," 142.

remained under the ownership of pre-colonial elites. The Company taxed landowners at rates determined by the size of land owned. Landowners divided their estates into plots and leased these out to multiple tenants. Tenants cultivated the land. The Company extended this tax structure to the Madras Presidency in 1802. However, under Munro's governorship, the company administration made changes to the tax structure in most parts of Madras from the 1820s. Munro's government excluded the intermediary and implemented a structure allowing the Company to tax the cultivator directly.

By 1900, three structures of tax and ownership operated in the province. First, the *Ryotwari* tenure provided ownership rights to the government. The government defined tax charges for a fixed term, periodically updated tax assessments and collected tax revenue directly from the cultivator.[20] Second, in *Zamindari* settlements, pre-colonial elites retained the proprietorship of landed estates during colonial rule. The government charged landowners a permanently fixed land tax or *peishkash*. *Zamindars* divided vast tracts of land into smaller plots and leased individual plots to tenants. Third, colonial governments granted proprietorship over tracts of land to regional nobility in the *Inam* or *Jagir* structure. *Inamdars* provided military and policing services to the colonial government in return while leasing plots of land to individual tenants. Property rights in colonial South India can otherwise be categorised into two broad systems. The government-cultivator system provided proprietorship to individual cultivators. The government-owner-tenant system provided proprietorship to non-cultivating landlords.

Land titles were comparatively more secure in the *ryotwari* system. The government divided land into fields. Each field varied in size and, as discussed in the previous chapter, landholding sizes were small in Madras.[21] Cultivators demarcated holdings or plots with physical boundaries. Local revenue departments taxed each plot. The government attached a title document or *patta* to each plot. The *patta* was a quasi-contract, confirming the farmer's fiscal obligation to the government.[22] Each *patta* specified the name of the occupant, size of plot and extent of tax assessment for the occupied holding.[23] *Pattas* ultimately acted as transferable property titles. Transfers in the occupation of land required revisions in this title to reflect the tax obligation of the new

---

[20] *Madras State Administration Report* (Madras, 1947), 87.
[21] *State Administration Report*, 87–88.
[22] Bahadur Rao and B. V. Narayanaswamy Naidu, *Report of the Economist for Enquiry into Rural Indebtedness* (Madras, 1945), 7.
[23] *State Administration Report*, 87–88.

landholder.[24] While the government *de jure* owned *ryotwari* lands, the exchange of *pattas* allowed for an active land market from the mid-nineteenth century. Cultivators *de facto* owned the land they cultivated. Farmers collateralised *pattas* to obtain credit.

Titles were more complicated in *zamindari* settlements. The government issued proprietary rights to landlords. The government attached one condition to this proprietorship, that the landlords met their tax obligation for the entire period of ownership.[25] The government issued *pattas* to landlords instead of issuing rights to the tenants who actually cultivated land. *Pattas* in the *zamindari* system were stronger than those provided to *ryotwaris*. Titles held by *zamindars* confirmed the land-owner's proprietorship of the estate, whereas titles held by *ryotwaris* inferred ownership by defining the tax obligations charged to the land-holder.[26] That the permanent occupiers of *zamindari* land were tenants complicated the transferability of land in these settlements.

Zamindars and *inamdars* profited from rent, rather than cultivation.[27] Landlords and tenants privately negotiated rents in these settlements. Rents were commonly higher than land tax bills. Landlords profited from the difference between the rent charged to their tenant and the tax paid to the government.[28] According to one government report, 'zamindars ordinarily lease out their villages yearly in auction to middle men who have no interest in the welfare of the ryots and try to rack rent them'.[29] As such, landowners were not incentivised to invest in improving land quality. Despite possessing transferrable titles, landowners in *zamindari* estates rarely mortgaged land or borrowed on the credit market.[30] Tenants in *zamindari* estates could not borrow credit easily in the late nineteenth and early twentieth century as titles owned by tenants were weak and less tradable than titles possessed by landowners.[31]

The regional composition of land tenure systems suggests that property rights were secure and tradable in most parts of Madras. Different

---

[24] Despite its primary function as a tax statement, the *patta* also served as the confirmation of a landholder's title. Transfers in ownership were reflected in this title.

[25] The *pattas* issued to *zamindars* were stronger than *ryotwari* settlements as they confirmed their proprietary ownership of the estate, rather than inferring ownership through the fiscal responsibility of the landholder.

[26] Rao and Naidu, *Report of the Economist*, 7.

[27] Roy and Swamy, *Law and the Economy*, suggest that *zamindars* made profits from the difference between rent charged to the tenant and tax paid to the government. Land revenue was a fixed annual cost while rent increased over time.

[28] A. M. Khusro, "Land Reforms since Independence." In *Economic History of India, 1857–1956*, edited by V. B. Singh (Bombay: Allied Publishers, 1965), 181.

[29] *A Statistical Atlas of the Madras Presidency* (Madras, 1936), 40.

[30] Roy and Swamy, *Law and the Economy*, 47.

[31] Rao and Naidu, *Report of the Economist*, 7–8.

Table 4.3 *Number of municipalities by land tenure arrangement, 1930*

Total Municipalities	Entirely Ryotwari	Majority Ryotwari	Entirely Zamindari	Majority Zamindari
241	32	149	8	52

Source: Statistical Atlas.
Notes: Data corresponds to the total number of acres owned, sub-classified by the type of land tenure arrangement within each municipality in the province. The source identifies the number of acres declared as 'owned' while reporting the number under each tax classification. 'Entirely *Ryotwari*' measures the number of municipalities where the ratio of ryotwari land to total land owned was 1. 'Majority *Ryotwari*' measures the number of municipalities where the ratio of ryotwari land to total land owned was above 0.5. The same exercise was constructed for *Zamindari* municipalities. *Zamindari* municipalities include *inam* tenure arrangements. The data includes semi-autonomous Agencies. These were tribal areas in the Vizagapatam district and a collection of *zamindari*-owned lands in the Ganjam district. Calculations made by the author.

tenure arrangements typically existed within municipalities and occasionally within villages.[32] Out of 241 recorded municipalities in 1930, 40 municipalities were reported to be aligned with just one tenure arrangement. The other 201 municipalities contained combinations of different tenure systems. Land ownership in the Berhampur municipality in the Ganjam district highlights the complex nature of this sub-district variation. In 1930, there were 230 *ryotwari* villages, 57 *imam* villages and 178 *zamindari* villages in Berhampur.[33] Despite complexity in the allocation of tenure systems, we can say with certainty that farmers in most villages across Madras owned land taxed under the *ryotwari* system. Table 4.3 assigns municipalities to tenure arrangements, basing the assignment on acreage under each system. The table assigns the vast majority of acreage and municipalities, approximately three-quarters of rural land, to the *ryotwari* tenure arrangement in 1930. *Ryotwari* or government-cultivator settlements formed the 'principal tenure of the province'.[34]

Provincial laws in the colonial and post-colonial period attempted to address the problem of opaque land titles in the remaining one-quarter of

---

[32] This challenges some existing literature that makes broad regional assumptions about regional variation in land tenure structure. Abhijit Banerjee and Lakshmi Iyer, "History, Institutions, and Economic Performance: The Legacy of Colonial Land Tenure Systems in India." *American Economic Review* 95, no. 4 (2005): 1190–213, for example, identify 'landlord' and 'non-landlord' land tenure arrangements by districts. This ignores large variation within municipalities and villages.
[33] *Statistical Atlas*, 17–62.   [34] *State Administration Report*, 87.

land classified under the *zamindari* arrangement. The provincial government enforced laws to strengthen the rights of tenants in *zamindari* settlements following legal disputes between tenants and landlords in the late nineteenth century. In these disputes, landlords approached courts to challenge the occupancy rights of tenants, following a period in which tenants attempted to collateralise leased land in return for credit. Judges ruled in favour of tenants as they were not 'tenants at will'. Judges believed that the occupation of *zamindari* land provided tenants cum farmers with stronger rights than tenants in *ryotwari* areas.[35]

The provincial government supported this view and enforced the Madras Estates Land Act in 1908. The Act provided tradable occupancy rights to tenants in *zamindari* areas.[36] According to section 6 of the act, occupiers or cultivators in 'possession' of land had the 'permanent right of occupancy in his holding'.[37] In terms of transferability, section 10 of the Act stated that 'all rights of occupancy shall be heritable and shall be transferable by sale, gift or otherwise'.[38] G. S. Forbes, a member of the provincial government, proposed the Madras Estates Land Bill in 1905.[39] Forbes believed that the Bill would allow tenants to leverage on their occupancy right to borrow and invest on cultivated land.[40] The aim of the legislation was to provide tenants on *zamindari* settlement with the equivalent protection as given to *ryotwari* landholders.[41] The act further strengthened tenancy protection by limiting the landlord's ability to exploit tenants through high rents. Sections 26, 27 and 28 of the Madras Estates Act exercised limitations to short-term rent increases.

In practice, absentee landlords were also present in *ryotwari* areas. Urban or non-cultivating landowners made higher profits from land rents, than from cultivation, though this system was less pervasive in the *ryotwari* settlements. The perverse incentives created by landlord-favouring property rights regimes restricted productive investment in rural areas, *zamindari* areas in particular. The Madras Estates Act

---

[35] Roy and Swamy, *Law and the Economy*, 46–47.
[36] The Madras Estates Land Act also strengthened tenancy protection by restricting the *zamindar's* ability to exploit tenants through high rents. Sections 26, 27 and 28 enforce restrictions on short-term rent increases.
[37] Section 6, Madras Estates Land Act 1908.
[38] Section 10, Madras Estates Land Act 1908.
[39] George Stuart Forbes graduated from Aberdeen University and joined the Indian Civil Service in 1871. Forbes held positions in the Madras administration, including Secretary to the British Resident in Hyderabad, Secretary to Berar and Chief Secretary to the Governor of Madras. Between 1906 and 1909, Forbes served on the Madras Legislative Council.
[40] *Proceedings of the Council of the Governor of Fort St. George* (Madras, 1905).
[41] Roy and Swamy, *Law and the Economy*, 62.

partially eroded this investment barrier as tenants benefitted from rent ceilings and were encouraged to access credit by collateralising their right to occupancy. Tenants in *zamindari* areas, at least in theory, could borrow more easily on the mortgage market after 1908.

Tenant protection laws eventually culminated in complete detachment from colonial land tenure arrangements after India gained independence. Nationalists and members of the newly formed Indian government believed that permanent occupiers continued to be exploited by rent-seeking *zamindars*.[42] The provincial government in Madras implemented land reforms that replaced the colonial Permanent Settlement system. The 1948 Madras Estates Act abolished the *zamindari* system entirely. The provincial government took temporary ownership of the estates under this category. Local government then redistributed holdings to permanent occupiers.[43] *Zamindars* were only entitled to continue owning the land they cultivated themselves. The government transferred ownership to tenants as long as they were the permanent occupiers and cultivated the land.[44] The government hoped that this redistributive legislation would diminish rent exploitation and incentivise new landowners to invest in land improvement. The government provided new landholders with stronger land titles. Section 12 of the 1948 Madras Estates Act stipulated that 'in the case of zamindari estate, the landholder shall with effect on and from notified date be entitled to a ryotwari patta'.[45] The provincial government converted the opaque ownership structure of *zamindari* settlements into more concrete property titles, as previously existed in *ryotwari* settlements. Greater clarity in titles, in the government's view, allowed farmers to collateralise land and borrow money.

As the *zamindari* system operated in a small part of the province and was eventually abolished, property titles were never much of a barrier to land

---

[42] Khusro, "Land Reforms since Independence," 181.
[43] The impact of this reform has inspired debate on inequality in post-colonial South India. For example, Suhas Chattopadhyay, "On the Class Nature of Land Reforms in India since Independence." *Social Scientist* 2, no. 4 (1973): 3–24, highlights the persistence in rural inequality as the share of land owned by smallholder cultivators did not increase after 1948. Chattopadhyay suggests that *zamindars* retained absentee landholdings through *benami* ownership. *Benami*, in this context, refers to a version of fraud where *zamindars* retained the ownership of land after land reform laws by registering titles under the ownership of their relatives or close friends. The widespread practice of this fraud, according to Chattopadhyay, restricted the impact of land reforms on wealth redistribution.
[44] Chattopadhyay, "On the Class Nature of Land Reforms," 3–5.
[45] Section 12, Madras Estates (Abolition and Conversion to Ryotwari) Act 1948.

purchases and mortgage lending in most of rural Madras.[46] As a deterrent to tax evasion, land disputes were taken seriously in courts.[47] Buyers and sellers of land registered ownership transfer with revenue and land registration offices in each district. In cases of outright sales and when ownership was not entirely clear, either because *pattas* did not confer the rightful owner or the title was disputed, judges authorised the transfer of ownership.[48] When titles were weak or unenforceable, agents exchanging the land approached courts for legal ratification. Judges could reject the sale or mortgage of disputed land. This practice was rare in Madras. Indeed, clarity in the title deed was rarely the point of contention in land disputes. Even in the early twentieth century, during the colonial period, the number of disputed land transfers due to the validity of titles was small. In 1928, for example, court judges reversed just seventy land purchases for invalid land titles. The government reported over 1 million mortgage and sale transactions in the same year.[49]

It is puzzling, then, that mortgages accounted for a small share of total credit transfers in colonial Madras. Creditors were generally reluctant to attach mortgage contracts to loans. Data from a survey of seventy-nine villages suggests that over half of rural lending did not have mortgage instruments attached in the late 1920s.[50] Data from the government's Justice Department shows that creditors were even more reluctant to attach mortgage instruments to loans than the data from village surveys suggest. The Civil Court Statistics series from Civil Justice Reports calculate the total number of civil disputes heard across the district courts and the High Court in Madras. The reports defined the number of disputes involving money and further categorised the number of disputes involving mortgage instruments. Based on these annual surveys,

---

[46] There was a connected barrier which is not discussed in the main text: land fragmentation. Misshapen plots or multiple and disconnected plots in a single holding were potential barriers to mortgage lending. Official reports suggest, however, that this problem was uncommon in Madras. On land fragmentation, the *Provincial Banking Enquiry* reports, 'These conditions, however, do not seem to prevail to any great extent in this Presidency. Holdings undoubtedly are fragmented and there is nothing uncommon about a *ryot* having half a dozen different plots but it is not the rule and though it is common for the *ryot* to have three plots it is uncommon to have many more.' The report proceeds to suggest that land sales consolidated landholdings in the nineteenth and early twentieth centuries. According to the report, the rich reported fragmentation, but this was because they owned multiple and cultivable plots of land in different parts of the village. See *Madras Provincial Banking Enquiry Committee Report*. Vols. I–V (Madras, 1930), 18–19.

[47] *Provincial Banking Enquiry*, 184.

[48] W. R. S. Sathyanathan, *Report on Agricultural Indebtedness* (Madras, 1935), 15.

[49] *Report on the Administration of the Registration Department* (Madras, 1929), 5.

[50] *Provincial Banking Enquiry*, 56–75.

creditors attached mortgage instruments to between 4 and 5 per cent of all the credit transactions under dispute between 1925 and 1935.[51] As discussed in the previous chapter, creditors were especially reluctant to attach mortgage instruments to loans in the high-risk, dry regions. Yet, cultivators owned, and were proprietors of, the majority of plots in the driest tracts. *Ryotwari* settlements constituted 100 per cent of total acreage in the Bellary district, with similar ratios of 96 and 99 per cent in the neighbouring dry districts of Anantapur and Kurnool.[52] A large number of *zamindari* estates were in municipalities near the Cauvery and Godavari deltas.[53]

Land tenure systems did affect land transfers, though not necessarily because of the tradability of land. The bigger problem was the tax obligation. Taxing land was a regressive policy choice, one that increased the farmer's exposure to volatility in climate and output. In good years, when output was high, tax obligations were met. In bad years, when output was low, revenue earned by peasants did not cover tax bills. When tax bills were not met, revenue officers auctioned land with tax payments attached. The price of tax-defaulted land was lower than market prices. Buyers acquiring unencumbered land paid a higher price than the buyers acquiring land with tax obligation attached. The Madras Estates Land Act Committee, set up for the purpose of reviewing the land tenure system in the province, reported in 1938 that 'for an arrear of one rupee, land worth Rs. 100 is brought to auction and taken for a very low price'.[54] According to the Deputy Registrar of the Bellary district in 1929, the sale price of red soil land in government auctions was between 5 and 25 rupees. This was between a half and a quarter of the market price, implying that potential buyers were reluctant to acquire tax-defaulted plots.[55] Indeed, labourers and tenants in colonial Bellary were discouraged from owning land in the 1920s as, in Washbrook's view,

---

[51] *Statistics of Civil Courts in the Madras Presidency* (Madras, 1925–1935).
[52] *Statistical Atlas*, 283–406.
[53] Ramnad, East and West Godavari as well as Vizagapatam districts housed several *zamindari* municipalities.
[54] *Madras Estates Land Act Committee Report: Part I* (Madras, 1939), 187. Hereafter source referred to as *MELAC Report*. Tanguturi Prakasam, chair of the committee that compiled the report, was a barrister in rural Madras until joining the Indian National Congress party in the early 1920s. Prakasam became an influential political figure in the province in the late colonial period, holding ministerial positions in the Legislative Assembly in the late 1930s and early 1940s. In the post-colonial period, Prakasam rose to leader of the Madras legislature until advocating for the partition of the province, following which he was elected as the leader of the Hyderabad legislature.
[55] *Provincial Banking Enquiry*, Vol. III, 1014.

'independent farm production brought only tax-bills'.[56] Creditors were equally reluctant to repossess property due to the possibility of inheriting overdue bills.

Because land was simultaneously taxed and collateralised to obtain credit, lenders faced possible conflict with government officials when recovering unpaid dues. Peasants could not easily borrow money to pay tax bills. The timing of credit disbursements did not coincide with payment of tax bills. The credit market operated seasonally, and the government demanded the payment of taxes annually. Peasants paid taxes when the credit market was lax. As reported in the Banking Enquiry Committee's survey of seventy-nine villages in 1929, borrowing to pay tax bills accounted for a small share of total borrowed, 2 and 4 per cent in wet and dry villages, respectively.[57] Nevertheless, credit defaulters were likely to have also been tax defaulters. When crops failed and earnings were low, peasants defaulting on credit bills also defaulted on tax bills. Tax and credit bills piled up at the same time for peasants, potentially creating frictions between debt and tax collectors. Moneylenders, however, recovered loans more easily than district government officials recovered unpaid tax dues. Revenue officials in the government regularly reported that borrowers prioritised the repayment of debts before the payment of tax.[58] When advancing mortgage loans, lenders were less concerned about chasing payments from clients and more concerned with the value of land, value derived from price minus inherited tax bill and transaction costs.

Moneylenders provided three types of mortgage instruments during the colonial period. First, lenders provided credit secured by mortgage without possession. Agents agreed to the transfer of land but lenders did not take possession until the borrower defaulted. Second, lenders provided usufructuary mortgages or loans secured by mortgage with possession. Borrowers transferred the ownership of land to lenders prior to loan disbursement. Third, borrowers provided lenders with a bond or promise of land transfer in the event of default. Mortgage without possession was the most common instrument used during the colonial period. Lenders rarely provided loans with the obligation of prior possession or bond. From a government survey of fifty-four villages in 1935, the number of loans secured by mortgage without possession was 2.5 times

---

[56] David A. Washbrook, "The Commercialization of Agriculture in Colonial India: Production, Subsistence and Reproduction in the 'Dry South', c. 1870–1930." *Modern Asian Studies* 28, no. 1 (1994): 129–64, 137.

[57] *Provincial Banking Enquiry*, 56–75. Calculations made by the author. The grouping of Mostly Wet and Mostly Dry conducted in the same format as Table 3.2.

[58] *MELAC Report*, Part I, 472; Baker, *An Indian Rural Economy*, 424.

Figure 4.1 Annual shifts in mortgage loans and commodity prices, 1911–33

Sources: Report on the Administration of the Registration Department 1911–1933; McAlpin, "Price Movements."

Notes: Annual number of mortgages is measured at the provincial level. The author calculates annual changes by taking the difference between the number of mortgage loans in year *n + 1* and the number of mortgage loans in year *n.* The same method is applied to calculating changes in the agricultural price index. Base year for mortgages and prices is 1911. The first point in the graph is the difference in mortgages and prices between 1911 and 1912. The graph stops at 1933 as recovery from the Depression began in 1934. The government installed a series of credit regulations from 1935 which affected the mortgage market. These factors are discussed in the next chapter.

higher than the number of loans secured by both possession and bonds.[59] Mortgage bonds were more common in loans provided for trade rather than cultivation, reflecting the different risks involved in each type of business. Bonds were less secure than other mortgage instruments, and revenue earned from cultivation was more volatile than revenue earned from trade.

Annual or short-term shifts in the number of mortgage loans in the early twentieth century seemed to respond to shifts in commodity prices. Figure 4.1 demonstrates that the difference in mortgages between year *n + 1* and year *n* closely followed changes in prices. The swift response of supply to price shocks was driven by the short-term structure of the credit market. There are two plausible, interconnected explanations for why lenders supplied a higher number of mortgage loans when commodity

[59] *Report on Agricultural Indebtedness,* 35.

prices rose. One is that increase in the value of commodities reflected an increase in the value of land, making mortgages a lucrative loan instrument. Another is that credit demand increased when prices were high. Bad years, or harvest failure after droughts or floods, caused commodity-supply shortages and inflated prices. Peasants struggled to meet credit bills in such years, defaulting on loans or demanding fresh loans to meet working capital requirements for the next season. In such cases, creditors either provided fresh mortgage loans or, more characteristically of the credit market in Madras, upgraded previously unsecured loans to mortgages.

Annual changes in prices and mortgage supply saw particularly large shifts after the First World War and during the Great Depression. Growth in demand for land and a series of crop failures inflated commodity prices and the value of land between 1918 and 1920. Peasants sought to renew unpaid loans and returning soldiers, with savings unspent during the war, sought to purchase land or expand existing holdings. In 1920, the Registration Department in the provincial government suggested that prices soared quickly because of widespread crop failure in 1918/19 as well as a 'revival in trade' and 'investment in land of the savings of a large number of demobilised men'.[60] This short period saw a surge in the number of mortgage loans.

Deflationary pressures during the global crisis drove down the number of mortgages in the province. Commodity prices declined by 20 per cent between 1929 and 1930, and 31 per cent between 1930 and 1931. The value of land declined due to deflationary pressures and unpaid tax burdens.[61] While the number of land auctions increased during the Depression, the government was the primary bidder for these plots. There was little interest among wealthier farmers in land auctions during the Depression period.[62] The waning interest in acquiring land is also evidenced in the supply of mortgage loans. The number of mortgage loans in 1933 was 27 per cent lower than the number provided in 1927. The Registration Department highlighted this trend of declining mortgages in the early 1930s, stating in 1931 that creditors did not renew a large portion of their outstanding debts and did not, 'have the courage to advance fresh loans' as commodity and land prices declined.[63]

---

[60] *Report on the Administration of the Registration Department* (1920), 4.
[61] *MELAC Report*, 187.
[62] K. A. Manikumar, *A Colonial Economy in the Great Depression, Madras (1929–1937)* (Chennai: Orient Longman, 2003), 63.
[63] *Report on the Administration of the Registration Department* (1931), 4.

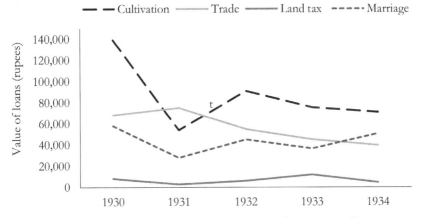

Figure 4.2 Nominal value of mortgage loans by purpose of borrowing, 1930–34
Source: Report on Agricultural Indebtedness, 35.
Notes: Government-commissioned surveyors collected data on mortgage loans in two villages per district, across twenty-seven districts in the province. The figure excludes data where the source reported the purpose of borrowing as either 'other' or unidentifiable. 'Cultivation' includes borrowing to finance production. 'Trade' includes borrowing to finance the transport of produce after the harvest. 'Land Tax' includes borrowing to specifically pay unpaid tax bills. 'Marriage' includes borrowing to finance a marriage ceremony. The graph excludes data on borrowings for the repayments of prior debts.

When mortgages were supplied, lenders commonly provided mortgage loans as secondary rather than primary loans. Secondary borrowing was a structural feature of the mortgage market, as the sheer scale of borrowing to finance defaulted loans suggests. Figures 4.2 and 4.3 report data collected on purposes of borrowing in the mortgage market during the early 1930s. The value of loans for cultivation and trade expenses, as reported in Figure 4.2, was higher than the value of loans borrowed to pay for marriage ceremonies. Yet, as illustrated in Figure 4.3, the most common purpose of borrowing in the mortgage market was for repayments of defaulted debt. At the start of the Depression in 1930, the value of borrowing to repay prior debts was fourteen times higher than the value of borrowing to finance cultivation expenses. During the Depression, deflationary pressures increased default rates. The supply of credit contracted, across borrowing categories, between 1930 and 1934. In this context, the rate of decline in credit used to meet production costs was high, especially in the first year of the crisis. Mortgage

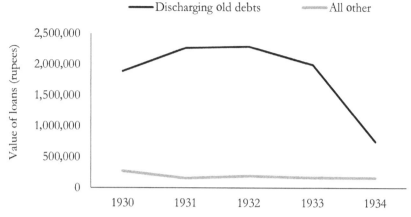

Figure 4.3 Nominal value of mortgage loans issued to discharge old debts, 1930–34
Source: Report on Agricultural Indebtedness, 35.
Notes: Data scope is similar to Figure 4.2. 'Discharging Old Debts' includes borrowing to repay previous loans. 'All Other' includes borrowing to finance cultivation, trade, land taxes and marriages. The graph excludes data where the source reported the purpose of borrowing as either 'other' or unidentifiable.

borrowing to meet cultivation expenses halved between 1930 and 1931. The nominal value of borrowings to finance defaulted debts increased between 1930 and 1932, then declined between 1932 and 1934. As borrowers started meeting their credit bills, the volume of debts borrowed to cover prior defaults expectedly decreased. However, in 1934, despite increasing prices and recovery from the crisis, the value of mortgage borrowing for the repayment of defaulted loans was still eleven times higher than the value of mortgage borrowing for production expenses, suggesting that the high ratio of secondary to primary borrowing in the mortgage market was not entirely a Depression-driven phenomenon. The data tells us that borrowers on the mortgage market were commonly defaulters. Lenders provided the majority of mortgage loans to clients topping up loans for the second or third time than they did to clients obtaining fresh loans. The crisis in the early 1930s only accentuated this pattern.

Data on the average loan terms, from when the loan was issued to when the loan contract expired or matured, of mortgage loans suggests that the main purpose of borrowing on the mortgage market was the repayment of defaulted loans. Government officials collected data on the time span (in years) of mortgage loans in two villages per district across twenty-seven districts. The source categorised data by the annual value of registered mortgages without possession, mortgages with possession and mortgage bonds between 1930 and 1934. The survey categorises volume of lending by contract period. In other words, it shows contract preferences among lenders by estimating the total amount of lending by contract type. Four contract types were chosen: less than one year, between one and three years, above three years and 'no term'. From the survey's findings, lenders provided long-term loans of between one and three years to high-income borrowers for the purchase of land or large capital expenses. Yet, these loans constituted the minority of total mortgage lending in rural Madras. 'No term' was specified on the majority of recorded mortgage loans between 1930 and 1934. Lenders deliberately avoided declaring specific time periods as a means of increasing their flexibility. As mortgages were secondary loans, lenders leveraged on undeclared loan terms to record defaults and register land transfers with short notice periods given to borrowers.[64]

In short, this section demonstrates that property titles were not a barrier to mortgage lending in most of rural Madras. When mortgages were supplied, lenders attached mortgage instruments to secondary loans, those loans to clients seeking to renew defaulted loans, rather than as primary loans to clients obtaining fresh debt. Transaction costs explain this feature of the mortgage market, as we will see later in the chapter. The role of alternative contractual arrangements and whether lenders secured primary loans with other types of contracts are questions that remain. To these questions, we now turn.

Contract Law and Rural Credit Markets

The change from Company to Crown rule in 1857 also changed the process of law-making. The colonial administration divided executive responsibilities between the central government and the provincial governments. Central and provincial governments designed laws while the judiciary enforced these laws. The colonial government established defined policy responsibilities for the central and provincial executives. The central government was responsible for the implementation of contract laws. The government designed contract laws in the late nineteenth century to regulate internal trade.

---

[64] *Report on Agricultural Indebtedness*, 36.

Prior to the design of contract laws, indigenous trading instruments or *hundis* were commonly used across rural India. *Hundis* were a variety of negotiated commercial instruments used in financial transactions throughout Indian history. There was non-uniformity in the design of *hundi* instruments, causing problems for the regulatory design of contract laws. The government tried designing contract laws to regulate the variety of indigenous trading instruments. The colonial government implemented a series of laws to regulate diverse *hundi* arrangements in the late nineteenth century.[65]

The government enforced two contract laws in the late nineteenth century, both of which contained instructions for the exchange of credit. The 1872 India Contract Act (ICA) and the 1881 Negotiable Instruments Act (NIA) encouraged and regulated the use of contracts in rural credit.[66] The NIA was the colonial government's attempt at regulating *hundi* transactions. The act refrained from the use of the word *hundi* but instead attempted to create an accessible law that uniformly regulated any negotiated instrument. The act defined a negotiable instrument as, 'a promissory note, a bill of exchange or cheque payable either to order or to bearer'.[67] The act further defines each instrument as follows:

A promissory note is an instrument in writing (not being a bank-note or a currency-note) containing an unconditional undertaking signed by the maker, to pay a certain sum of money only to, or to the order of, a certain person, or to the bearer of the instrument.

A bill of exchange is an instrument in writing containing an unconditional order, signed by the maker, directing a certain person to pay a certain sum of money only to, or to the order of, a certain person or to the bearer of the instrument.

A cheque is a bill of exchange drawn on a specified banker and not expressed to be payable otherwise than on demand.[68]

The challenge for the colonial government was to design a comprehensive law that regulated the variety of indigenous contracts. At first sight, it would seem that the colonial state failed to properly integrate the myriad

---

[65] See Abraham, "Colonial Law in Early British Malabar" and Marina Martin, "Project Codification: Legal Legacies of the British Raj on the Indian Mercantile Credit Institution Hundi." *Contemporary South Asia* 23, no. 1 (2015): 67–84, for an assessment of these laws in failing to account for the diversity of indigenous commercial instruments.

[66] Section 10 of the India Contract Act defined a contract as, 'All agreements are contracts if they are made by the free consent of parties competent to contract for a lawful consideration and with a lawful object, and are not hereby expressly declared to be void.'

[67] Section 13, Negotiable Instruments Act 1881.

[68] Sections 4–7, Negotiable Instruments Act 1881.

of indigenous instruments under the purview of contract laws.[69] The colonial period was one of legal 'discontinuity' as contract laws did not regulate, and even marginalised, indigenous *hundi* instruments. Judges faced difficulties in hearing disputes involving *hundi* transactions that were not explicitly regulated in the NIA. Judges had a choice between arbitrating based on an applied judicial structure from Britain or to use local precedent to deal with disputes involving *hundi* instruments.[70] A part of the problem was defining an appropriate contract, owing to the multiple types of contracts used. The Chettiar bankers, for example, used three different types of credit instruments. The *Darshani* instrument was payable on sight, the *Muttadi* instrument defined a specific period of payment on paper and, what was commonly used by Chettiar bankers in this period, the *Nadappu* instrument provided agents flexible periods of repayment. With each *hundi* displaying levels of complexity beyond the direction defined in the NIA, judges were unprepared to regulate *hundis*.[71]

Colonial administrators seemed aware of this problem. However, the government's solution was to empower agents and judges to group the ambiguous instrument under one of the three instruments defined in the NIA. Section 17 of the NIA contained a provision for 'Ambiguous Instruments' where, 'an instrument may be construed either as a promissory note or a bill of exchange, and the holder may at his election treat it as either and the instrument shall be thenceforth treated accordingly'.[72] The provision recognized the diversity in *hundi* instruments, though provided vague directions to judges. Interpreting section 17 was tricky. It suggested the three instrument types as points of comparison, maintaining that any *hundi* instrument could be classified as one of either a bill of exchange, cheque or promissory note. In this context, the law designated promissory notes as the model debt instrument in rural credit markets.

The key difference between promissory notes and bills of exchange was their tradability. Promissory notes were fixed contracts. The NIA designed the appropriate debt contract in two stages. In the first stage, the act defined the purpose of a credit contract as an instrument that protected the interests of borrowers when debts were repaid. The act

[69] Abraham, "Colonial Law in Early British Malabar," and Martin, "Project Codification," argue that contract law failed to regulate the diversity of indigenous instruments used in colonial India.

[70] Martin, "Project Codification," 70–73.

[71] Tirthankar Roy, "The Monsoon and the Market for Money in Late-colonial India." *Enterprise & Society* 17, no. 2 (2016): 324–57, 345–47.

[72] Section 17, Negotiable Instruments Act 1881.

stated that 'where a debtor, owing several distinct debts to one person, makes a payment to him, either with the express intimation or under circumstances implying, that the payment is to be applied to the discharge of some particular debt, they payment if accepted, must be applied accordingly'.[73] In the second stage, the act defined features of a sample debt contract and explicitly noted promissory notes as the model to follow. The NIA described the contractual setting as,

A owes B, among other debts, 1,000 rupees upon a promissory note, which falls due on the first June. He owes B no other debt of the amount. On the first June A pays to B 1,000 rupees. The payment is to be applied to the discharge of the promissory note.[74]

By simplifying features of the appropriate contract, the colonial government directed judges to accept different types of promissory notes, as long as the basic conditions of a debt contract were fulfilled, basic conditions referring to mutual recognition of both repayment amount and date of expected repayment.

Promissory notes, being fixed contracts, were easier to regulate than the other contract types. Despite the varied design of pro-notes, some similar features unified the different instruments used and brought them under the purview of nineteenth-century contract laws. Figure 4.4 is a sample promissory note from one transaction in 1929. It contained the key features of commonly used promissory notes at the time and went beyond the basic conditions of debt contracts prescribed in the NIA. Defined in pro-notes were lending terms including the loan principal, rate of interest and repayment or maturity date. Signatures or thumb-prints from lenders, borrowers and co-applicants were universal features of these contracts. The obligation to repay fell on both the borrower and guarantor, as illustrated by the wording of 'me/us' and 'I/we' in Figure 4.4. Borrowers that did not have the skills to read promissory notes typically relied on the assistance of teachers in local schools as well as village accountants and clerks. Surveyors in the Provincial Banking Enquiry Committee found that borrowers commonly approached *karnams*, or local accountants, 'village schoolmasters' and friends 'conversant with arithmetic', to interpret promissory notes and ensure that borrowers had 'not been cheated'.[75]

Promissory notes were more popularly used than mortgage instruments in colonial Madras. Creditors presented pro-notes, similar to the illustration in Figure 4.4, to local courts as evidence that borrowers had defaulted

---

[73] Section 59, Negotiable Instruments Act 1881.
[74] Section 59, Negotiable Instruments Act 1881.   [75] *Provincial Banking Enquiry*, 220.

1215

APPENDIX F-IV-2.
(Form of Pronote)

உ.

சிவமயம்.

No._____   Rs._____

198   ஹ்ரூ_____ மீ_____ உக்கு_____ ஹ்ரூ_____ மீ_____ உ.

நிண்டுக்கல்லில் கடைவைத்திருக்கும்
தேவகோட்டை வெ. ஆ.தி. க. கடேசன் செட்டயாா் அவா்களுக்கு

_____

_____

_____

_____

_____

_____

_____எழுதிக்கொடுத்த பிரும்சசிடோட்

_____

_____

_____

தங்கள் வஙக_____ ரிடம் நா_____கடஙக வட்டிக்கி வாங
கியது ரொக்கம் ரூ._____இந்த ரூபாய்_____க்கும்
நாளது தேதிமுதல் மாதம் 1-க்கு 100-க்கு வட்டி ரூபாய்_____வீதம்
வட்டி சோ்த்துக கூடியவட்டியும் முதலையும் தாங்கள் வேண்யும்போது தங்க
ளுக்காவது அல்லது தங்கள் ஆா்டருக்காவது ரொக்கம் செலுத்திவைப்பே

சாகூ்கள்.
எழுதியதமான சாக்ஷியுமான

Translation.

' No.   ' Rs.   . . . . '
      (Tamil) date .   .   .   .   corresponding to (English),
                                                    date   . . .19 . .

    The promissory note executed in favour of Devekottai V. At. N. Natesan
Chettiyar Avargal, who has got a firm in Dindigul, by

is as follows : —

    The amount received by $\frac{me}{us}$ in cash as loan bearing interest from
                                  of your firm is Rs.   . On
demand, $\frac{I}{we}$ promise to pay to you or to your order in cash the principal
together with interest from this date on this sum of Rupees   at
                            per cent per mensem.
      Witnesses ~
      Written and attested by—

158

Figure 4.4 Model promissory note in 1929
Source: Provincial Banking Enquiry, Vol. III, 1215.

Table 4.4 *Credit disputes in thirteen district courts, 1930–1934*

Year	Disputes (1)	Disputes with Pro-Notes (2)	Disputes with Mortgages (3)	Ratio 2 to 1 (per cent)	Ratio 3 to 1 (per cent)
1930	47,975	37,859	6,096	78.9	12.7
1931	53,620	44,772	5,953	83.5	11.1
1932	55,857	49,462	9,081	88.6	16.3
1933	52,881	42,918	7,442	81.2	14.1
1934	47,394	37,608	7,151	79.4	15.1

Source: *Report on Agricultural Indebtedness*, 44.
Notes: The data refers to cases in lower courts involving moneylenders and borrowers who listed their profession as agriculture or cultivation. Data for columns (1) and (2) presented exactly as they are in the source. The ratios for 1932 do not add up to 100 per cent, possibly reflecting an error in the source. The total number of disputes were classified according to the security provided on loans. The cases involving promissory notes (2) were not secured against any form of physical collateral. The data constitutes approximately 10 per cent of the total number of credit disputes in the same time period. According to civil court statistics, the number of cases involving money or movable property was 478,404, 541,486, 554,394, 556,815 and 499,013 in the years 1930–1934. See *Statistics of Civil Courts 1930–1934*.

on their debt obligations. Judges adjudicated such disputes by interpreting contract laws and applying their interpretation to the conditions attached in promissory notes. Judges seemed to have little difficulty in interpreting contract laws to adjudicate disputes involving promissory notes, much to the advantage of the contract holder. Indeed, data from thirteen district courts in the early 1930s demonstrate that creditors more commonly attached promissory notes to credit disputes. As illustrated in Table 4.4, of the surveyed 257,727 credit transactions in dispute between 1930 and 1934, creditors attached promissory notes to 212,619 transactions and mortgages to 35,723 transactions. In approximately eight out of ten disputed transactions in any given year, creditors secured contested debts with signed promissory notes. Put differently, moneylenders frequently brought signed promissory notes to disputed credit transactions in courts.

Why were promissory notes more common than mortgages in the rural credit market? An explanation for the persistence in preferences for types of contracts, and the focus of the next section of this chapter, is that creditors relied on credit instruments that were most cost-efficient, relative to the value of loans. The use of promissory notes incurred lower transaction costs, relative to mortgages. The design of contract laws made the use of promissory notes lucrative for the moneylender. Court judgements were expedited in cases with signed promissory notes. Lenders were presented with an accelerated forum of appeal to enforce the repayment of loans. This was supplemented by lower fees when creditors presented pro-notes, rather than mortgage contracts in courts. The next section analyses the costs of enforcing different contracts and demonstrates the modes of transmission of these costs on the price of credit.

Contract Enforcement and Credit Pricing

Enforcing credit contracts was complex when defaults were not strategic and instead occurred due to weather-induced crop failure. The question of liability was unclear when volatile climate was the underlying cause of loan defaults. When crops failed, debt defaulters petitioned courts to evaluate their contractual obligation. Mortgage registrations, for example, were regularly disputed and brought to courts as defaulters requested Judges to administer loan extensions and restructure repayment schedules, accounting for threats imposed by volatile climate.

That borrowers rarely defaulted on contracts wilfully weakened the penalties imposed on defaulters by judges. Climate risk was not insured against and, therefore, weather shocks and crop failures had significant short-term effects on the repayment capacity of peasants. This was not just a problem for tenants and labourers but also a challenge for holders of small land parcels, especially those smallholders in the dry districts. Smallholders, in this case referring to cultivators owning less than 5 acres of land, commonly approached famine camps and relied on food welfare entitlements as they were barely able to subsist in drought years.[76] In such cases, *force majeure* clauses in contract laws acknowledged the problem and instructed judges to alter contractual terms to ensure fairness between contracting agents. Section 36 of the India Contract Act voided contracts that were 'contingent on impossible event ... whether the impossibility of the event is known or not to the parties to the agreement at the time when it is made'.[77] The ICA further empowered judges to protect agents from coercion and undue influence.[78] Judges invoked these clauses when creditors with disposable income attempted to collect penalties from poor borrowers.

There was precedent for judges to interfere in tenancy and credit disputes to enact 'the principles of natural justice and equity' following harsh conditions imposed by 'acts of god'.[79] In credit disputes, judges

---

[76] *Report on Agricultural Indebtedness*, 11–12.   [77] Section 36, India Contract Act.
[78] See sections 16 and 19 of the India Contract Act.
[79] See the list of referred tenancy cases in the court judgement, Kondnath Chathoth Kunhi Raman Nambiar v. Cheriyalanthot Aniyath Elambilan Kunhi Kannan Nambiar (1936 71 MLJ 352, Madras, 14 February 1936).

enforced moratoriums and reduced rates of interest to allow for easier repayment. In one case, a farmer borrowed 71 rupees from a local moneylender in 1907. The terms of the contract stipulated that the borrower repaid the loan in 142 monthly instalments. The borrower paid 29 instalments and defaulted on subsequent ones. The contract stipulated a daily penalty for non-payment. The creditors sued to collect 52 rupees of the original principal and 154 rupees for 19 months of defaulted interest which amounted to penal interest of 190 per cent per annum. The lower and high courts reduced the rate of interest to 24 per cent, a commonly charged rate for the recovery of defaulted loans in courts, and stipulated a flexible repayment schedule for the borrower, considering the willingness to repay the loan when there was income available to repay. The judges justified their position by stating that contracts need judicial interference, not only in cases of fraud and misrepresentation but also 'because of the borrower's extreme necessity and helplessness'.[80]

Partly reflecting the inherent problems in fixing liability when defaults happened due to 'acts of god', cases could take a long time to settle. This posed a problem when the moneylender's incentive to link credit and land markets was tied to the productivity of legal institutions. Timely and inexpensive proceedings could ensure a more effective execution of land transfers as an enforced penalty on defaulted borrowers. In contrast, lengthy and expensive proceedings incentivised defaulters to extend disputes to delay or reverse the transfer of mortgaged land.

How long did average credit disputes take to reach settlement in Madras? As previously mentioned, creditors typically provided short-term, four- to six-month loans to peasants. Credit disputes in courts lasted much longer.[81] In 1922, the *munsiff* courts, the lowest courts in the province, reported a backlog of 52,559 cases of which 11,990 cases were pending for over one year.[82] With every appeal, the duration of disputes grew disproportionately longer. Credit disputes were generally heard over a period of one to two years in District Courts. The duration of disputes in the High Court showed even greater unpredictability. Data recorded by the provincial government suggests that high court proceedings lasted between twenty-four and thirty-six months between the 1920s and 1940s.[83] The problem was potentially more severe, with some surveys

---

[80] Avathani Muthukrishnier v. Sankaralingam Pillai (1912 24 MLJ 135, Madras, 10 September 1912).

[81] Duration measured as the average number of days taken between initial hearing and final judgement for civil cases.

[82] G. F. F. Foulkes, *Local Autonomy* (Madras, 1937), 105.

[83] *Statistics of Civil Courts* (1920–45). Data is not available for the years 1940–44, 1948–53.

suggesting that several cases appealed in the Madras High Court in 1923 lay idle for twenty-four months.[84] The decade after 1947 saw a crisis in the caseload across provincial courts. By 1957, it was common for disputes in the Madras High Court to last between six and eight years.[85]

The aforementioned data provides an understated account of the duration of cases in provincial courts. The data refers to appellate forums and has not considered the duration of cases in lower rural courts. Indeed, disputes in *munsiff*, or village, courts, subdivisional tribunals and small cause courts were equally time consuming while the process of appeals added to these already time-intensive procedures. Furthermore, the execution of judgement and transfer of assets were additional time-demanding procedures. The sale and registration of new land titles, for instance, was a lengthy process. An all-inclusive estimation widens the difference between the duration of court disputes and the time span of agricultural loans. Loan recovery in courts, as a result, was an expensive task in time and money for moneylenders, an issue recognised by official surveyors of rural credit. As stated by the Provincial Banking Enquiry Committee, 'it is uncommon for the ryot to go out of his way to repay a money-lender and the fullest possible advantage is taken of the law's delays by procrastination in court and by evading or circumventing the court's efforts on behalf of the decree holder'.[86]

The Provincial Banking Enquiry Committee went further and provided a model estimate of the costs incurred by litigants in a 'City Civil Court' and the Madras High Court in 1930. The model includes an estimate of the bills raised by courts and the fees that clients paid to lawyers. Court fees in the lower courts included stamp charges on the plaint and the costs incurred to process the following documents: the *vakalat* or affidavits between clients and lawyers, summons to the defendant, subpoenas and witness documents, the application documents and the copy of the decree. This, according to the Banking Enquiry, cost disputants 220 rupees and 15 annas. Clients paid, on average, 118 rupees to lawyers to litigate in civil courts. The model cost of dispute in the civil court added up to 338 rupees and 15 annas.[87] Disputants at the High Court level incurred higher costs. Stamp charges were similar to the civil court but, according to the Banking Enquiry, plaintiffs and defendants incurred higher charges for the processing of court documents. Disputing parties also paid higher fees to lawyers and paid the High Court a one-time fee for the processing of documents for 'first day hearing'. The High Court charges included 235 rupees and

---

[84] Foulkes, *Local Autonomy*, 117–18.   [85] *Statistics of Civil Courts* (1959).
[86] *Provincial Banking Enquiry*, 84.   [87] *Provincial Banking Enquiry*, 183.

7 annas for the court fees and 165 rupees and 3 annas for the bills raised by lawyers. In total, litigating in the High Court in 1930 cost approximately 400 rupees and 10 annas. Assuming agents registered credit disputes in the civil court and appealed the verdict in the High Court, they incurred an estimated cost of 739 rupees.[88]

These model costs do not account for additional expenses, including transport costs, the costs of litigating in lower courts and the bills incurred in the appeals process. The cost of title transfer and land registration generated a set of expenses that are also not presented in the cost tables.[89] Reviewing the costs, in time and money, incurred by moneylenders, and why lenders one official report commented in 1935 that,

The average duration of suits is startlingly high, exceeding 400 days or approaching a period of two years. One can imagine the great cost to the parties, incurred in travelling long distances to appear at these courts over and over again for a single suit, often to waste their time and money in idle waiting because of inevitable adjournments.[90]

Enforcing promissory notes generated lower legal costs than enforcing mortgages. Loans declared on signed promissory notes were charged a flat court fee which was lower than the costs of court disputes on mortgage loans. Litigants incurred a flat cost of 270 rupees inclusive of decree execution and advocate fees if they presented judges with signed promissory notes.[91] Enforcing mortgage contracts in civil courts was 30 per cent more expensive than enforcing promissory notes in the same forum. Mortgage disputes in the High Court cost lenders and borrowers 1.5 times more than promissory note disputes in the same forum. As recorded in the previous chapter, from the Provincial Banking Enquiry's estimates, the average debt per acre was 58 rupees for the province in 1929. The costs of enforcing promissory notes and mortgage contracts were five and seven times higher than the average debt per acre in the province. These enforcement costs were more comparable, being only marginally higher, than the costs of purchasing working cattle in the late colonial period.[92] In other words, enforcement costs were significantly higher than the average size of small working capital loans in the 1920s and 1930s.

In cases where the courts ruled in favour of the lender, judges typically ordered for borrowers to bear some or all of the court fees. Judges

[88] *Provincial Banking Enquiry*, 183.
[89] The Provincial Banking Enquiry Committee's estimated cost of land registration was 26 rupees and 6 annas. See *Provincial Banking Enquiry*, 183.
[90] *Report on Agricultural Indebtedness*, 45.   [91] *Provincial Banking Enquiry*, 183.
[92] These costs are mentioned in Chapter 3. The costs of purchasing working cattle generally varied between 200 and 400 rupees in the late 1930s.

determined the allocation of costs to plaintiffs and defendants, and this allocation differed on a case-by-case basis. Judges could dismiss cases with some or all the costs charged to the plaintiff or the defendant. Itemised billing and the charges placed by the courts on the litigants were not discussed in the individual case judgements. When courts raised bills on the litigants, this only included court fees and fees for document processing. Even when confident of victory, creditors needed to budget for other costs, including lawyer fees, transport costs and registration charges.

The incentive structure of the moneylender can be measured by the difference between the term of borrowing, between issue and maturity, in year n and the expected duration of legal dispute in year $n + 1$. Alternatively, the lender's incentive to provide a contract-backed loan can be measured by the ratio of the expected cost of enforcement to size of the loan. Moneylenders provided contracted loans if the cost of enforcing land transfers in court was lower than the size of the loan. In combination, creditors provided contracted loans if the term of borrowing and size of loans exceeded the time required and costs incurred to enforce contracts and the transfer of land in courts. This justified the composition of loans that were secured by court-enforced contracts. Loans of a certain value, which exceeded the provincial average, satisfied the high enforcement costs in courts.

Moneylenders interviewed in government reports highlighted the relationship between the size of loans and enforcement costs. A government-employed surveyor, as part of the task of reporting on village credit markets in 1935, recorded one moneylender from the Ramnad district saying that, 'decisions in civil courts are often so frivolous and arbitrary'. The surveyor, following the discussion with the moneylender, reported that 'court-fees and court costs are extravagant and the law's delays are tremendous'. The anonymised moneylender from Ramnad, according to the surveyor, incurred, 'as much as Rs. 50 to Rs. 100 in costs', for a suit worth 100 rupees. The lender claimed that the decision to initiate legal proceedings depended on whether the size of loan exceeded legal costs, indicating that they avoided courts when the value of disputed loans was small.[93]

The costs of judicial proceedings incentivised moneylenders to operate a multi-layered enforcement structure in Madras. Primary loans were unsecured. First- and second-time defaults changed the contractual nature of loans. Following a first round of default, lenders upgraded

---

[93] *Report on Agricultural Indebtedness*, 17.

unsecured loans to loans secured by promissory notes. Short periods of repayment were fixed on pro-notes. Interest rates compounded following rounds of default. The law stipulated a maximum three-year limitation on each pro-note, which necessitated a fresh renewal of a previous note following its expiry. With each renewal, lenders added the compounded interest from previous defaults into the unpaid principal. This process continued until creditors upgraded the initial promissory note into a mortgage-backed loan.[94]

Lenders choosing promissory notes in the first contractual stage was logical. Enforcing promissory notes cost less than enforcing mortgages, though was equally enforceable. Judgements were issued based on terms in signed contracts. Signed pro-notes demonstrated a mutual recognition of default, offering lenders sufficient evidence for demanding repayment in courts. Lenders used mortgage instruments as a last resort. Land transfer was a repayment option when multiple defaults signalled the borrower's inability to repay.[95] Put differently, mortgages were cost-effective when the size of compounded debt matched the cost of enforcing land transfers in court.

Moneylenders used pricing strategies to compensate for the high costs of contract enforcement. Contract laws allowed lenders the flexibility to transmit the cost of enforcement into higher interest rates in pro-notes. According to section 79 of the NIA,

When interest at a specified rate is expressly made payable on a promissory note or bill of exchange, interest shall be calculated at the rate specified, on the amount of the principal money due thereon, from the date of the instrument, until tender or realization of such amount, or until such date after the institution of a suit to recover such amount as the court directs.[96]

Data from a survey of mortgage loans in 1935 shows that lenders coordinated loan principals and interest rates to match the cost of enforcement. Lenders added enforcement costs to the loan principals, interest rates or both. Interest rates were low on large loans and high on small

---

[94] *Report on Agricultural Indebtedness*, 15.   [95] *Report on Agricultural Indebtedness*, 15.
[96] Section 80 of the NIA recommended that judges enforce interest rates of 18 per cent when pro-notes did not declare a specified rate. According to the Act,

When no rate of interest is specified in the instrument, interest on the amount due thereon shall, [notwithstanding any agreement relating to interest between any parties to the instrument], be calculated at the rate of 18[eighteen per centum] per annum, from the date at which the same ought to have been paid by the party charged, until tender or realization of the amount due thereon, or until such date after the institution of a suit to recover such amount as the court directs.

Judges rarely had to follow this recommendation in the unregulated market as pro-notes typically defined rates charged on loans.

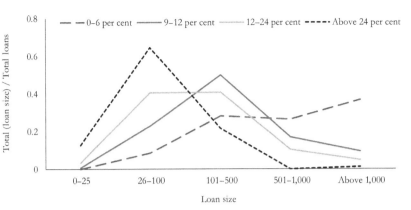

Figure 4.5 Mortgage loans by size and interest rate, 1930–34
Source: *Report on Agricultural Indebtedness*, 36.
Notes: Government-commissioned surveyors collected data on mortgage loans in two villages per district, across twenty-seven districts. The source categorised data by the annual number of mortgages without possession, mortgages with possession and mortgage bonds between 1930 and 1934. This allows an analysis of 12,503 mortgage transactions, valued at 6.9 million rupees. The source measures two variables: the number of loans of a certain size and the interest rates attached to those loans. The source identifies five loan size categories and four interest rate categories. The graph matches the size of loan to interest rates. The author measures the importance of each loan size category, relative to the interest rate charged. For example, if 60 per cent of loans priced above 24 per cent were between 26 and 100 rupees, that is relative to all loans priced above 24 per cent. Therefore, the majority of loans between 26 and 100 rupees yielded interest rates above 24 per cent. The opposite is the case for loans above 1,000 rupees. The source provides annual data between 1930 and 1934. The author aggregates the data and does not account for temporal variations.

loans. The number of loans below 100 rupees and yielding rates below 6 per cent were low. Conversely, the number of loans between 26 and 100 rupees and yielding rates above 24 per cent were high. As shown in Figure 4.5, there was a linear increase in the number of lowest-priced loans across size categories. The number of loans priced 9 per cent and higher presented inverted-U graphs. The peak number of loans yielding rates between 9 and 12 per cent were sized between 100 and 500 rupees. The peak number of loans yielding rates above 24 per cent was sized between 26 and 100 rupees. Creditors charged low interest rates of between 0 and 6 per cent on loans above 1,000 rupees.

The pricing strategies adopted by select moneylenders in the early 1930s show that creditors adjusted the price of credit depending on the size and duration of loans. Seasonality in the credit market complicated loan recovery in courts, adding to enforcement costs. Small working capital loans for cultivation expenses were typically short term arrangements, increasing the lender's costs in times of default. Creditors usually provided longer-term loans to borrowers purchasing land or making improvements to land. In such cases, lenders were more willing to collateralise land and charge lower rates of interest. Loans for cultivation expenses were, according to the Banking Enquiry, 'only six months' while loans for larger expenditures were 'more than one year'. In the case of the former, one landowner reported to the Banking Enquiry that they charged interest rates of '2 to 3 per cent per *mensem*'. The same landowner reported charging rates of '1.5 per cent per *mensem*' in the case of the latter.[97] Creditors created a minimum cost barrier to compensate for the expensive legal proceedings following defaults. Substantial loans over long periods surpassed the barrier. Petty, short-term credit did not in the first instance. Secondary and tertiary defaults compounded the value of these loans till repayment crossed the barrier. According to an interview of one borrower in 1935, an initial loan of 40 rupees compounded to 400 rupees after a 'few years'. At this point, the creditor took possession of the borrower's land, worth 1,000 rupees, in court.[98]

The account books of two moneylenders in the Chingleput district show that creditors adjusted the price of credit at each stage of the loan upgrading process. A government report in 1935 summarised the amount of lending, type of credit instrument used and price of loans from the two lenders. Both creditors provided loans to cultivators in the same village. One had an exposure of over 100,000 rupees and the other of between 40,000 and 45,000 rupees. Both lenders executed promissory notes with defaulting borrowers. The interest rates mentioned on signed pro-notes exceeded the rates charged on credit repaid. As recorded in Table 4.5, both creditors charged different interest rates for out-of-court settlements and court disputes. Lenders accepted non-court-enforced contracts, where they charged lower interest rates on loans repaid out of court. When informal arbitration failed, both lenders charged a 'penal interest' on defaulted loans that were recovered in court. According to one moneylender, the Depression and subsequent wave of defaults compel them to 'to take his clients to court … which means that the penal rate of interest of 24 per cent comes into operation'.[99]

Moneylenders, from the case study presented in Table 4.5, provided loans for a period of ten months. Each lender attached pro-notes defining

---

[97] *Provincial Banking Enquiry*, Vol. III, 621.   [98] *Report on Agricultural Indebtedness*, 18.
[99] *Report on Agricultural Indebtedness*, 16.

Table 4.5 *Price of credit from two lenders, 1935*

Lender	Lending Exposure (rupees)	Contracted Loans (per cent)	Contracted Interest (annual)	Settled Interest (annual)
Lender A	100,000	66	18–24	10.5–12
Lender B	40,000–45,000	100	18–24	10

Source: *Report on Agricultural Indebtedness*, 15–16.
Notes: Data extrapolated from qualitative evidence in the source. Contracted loans refer to the ratio of pro-note loans to total. Contracted interest refers to the penal rate charged by the moneylender to account for the costs of enforcement in court. Settled interest refers to prices charged if borrowers repaid loans out of court.

the repayment of loans in monthly instalments. Borrowers defaulted on the majority of the loans provided by both lenders between 1925 and 1935. Filtered down, the monthly interest rate on privately settled loans was between 1 and 1.2 per cent. The monthly rate on court-disputed defaults was between 1.8 and 2.4 per cent, or between 50 and 140 per cent higher than rates on undisputed credit. In other words, the varied costs of enforcing different credit contract types explain the variation in the prices of credit at the level of the individual loan. Creditors increased interest rates with primary and secondary defaults to compensate for the costs of enforcing contracts in court and court-ordered transfers of the borrower's assets.

The cost structure of credit proceedings impacted regional and household variations in credit access within the province. Creditors granted extensions to landholders as land transfers were an insurance against enforcement costs. As such, landless borrowers were most affected by enforcement costs. Poor peasants in dry areas, especially tenants and the smallholders who owned low-value land, were less likely to receive loan extensions as enforcement costs were too high. Creditors were less likely to approach courts in famine-prone districts, such as Bellary, than in the deltas. The average size of loans in dry districts was significantly lower than the size of loans in the deltas. As recorded in the previous chapter, the Provincial Banking Enquiry's survey of select villages shows that the average debt per acre was 17 rupees in Bellary and 116 rupees in Tanjore in 1929. Enforcing contracts in courts was between sixteen and twenty-four times the value of the debt per acre in Bellary. As recorded in one survey of the Bellary district, poor peasants 'can seldom indulge in the delights of civil litigation'.[100]

Loan extensions were less likely and credit terms were harsher for poor peasants in the dry districts. This was evident in the methods adopted by creditors to recover loans from the poor in famine-prone areas. Following a bad year, the district government established a committee to oversee famine relief in Bellary in the 1930s. Commenting on one group of moneylenders and their methods to recover loans, one member of the District Famine Relief Committee reported, 'They have lent money to people and collect it probably using much more coercion than the courts would allow'.[101] District officials found creditors using unscrupulous ways of retrieving unpaid loans from smallholders, including 'hovering about (famine) camps' to seize the welfare entitlements of peasants in bad years.[102] Famine reports advised government officials to enforce moratoriums on unpaid credit as a method of alleviating peasant distress in dry districts.[103] In better years, poor borrowers parted with crop or, in some cases, jewellery and furniture to repay loans in the dry areas. Creditors used these informal methods to both recover loans and enforce penalty interest charges on defaulters in the absence of court supervision.

In some cases, moneylenders approached courts and compensated for the costs of enforcing contracts by manipulating the terms in promissory notes. Lenders inflated loan principals in contracts to compensate for charging lower-than-desired interest rates. Put differently, lenders attached contracts which declared higher loan principals than the principal in the physical transaction. By doing this, lenders could declare low interest rates in contracts. As such, the interest rates that moneylenders reported to government surveys and other sources were possibly lower than the actual rates charged. One reason for this contract manipulation was that moneylenders presented contracts with low interest rates in courts to obtain favourable judgements. Indeed, large loans with low interest rates seemed less exploitative than vice versa. Sources recorded this method of contract manipulation more regularly in the 1940s, following government intervention in the late 1930s. To evade the interest rate ceiling, moneylenders inflated loan principals on contracts. This practice is discussed in the next chapter.

---

[100] *Madras District Gazetteers: Bellary.* Part I (Madras, 1915), 101.
[101] *Report of the Madras Famine Code Revision Committee.* Vols. I, II. (Madras, 1938), 226–27.
[102] *Report of the Madras Famine Code Revision Committee*, 224.
[103] *Famine Commission Inquiry* (Madras, 1945).

In short, the size of loans to the rich in dry districts and to a wider spectrum of borrowers in the wet districts exceeded the costs of court enforcement. In these cases, creditors operated a multi-layered enforcement structure. First- and second-time defaults changed the contractual nature of loans. Following a first round of default, lenders upgraded unsecured loans to loans secured by promissory notes. Following second and third rounds of default, creditors upgraded the initial promissory note into a mortgage-backed loan, compensating for the rising costs of enforcement by increasing interest rates.[104] On first issue and after several defaults, some loans, particularly loans to smallholders and tenants in the dry areas, were never large enough to compensate lenders for the costs of approaching courts. In such cases, contracts were rarely used, loan extensions were unlikely, and enforcement methods were informal and inflexible.

Conclusion

Moneylenders faced an enforcement cost conundrum in Madras. Whereas banks relied on contracts and courts to recover unpaid loans, these proceedings were expensive solutions for moneylenders. Yet, in the unregulated credit market in Madras, contract laws let moneylenders price credit freely, allowing for some element of leniency as lenders granted loan extensions to defaulting borrowers. When unsecured loans remained unpaid for long periods, moneylenders attached contracts to these loans while adding the costs of judicial proceedings to the interest rates charged. This chapter records the relationship between contract enforcement and credit pricing and finds evidence that creditors adopted a three-stage loan upgrading arrangement to enforce the repayment of defaulted loans.

The size of loans was a decisive factor in determining the use of credit contracts in Madras. When the combination of principal and interest exceeded legal costs, moneylenders attached contracts to loans. Put differently, creditors increased the price of contracted loans to compensate for the costs of enforcing contracts. Two commonly used contracts in the 1930s were mortgage instruments and promissory notes. Each instrument was governed by a different set of laws. Land laws, enforced in the nineteenth and early twentieth centuries, regulated the use of mortgages while the 1881 Negotiable Instruments Act regulated the use of promissory notes. Promissory notes were cheaper to enforce and more

---

[104] *Report on Agricultural Indebtedness*, 15.

commonly used than mortgages. Creditors upgraded loans following first- and second-time defaults, attaching promissory notes following the first stage and mortgage instruments following the second stage.

The chapter has lessons for the design of institutions, and its impact on credit supply. The combination of expensive judicial proceedings and high credit prices in colonial Madras highlights the inverse relationship between transaction costs and equity in rural credit. The higher the transaction cost, the more inequitable the exchange. The problem was more severe for peasants in drier and poorer districts. When loans were small and seasonal, the use of contracts was unlucrative. Enforcement was through private negotiations and credit terms were harsh for the borrowers. The chapter further demonstrates that the isolated act to strengthen property rights had an insignificant impact when courts were unproductive. Enforcement was problematic when the costs to enforce contracts exceeded the size of loans.

5 . Regulating Moneylenders

When studying markets for microloans, economists tend to ask the following question: Do credit markets operate efficiently or as vehicles of exploitation? One interpretation holds that high interest rates signal market failure.[1] In the absence of competition, lenders use monopoly power to arbitrarily charge high rates, extracting rents from borrowers. Another interpretation suggests that lenders responded to market incentives such that lending arrangements, including high interest rates, reflect the costs of exchange.[2]

The provincial government asked a similar question about rural credit markets in Madras. They answered the question by promoting the first interpretation of market exploitation. Explaining the key factor driving high interest rates in the rural credit market, Indian economists and politicians suggested that in villages without banks and few moneylenders, credit markets were non-competitive in the 1930s. In their view, moneylenders deliberately priced loans higher than the cost of providing them to extract rents at the expense of the borrower. When the Great Depression hit and the wave of credit defaults made the market seem especially inequitable to the borrower, lawmakers in colonial Madras used this version of market failure to justify enforcing artificial price controls, in the form of interest rate ceilings, in the late 1930s. In 1937,

---

[1] Amit Bhaduri, "A Study in Agricultural Backwardness under Semi-Feudalism." *The Economic Journal* 83, no. 329 (1973): 120–37; Utsa Patnaik, "The Agrarian Question and Development of Capitalism in India." *Economic and Political Weekly* 21, no. 18 (1986): 781–93; Alice Thorner, "Semi-Feudalism or Capitalism? Contemporary Debate on Classes and Modes of Production in India." *Economic and Political Weekly* 17, no. 50 (1982): 1993–99.

[2] Joseph E. Stiglitz, "Chapter 5: Economic Organization, Information, and Development." In *Handbook of Development Economics*, edited by T. Paul Schultz and John Strauss, 93–160, Vol. 1 (Amsterdam: Elsevier B.V., 1988); Timothy Besley, "How Do Market Failures Justify Interventions in the Rural Credit Market?." *The World Bank Research Observer* 9, no. 1 (1994): 27–47; Parikshit Ghosh and Debraj Ray, "Information and Enforcement in Informal Credit Markets." *Economica* 83, no. 329 (2016): 59–90.

the government implemented an interest rate ceiling of 6.25 per cent (annualised) on all loans provided by rural moneylenders.

The success of artificial price controls hinged on the cooperation of moneylenders. Moneylenders could have responded to the interest rate ceiling in three ways. First, they could have followed the law and provided credit at lower prices. Second, they could have supplied less credit as it was unprofitable to lend at low rates. Third, they could have evaded the law altogether and continued providing credit at high prices. The chapter shows that creditors in Madras opted for versions of the second and third responses. Evidence shows that the market contracted and remaining lenders evaded the law.

The impact of credit intervention was a contraction in the supply of credit and the emergence of a black market for loans priced above the ceiling. The region-specific features of the credit market in Madras allowed creditors to make swift supply changes. The market functioned seasonally, enabling creditors to issue fresh loans in one year but withdraw from issuing new loans in the following year. From the start of credit legislation in the mid-1930s, and in expectation of stronger regulation in the late 1930s, some cultivators stopped allocating disposable income to lending in the mortgage and contracted-credit market in the short term. While data shows a contraction in credit supply, primary sources also indicate that creditors continued to lend but outside the scope of laws and legal procedures. The interest rate ceiling was only enforceable by court judges. Judges lowered the interest rates in credit disputes to the legal limit. To avoid the law, creditors resorted to enforcement arrangements that circumvented courts.

This accent on enforcement is a particular contribution of the chapter. Economists and economic historians study enforcement mechanisms in isolated spheres of courts and banking or crop-sharing and non-banking creditors.[3] The chapter demonstrates that when cultivators were also village bankers, crop-sharing arrangements were as viable an enforcement option as courts. Intervention increased the costs of formal enforcement but not

---

[3] For formal credit and courts, see Rafael La Porta, Florencio Lopez-De-Silanes, Andrei Shleifer, and Robert W. Vishny, "Law and Finance." *Journal of Political Economy* 106, no. 6 (1998): 1113–55; Simeon Djankov, Rafael La Porta, Florencio Lopez-De-Silanes, and Andrei Shleifer, "Courts." *The Quarterly Journal of Economics* 118, no. 2 (2003): 453–517; Andrea Moro, Daniela Maresch, and Annalisa Ferrando, "Creditor Protection, Judicial Enforcement and Credit Access." *The European Journal of Finance* 24, no. 3 (2018): 250–81. For informal enforcement and interlinked factor markets, see Pranab K. Bardhan, "Interlocking Factor Markets and Agrarian Development: A Review of Issues." *Oxford Economic Papers* 32, no. 1 (1980): 82–98; Avishay Braverman and Joseph E. Stiglitz, "Sharecropping and the Interlinking of Agrarian Markets." *The American Economic Review* 72, no. 4 (1982): 695–715.

informal enforcement systems, resulting in a transition in the preferred contract arrangement. The attempt to formally regulate the credit market, paradoxically, aided the shift of the market from formal to informal.[4]

If the goal was to create a more equal footing between moneylenders and borrowers, then results from 1930s credit intervention were disappointing. There were few winners and several losers from credit intervention in Madras. Creditors who exited the market potentially lost, especially as the period after intervention was more economically stable than the period before. The borrowers lost as an already liquidity-constrained credit market became more inaccessible after intervention. The borrowers who accessed credit following intervention continued to pay high prices. The only potential winners were the lenders who operated outside the law. This situation resembles the type of welfare loss economists describe as 'deadweight loss'. Following the artificial price ceiling, the market operated less efficiently as credit supply declined and prices were less transparent than before. The market also operated either as or more inequitably as the remaining creditors provided loans at pre-intervention prices.

The chapter proceeds in four stages. The first looks at debates in the Legislative Council and key publications from economists and policy-makers in colonial Madras to discuss the design of credit intervention, focusing on the arguments made by key political actors justifying the importance of the interest rate ceiling. The second examines the impact of intervention on the market for mortgage loans. The third explores conflicts between the interest rate ceiling and nineteenth-century contract laws, and its resulting impact on the supply of contracted loans. The fourth considers the relationship between enforcement costs and the shift in lending arrangements after intervention.

Designing Credit Intervention

The colonial government protected borrowers through various measures at the federal and provincial levels. The government perceived high 'agricultural indebtedness' a barrier to development and effective governance

---

[4] Schwecke, in a recent article on moneylending in nineteenth-century Banares, distinguishes between a 'monetary inside' and a 'monetary outside'. Regulation seems to be at the centre of this distinction. Regulated capital markets where the law defined money transactions, in this case the monetary inside, co-existed with unregulated 'economic arenas' where money transactions occurred outside the scope of the administrative machinery. See Sebastian Schwecke, "A Tangled Jungle of Disorderly Transactions? The Production of a Monetary outside in a North Indian Town." *Modern Asian Studies* 52, no. 4 (2018): 1375–419.

in rural areas. State officials believed that peasants needed to moderate their exposure to credit. From the mid-nineteenth century, the colonial headquarters delegated policymaking in rural credit to governments in the individual provinces. The government in Madras did not regulate rural credit until the 1930s.

The 1875 Deccan Riots marked a transition in colonial attitudes towards moneylenders. The riots occurred not long after the 1857 rebellion, a time in which the colonial government feared peasant uprisings. Colonial officials reported that the exploitation of poor borrowers by urban moneylenders sparked a series of riots in the Bombay Deccan. The riots encouraged the first of many legislative measures to counter the market power of moneylenders and protect borrowers.[5] Safeguarding the interests of the peasant was determined a necessity to maintain peace in colonial India. As summarised by G. S. Forbes, member of the Madras Legislative Council in the early 1900s, 'it is a universal proverb in this country that the prosperity of the ryot is the prosperity of the raja.'[6] In this context, the *ryot* refers to the cultivator while the *raja*, literally translating to 'ruler', refers to the colonial administration.

Governments in Bombay and Punjab regulated rural credit in the late nineteenth century. The provincial government in Bombay enforced the 1879 Deccan Agriculturists Relief Act (DARA) in response to the riots. The DARA regulated rural credit in two ways. First, the government regulated land alienation. Urban traders provided credit to farmers growing cash crops in parts of Bombay in the 1860s. Default rates were high and policymakers were concerned about the frequency of land transfers from farmers to moneylenders that did not cultivate land. The government in late nineteenth-century Punjab followed a similar strategy to the one in Bombay, enforcing the Punjab Land Alienation Act in 1900. Both provinces restricted the transfer of mortgaged land from farmers to professional moneylenders.[7] Second, and a common theme of credit intervention in colonial India, the government empowered court judges to protect borrowers when credit terms favoured the moneylenders.[8] Judges granted loan extensions and imposed interest rate reductions in credit disputes.

---

[5] C. F. Strickland, "Cooperation and the Rural Problem of India." *The Quarterly Journal of Economics* 43, no. 3 (1929): 500–31, 510–11.

[6] *Proceedings of the Council of the Governor of Fort St George* (Madras, 1905), appendix III.

[7] Latika Chaudhary and Anand V. Swamy, "A Policy of Credit Disruption: The Punjab Land Alienation Act of 1900." *Economic History Review* 73, no. 1 (2020): 134–58, shows that the law led to a reduction in the supply of credit in the short term but had a limited impact on private investment in rural Punjab.

[8] Latika Chaudhary and Anand V. Swamy, "Protecting the Borrower: An Experiment in Colonial India." *Explorations in Economic History* 65, no. C (2017): 36–54, shows that the 1879 Act led to a significant contraction in credit available to smallholder and tenant

The government in Madras did not directly regulate rural credit markets until the 1930s. Rural credit did not worry colonial officials in nineteenth-century Madras the same way it did in Bombay or Punjab. The governments in Bombay and Punjab regulated credit to regulate land alienation. They acted on a belief that investment in land was low because urban moneylenders took ownership and leased land to tenants at high rents.[9] In Madras, farmers were the moneylenders. Colonial officials did not regulate the market in the late nineteenth and early twentieth century as mortgaged land transferred from one farmer to another.

The first attempt at regulating moneylenders in this region was in response to the impact of the Depression in the 1930s. Wholesale prices of rice, cotton and groundnut declined by 52, 42 and 61 per cent, respectively, between 1928 and 1933.[10] A shock to the market for credit, the halving of commodity prices in the early 1930s increased the number of defaults on agricultural loans. Peasants were unable to repay credit bills as income from farming saw significant decline in the early 1930s. In order to finance this defaulted debt, farmers supplemented ongoing obligations with extensions or secondary loans while the instability of prices persisted until the mid-1930s.[11] A government-commissioned survey of 141 villages in 1935 warned about the dangers of the post-Depression rural credit market. The survey reported the rising number of over-leveraged borrowers with unrepayable debt obligations.[12] As shown in previous chapters, borrowing for the purpose of repaying previously undertaken debt increased in the Depression period. Price deflation in the early 1930s had an especially detrimental impact on borrowers with pre-1930 debt obligations. The halving of commodity prices doubled the real value of debts between 1930 and 1935.[13] The crash in prices of commodities and subsequent defaults on loans prompted the provincial

cultivators in the short and medium terms. Rachel E. Kranton and Anand V. Swamy, "The Hazards of Piecemeal Reform: British Civil Courts and the Credit Market in Colonial India." *Journal of Development Economics* 58, no. 1 (1999): 1–24, shows that court protection disincentivised lenders from granting loan extensions to defaulters. Lenders preferred recovering loans in courts instead.

[9] The Epilogue has a longer discussion of credit regulation in nineteenth-century Bombay and Punjab.

[10] Bijayeti Venkata Narayanaswami Naidu and P. Vaidyanathan, *The Madras Agriculturists Relief Act: A Study* (Annamalainagar: Annamalai University, 1939), 18.

[11] W. R. S. Sathyanathan, *Report on Agricultural Indebtedness* (Madras, 1935), 42.

[12] Following a survey of credit markets across 141 villages in 1935, authors of the *Report on Agricultural Indebtedness* showed that the majority of loans went towards the financing of previously defaulted debt.

[13] K. A. Manikumar, *A Colonial Economy in the Great Depression, Madras (1929–1937)* (Chennai: Orient Longman, 2003), 18.

government to implement a series of legislative measures to shield borrowers from compounding debt burdens.

Political changes, including the devolution of powers to Indian governments, further explain the timing of intervention. The inclusion of Indian policymakers in the provincial government in phases from 1909 motivated a more interventionist state. The colonial government devolved policymaking in select sectors to legislatures run by elected officials from Indian political parties. Rural credit was part of the devolved policy sector. There were three key political transitions in the early twentieth century: the 1909 India Councils Act (Morley-Minto Reforms), the 1919 Government of India Act (Montagu-Chelmsford Reforms) and the 1935 Government of India Act. The 1919 and 1935 reforms substantially increased the administrative powers of local government. Prior to 1919, the provincial government constituted a unicameral legislature. The legislature operated as a board of governors and the British government appointed members to the Madras Legislative Council. The reforms in 1919 created a quota for elected members, reserving a number of seats for members from local political parties to sit on the Council. The first Council elections took place in 1920. The 1935 reforms created bicameral legislatures in the provinces. The Madras Legislative Assembly was the lower house and constituted elected members from local political parties. The government ran the first Provincial Legislative Assembly Election in 1937. The Legislative Council remained and formed the upper house.

Two political parties, the Justice Party and the Indian National Congress, competed for elected positions in the provincial legislature during the colonial period. Both parties put forward different profiles, ran dissimilar campaigns and sought distinctive mandates between 1920 and 1937. The Justice Party was founded in 1916 and ran campaigns to diminish caste prejudices in local government. The party aimed to disconnect from broader nationalist campaigns in a bid to draw attention to Tamil- and Telugu-specific interests, and to detach from its perception of the Congress' nationalist campaign as a proponent of upper caste, Brahmin interests.[14] The Justice Party won the majority of

---

[14] See Eugene F. Irschick, *Politics and Social Conflict in South India: The Non-Brahman Movement and Tamil Separatism, 1916–1929* (Berkeley: University of California Press, 1969); Christopher John Baker, *The Politics of South India 1920–1937* (Cambridge: Cambridge University Press, 1976); David A. Washbrook, *The Emergence of Provincial Politics: The Madras Presidency, 1870–1920* (Cambridge: Cambridge University Press, 1976); Pamela G. Price, "Ideology and Ethnicity under British Imperial Rule: 'Brahmans', Lawyers and Kin-Caste Rules in Madras Presidency." *Modern Asian Studies* 23, no. 1 (1989): 151–77.

seats reserved for local parties in the Council from 1920 to 1937. *Zamindars* and landowners dominated the leadership of the Justice Party which invited criticism and claims of hypocrisy in the contradiction between its anti-elite campaign and its disregard for peasant interests in the early 1930s. The Indian National Congress extended its *Swaraj* or Indian self-rule promotion to its campaign expansion in Madras. In the 1920s and 1930s, the party extended its campaign in the south by criticising the synonymity between colonial policy and the vested interests of elite landowners. In doing so, Congress leaders claimed the leaders of the Justice Party supported the aims of colonial rulers. From the early 1930s, Congress leaders established a large support base in rural districts by promoting tenancy reforms and debt relief laws in a larger campaign to rid the province of colonial rulers.[15] The party legitimised itself as a representative of peasant interests in the fight against the British and their landowner allies. Following the 1935 Government of India reforms, the Indian National Congress party won the majority of seats in the Assembly elections in 1937. The Congress won 159 out of the contested 215 seats in the Legislative Assembly.

The focus on reducing economic inequality in villages cut across party lines, to some extent. A speech delivered by K. V. Reddy Naidu, a member of the Justice Party in 1924, emphasised the dangers of colonial forms of property rights. In Naidu's view, 'the English and Scotch land systems were based upon the Roman conception of Dominium. According to these systems, the landlord is the absolute owner of the soil. The tenant has no proprietary interest in it, and has no rights whatsoever.'[16] P. J. Thomas, a member of the Indian National Congress, echoed the need for dual intervention in land and credit markets.[17] Prior to winning a seat in the Madras Legislative Assembly Election in 1937, Thomas argued,

The Indian Banking Committee points out that where the moneylenders are mostly landholders (chiefly in the Punjab and Madras), changes in the

---

[15] David A. Washbrook, "Country Politics: Madras 1880 to 1930." *Modern Asian Studies* 7, no. 3 (1973): 475–531; Christopher John Baker, "The Congress at the 1937 Elections in Madras." *Modern Asian Studies* 10, no. 4 (1976): 557–89.

[16] K. Venkata Reddy Naidu, *Presidential Address*, The Second Malabar Tenant's Conference, 1924.

[17] P. J. Thomas was a lecturer in the Economics Department at the University of Madras between 1927 and 1942. Thomas was elected as a member of the Madras Legislative Assembly in 1937 and contributed to governance in the province till 1942. At this point, Thomas began a twenty-year career as an advisor to the Indian government in Delhi. Thomas published extensively on all areas of the Indian economy.

ownership of land are not detrimental to agricultural efficiency, but this is a highly questionable view, seeing that such transfers lead to the increase in tenants and tenant-farming, which is not desirable in many ways.[18]

In Reddy Naidu's and Thomas's view, the exploitation of peasants persisted through inequities in factor markets. The view, agreed by members of the different political parties, concluded that landowners extracted from permanent tenants through their control on the supply of credit. The Congress party, however, enforced stronger borrower protection measures after their electoral victory in 1937. Indeed, rural voters considered the Justice Party more elite-favouring than the Indian National Congress. As a result, the Justice Party lost favour in the rural districts during the 1920s and 1930s. Rural voters believed that the Congress would implement policies that protected the interests of poor peasants against rent-seeking landowners.[19] The protection of borrowers from harsh credit terms imposed by rich moneylenders was one example of this policy approach.

The Justice Party-controlled provincial legislature regulated credit markets but with limited impact on protecting borrowers. Few credit-related policies were introduced in the 1920s. The Justice Party let the rural credit market operate without interventions, until the early 1930s. Official reports in the early 1930s recommended stronger credit intervention. The Provincial Banking Enquiry Committee in 1930 and the Report on Agricultural Indebtedness in 1935 recommended new policy measures to protect borrowers from credit exploitation. The first in a series of legislative measures by the Madras provincial government was the 1936 Debtors Protection Act. C. Basudev, a member of the Justice Party-controlled legislature, introduced the Debtors Protection Bill in 1932. The Bill underwent several revisions and, when enacted, eventually enforced an interest rate ceiling of 9 per cent on secured and 15 per cent on unsecured loans.[20] The Debtors Protection Act also recommended that lenders present courts with ledgers and more formal accounting methods in credit disputes.[21] The law only regulated loans below 500 rupees.

Following the Debtors Protection Act, policymakers designed a judicial forum dedicated to credit dispute resolution. As directed in the 1936 Debt Conciliation Act, the government formed a board of judges in the Madras High Court to 'amicably' resolve disputes on loans above

---

[18] P. J. Thomas, *The Problem of Rural Indebtedness* (Madras: Diocesan Press, 1934), 13.
[19] Washbrook, "Country Politics."   [20] Manikumar, *A Colonial Economy*, 150–52.
[21] S. Y. Krishnaswamy, *Rural Problems in Madras: Monograph* (Madras, 1947), 370–75.

100 rupees.[22] The Conciliation Act empowered debt conciliation boards to enforce the interest rate ceilings prescribed in the Debtors Protection Act and to limit the total repayment of loans to double the initial principal loaned, restating the ancient Hindu law of *Damdupat*.[23] First located in ancient Hindu texts, the law of *Damdupat* was originally practised to protect borrowers against usury and exploitative credit arrangements.[24] By placing a cap on the total value of repayment, the colonial government believed that the law restricted the scope for lenders to extract rents through compounding debts. However, the Conciliation Act did not give judges on the conciliation boards the power to actually enforce changes to credit contracts. Debt conciliation boards dismissed cases with suggested remedies that were not legally enforceable. In practice, creditors typically did not implement the changes recommended by judges. Recognising the law's failure to have the desired impact, the Congress-led provincial government dissolved debt conciliation boards in 1942.[25]

The Indian National Congress' electoral victory in 1937 gave policy-makers a stronger mandate to act on their promise of providing peasants protection against market exploitation, particularly protection against predatory pricing in the credit market. Following the Congress' landslide victory, the government designed, and later enforced, the Moratorium Bill in September 1937. The law banned creditors from suing borrowers with unpaid credit bills for one year. T. S. S. Rajan, a member of the Congress party and Minister for Public Health in the provincial Assembly, went further to carry out the party's campaign promise to aggressively intervene and protect poor borrowers in credit markets. Rajan introduced the Debt Relief Bill in December 1937. The Bill carried stronger regulation of market power than previous policies. When introducing the Bill in the Assembly, Rajan stated,

---

[22] *Rural Problems in Madras*, 370–75.
[23] The law of *Damdupat* dictated that repayments are not to exceed double of the initial principal loaned. *Damdupat* regulation was recommended in a Bill that was eventually rejected in the early nineteenth century. A vocal opponent of this Bill was Jeremy Bentham, who wrote of expected problems when enforcing a ceiling on interest rates. Bentham's argument highlighted the potential ways for lenders to deceive borrowers and law enforcement. Bentham emphasized the incentive for lenders to charge higher rates of interest by inflating the loan principal in contracts. See Jeremy Bentham, "ART. VII.-USURY LAWS." *Calcutta Review* 101, no. 201 (1895): 150–67, 163–64.
[24] For the history of *Damdupat* legislation, see Mandar Oak and Anand Swamy, "Only Twice as Much: A Rule for Regulating Lenders." *Economic Development and Cultural Change* 58, no. 4 (2010): 775–803.
[25] *Rural Problems in Madras*, 370–75.

Now we have been returned by a large number of voters many of whom are preeminently agriculturists and to whom we have given the word of honour and to keep the word of honour we put before the two Houses of legislature this Bill which is intended to relieve the agriculturists of his debts.[26]

The Bill progressed and the Congress-led government eventually enforced the landmark Madras Agriculturists Relief Act (MARA) in September 1938. The primary objective of the MARA was to reduce the value of compounding debts accumulated during and immediately after the Great Depression. The provincial government believed that amicable and voluntary settlements, such as those encouraged by the Debtors Protection Act, did not go far enough. Stronger intervention was needed to see results in the market. The MARA directed judges to discipline moneylenders and alter contracts to include fair credit terms for borrowers.

The MARA placed an interest rate ceiling on loans to farmers and included different provisions for loans borrowed during and after the Depression period. When designing the law, the government deliberated how best to arrive at a ceiling price. The government decided to enforce an interest rate ceiling that was marginally above the rate at which local government borrowed but below the rate at which cooperative banks were lending. Pricing below the rate charged by cooperative banks was strategic. The fear, according to government officials, was that moneylenders could borrow at low rates from cooperatives and charge a higher rate to their clients.[27] In doing so, moneylenders could continue to corner the credit market, and charge poor peasants high interest rates. The government arrived at the rate of 6 per cent per annum, marginally above the 5 per cent that local government borrowed at and below the rates that cooperatives charged in the same period.[28] The Congress Party then increased the rate to 6.25 per cent per annum.[29] Officials in the party believed that this rate was easier to calculate as it translated, in currency terms, to one pie per rupee borrowed.[30] The law also distinguished between debts borrowed before and after 1 October 1932. The government enforced different ceilings to account for deflationary pressures during the Depression. The MARA enforced a ceiling of 5 per cent annual interest on all loans undertaken between 1932 and

---

[26] *Madras Legislative Assembly Debates*, Vol. I (Madras, 1937).

[27] Kodaganallur Ganapattri Sivaswamy, *Legislative Protection and Relief of Agriculturist Debtors in India* (Poona: Gokhale Institute of Politics and Economics, 1939), 204–5.

[28] Cooperatives charged rates above 7 per cent. Chapter 6 discusses cooperatives in greater detail.

[29] Section 12, Madras Agriculturists Relief Act 1938.

[30] Pie was the smallest currency unit in colonial India.

the implementation of the Act in 1938. In an attempt to cement the *Damdupat* rule, the law wrote off partially repaid debts if the amount repaid matched double the initial principal loaned. The government enforced the *Damdupat* rule to moderate the size of compounding interest following multiple defaults. The government administered the MARA through the judiciary. The law directed courts to intervene in credit disputes and adjust lending terms when interest rates charged exceeded the legal limit.

Congress-led intervention in the late 1930s invited criticism from political opposition and some provincial lobbyists. When the Congress party introduced the Madras Agriculturists Relief Bill in 1937, serious debates ensued in the lower house. Opponents to credit intervention can be placed in two groups. The first group consisted of landowners resisting the government's assumption that landlords exploited tenants, the assumption that was the basis for market regulation. Officials representing the interests of landowners in the Assembly demanded less radical legislation on the grounds that landowners showed leniency to rent defaulters in the unregulated market. Supporters of the landowners' position disagreed with any existence of market exploitation as they believed that landlords in Madras had a 'hereditary love for their tenantry'. C. Muttukumaraswami Mudaliyar, a landowner and *zamindar* in the Chunampet village, opposed the Debt Relief Bill on the grounds that it unfairly presumes that 'the interests of the *zamidnars* and those of the tenants are antagonistic'. Mudaliyar fervently appealed to elected officials to redesign the accepted narrative that 'the *zamindar* is ever bent upon encroaching upon the rights of the tenants and unless the rights of the tenants are buttressed by all the safeguards which the legislature can devise, they will be annihilated by the insatiable ambition and cruel exactions of the zamindar'. Landowners in the Assembly believed that the feeling of 'distrust' was 'unjustly entertained towards the *zamindars* as a class', and that interventions to protect peasants were unnecessary.[31]

The second group consisted of pro-market enthusiasts, claiming that the Relief Bill was too interventionist. Pro-market officials considered the Relief Bill a move towards socialist intervention, an issue that provoked widespread concern on the future legislative capacity of government. That the Congress won a large majority of seats in the first legislative assembly and was the first Indian political party to receive a mandate of this size in Madras, worried the opposition. Pro-market members from the Justice Party pointed to the conflict between debt relief and the

---

[31] *Madras Legislative Debates.*

nineteenth-century laws that protected the freedom of contract. Reddi Nayudu, for example, echoed this hesitation by stating, 'The Bill treats the sanctity of contracts with contempt ... there are large amounts of debts on promissory notes and the contention has been raised, and I believe there is a good deal of force in that contention.'[32] Members of the ruling administration also recognised the potential contradictions between the MARA and contract laws. Rajan, who introduced the Relief Bill, acknowledged the infringement of borrower protection on the freedom of contract. During an eight-hour debate among legislators on the Relief Bill, Rajan conceded that the law might conflict with existing contract laws that supported free enterprise. According to Rajan,

As regards sanctity of contracts, this question has been discussed threadbare. I am not speaking as a lawyer but I am going to speak as an ordinary citizen and I know certainly the obligations of a contract. That a man who has borrowed has got to pay back what he has borrowed is a fundamental law which even the meanest of our citizens does understand and which even the most ignorant citizen will not repudiate.[33]

However, the debate was won by interventionists. Key members of the Congress believed more strongly in regulating market exploitation than in supporting free enterprise. According to Congress officials, contract laws protected moneylenders at the expense of the borrowers. Moneylenders, in the view of officials, used contracts, and the judicial protection contracts carried, to charge high credit prices.[34] C. Rajagopalachariar, leader of the Congress government in the 1930s, supported the pro-borrower stance and believed that market intervention was more important than the protection of contract laws.[35] Responding to wider criticisms over credit intervention across provinces, Rajagopalachariar believed that 'credit will not be lost. The scare will disappear and the country will have the previous industry standing on its own legs'.[36] Rajagopalachariar, in other words, recognised the dangers of regulation affecting the supply of credit but predicted that the market would return to its original state following an initial shock.

Left-leaning activists and politicians serving in the legislature supported the government's approach. Despite the recognition that lenders

---

[32] *Madras Legislative Debates.*   [33] *Madras Legislative Debates.*

[34] Naidu and Vaidyanathan, *The Madras Agriculturists Relief Act,* 20–25.

[35] Rajagopalachariar was an influential policymaker in India. He was elected Chief Minister of the Madras Legislative Assembly in 1937, appointed Governor of West Bengal in 1947 and served as Governor General of India after the end of colonialism in 1948 until 1950. Rajagopalachariar returned to Madras as Chief Minister of the state between 1952 and 1954.

[36] *Madras Legislative Debates.*

could withhold credit as market monopolists, some legislators believed that laws in the joint spheres of land and credit was a solution to the trade-off between efficiency and equity. Sivaswamy, a member of the Legislative Council and later member of the Socialist Party in post-colonial Madras, praised the Congress government's design of credit intervention.[37] Sivaswamy wrote in favour of the MARA in 1937, predicting that the law would successfully regulate exploitation without affecting the peasant's access to credit.[38] According to Sivaswamy, the strengthening of property rights in the early twentieth century incentivised creditors to lend despite restrictions on interest rates. In other words, Sivaswamy speculated that stronger property rights allowed lenders to manage default risk through imposing collateral requirements on loans, avoiding disruptions in the supply of loans after regulation.

Did intervention restrict the supply of credit in Madras? Was the credit market more equitable in the short term? These are the central questions dismissed by policymakers in the late 1930s. The chapter tackles these questions and shows that the design of intervention made credit arrangements in the unregulated market unprofitable after regulations were enforced. The credit market contracted and moneylenders evaded the law in the short term.

Intervention and the Mortgage Market

Recovery from the Depression began in the mid-1930s. Commodity prices and the number of mortgage loans started to increase from 1934. However, the mortgage market was exposed to a second shock in the form of state intervention. Mortgage lenders faced three choices following the intervention. First, lenders could follow the law and continue to provide credit that met the legally imposed conditions. Annual changes in the supply of credit would continue to respond to prices under this regime. Second, lenders could reject the law and stop lending to peasants. Commodity prices would have limited bearing on

---

[37] K. G. Sivaswamy was among the less familiar historical figures that shaped the evolution of the Indian independence movement. He was an active member of both the Servants of India Society and the Agricultural Workers Union prior to independence. Sivaswamy's ideological leanings eventually inspired his membership of the Madras Socialist Party in the early 1950s, where he advocated for the benefits of collective farming in India. Sivaswamy encouraged a practical approach to regulating informal lending in rural India. He criticised the 1879 Deccan Agriculturists Relief Act, which restricted the transfer of land from borrower to moneylender in agricultural Bombay, for causing an immediate contraction in the supply of credit for smallholder cultivators.

[38] Sivaswamy, *Legislative Protection*, 97–102.

the supply of mortgage credit under this regime. Third, lenders could evade the law and continue to provide credit on the same terms as the pre-regulated market.

Mortgage lending did not respond to the upward swing in prices in the late 1930s. McAlpin's agricultural price index indicates a 28 per cent increase in prices between 1934 and 1941.[39] An official report commissioned by the provincial government estimated an increase in the prices of rice, cotton and groundnut by 2.2, 2.3 and 4.8 times between 1939 and 1944.[40] However, the number of mortgage loans, in wet and dry districts combined, in 1941 was 10 per cent lower than the same number in 1930. The steepest decline in the annual number of mortgages was between 1937 and 1938, coinciding with the enforcement of the Madras Agriculturists Relief Act. The number of mortgagors in wet districts declined by 14 per cent between 1937 and 1938. The same number declined by 16 per cent in dry districts.[41] If adjusted for population changes in each district, we should expect to observe an even greater annual decline, in percentage terms, of the number of mortgagors in both wet and dry districts. Trends in the *value* of mortgage loans corroborate this intuition.

As shown in Table 5.1, debt relief laws had a significant impact on mortgage registrations. In nominal terms, the value of mortgages supplied declined across agroecological zones between 1936 and 1941. Dry districts fared especially poorly. Against rising prices of cereals and cotton, the nominal value of mortgage loans supplied in Bellary declined at an increasing rate between 1936 and 1941. The value of registrations declined by 7 per cent between 1936 and 1937. The same number declined by 15 per cent between 1937 and 1938, and declined by 25 per cent between 1938 and 1939. More surprisingly, the number and nominal value of mortgage loans registered in Bellary were 23 and 27 per cent lower in 1941 than in 1933, the peak of the Great Depression.

Mortgage lending declined at a similarly fast rate for the first couple of years in the wet districts, though less substantially from 1939. Nominal value of mortgage registrations in West Godavari, for instance, declined by 30 per cent between 1937 and 1938, then increased slightly and

[39] Michelle McAlpin, "Price Movements and Fluctuations in Economic Activity (1860–1947)." In *The Cambridge Economic History of India*, edited by Dharma Kumar and Meghnad Desai, 2: 878–904 (Cambridge: Cambridge University Press, 1983).

[40] Bahadur Rao and B. V. Narayanaswamy Naidu, *Report of the Economist for Enquiry into Rural Indebtedness* (Madras, 1945), 47.

[41] Division between wet and dry districts conducted in the same format as Table 3.2 in Chapter 3. South Arcot, Malabar, South Kanara and Nilgiris districts excluded from this analysis. *Report on the Administration of the Registration Department* (Madras, 1937–38).

Table 5.1 *Difference (in per cent) in the value of mortgages and sales between 1936 and 1941*

District	Mortgages (nominal)	Mortgages (real)	Sales (nominal)	Sales (real)
Bellary	−33	−41	17	7
Cuddapah	−13	−22	0.4	−10
Kurnool	−36	−44	−10	−19
Tinnevelly	−9	−17	20	8
West Godavari	−12	−20	6	−5

Sources: *Report on the Administration of the Registration Department* (1934–41); McAlpin, "Price Movements".

Notes: The table shows change in the value of mortgages and sales registered in select districts. *Real* values are estimated by price adjusting nominal loans to 1936 prices, using McAlpin's agricultural price index. The districts are a sample of different agroecological zones. The land tenure system across the majority of the acreage in each district was *ryotwari* or government-cultivator. As such, the data is not affected by inconsistencies in land titles within and across the sample districts.

stagnated in the following years. Nominal value of mortgage registrations in Tanjore declined by 20 per cent between 1937 and 1939.[42] The land registration department in the provincial government attributed the decline in mortgage registrations to credit intervention. Explaining the causes of the decline in mortgage lending, the department's annual report in 1938 suggested, 'the fall is attributed to the reluctance of the moneyed class of people to advance loans consequent on the operations of the Madras Agriculturists Relief Act 1938'.[43]

Due to gaps in source material, it is difficult to predict the duration of this supply-side shock. Land registration records from the early 1940s are unavailable. However, data from 1947 suggests that the trend of declining mortgage supply persisted. The number of mortgage loans in wet districts declined by 13 per cent between 1941 and 1947. The number of loans in the dry districts declined by 10 per cent in the same period. The real value of mortgage loans also declined between 1941 and 1947. The value of mortgage loans was 40 per cent lower in both wet and dry districts.[44]

[42] *Report on the Administration of the Registration Department* (1936–41). The data for Tanjore is not presented in the table due to inconsistencies in data recording during the 1930s.
[43] *Report on the Administration of the Registration Department* (1938).
[44] *Report on the Administration of the Registration Department* (1941–47).

How did credit intervention affect the settlement of old debts? An outcome of the MARA was an increase in the number and value of land sales. The number of land sales increased consistently between 1935 and 1941, with a particularly large rise after 1938. The number of sales, across the province, in 1941 was 12 per cent higher than the number of sales in 1929 and 15 per cent higher than the same measure in 1934. Sales registrations saw a small increase between 1936 and 1938, and a noticeable rise between 1938 and 1941. The number of sales rose by 37 per cent and the nominal value of sales by 33 per cent between 1938 and 1940. In the same period, the number and nominal value of land sales increased by 15 per cent each in West Godavari. In areas where sales registrations saw a smaller increase, or declined in real terms, the extent of the decline was smaller than the equivalent change in mortgage registrations. As shown in Table 5.1, land sales in Kurnool declined in the late 1930s, though at a much smaller rate than the decline in mortgage registrations. That the MARA had disproportional effects on sales and mortgages in Kurnool is reflected in a comparison of the land market between early and late 1930s. In nominal terms, the value of mortgage loans was 9 per cent higher, whereas the value of sales was 60 per cent higher in 1939 relative to Depression-era levels in Kurnool. Officials in charge of land registrations acknowledged the contrast in declining mortgages and rising sales, though failed to provide thorough explanations of this trend. The Registration Department stated in 1940 that the mortgage market saturated while the 'rise in the number of sales' was 'due to the Madras Debt Conciliation Act, 1936, and the Madras Agriculturists Relief Act, 1938'.[45] A closer look at disputes in court provides more detailed explanation for why the MARA affected sales registrations.

The MARA incentivised rising land sales by encouraging creditors to recover unpaid debts through court-mandated sale settlements. Courts ordered the transfer of land where borrowers were unable to repay loans under the interest rates specified in the MARA. As protection for the lender, rules in the MARA allowed one-time settlements for previously unpaid loans. The MARA did not contain provisions for the repayment of loans in instalments. While interest rates were capped and loan sizes amended by judges, the law expected swift rather than drawn-out settlements. Under these conditions, judges ordered debtors, without the capacity to repay their scaled-down debts, to transfer land to lenders as a method of repayment.[46] Section 7 of the MARA allowed for land sales

[45] *Report on the Administration of the Registration Department* (1940).
[46] Naidu and Vaidyanathan, *The Madras Agriculturists Relief Act*, 21–22.

as long as the quantity of land transferred matched the value of the reconfigured, discharged loan.[47] This design changed the incentive structure for lenders in the short term. Whereas lenders in the pre-regulated market commonly extended defaulted loans or agreed instalments out of court, the MARA encouraged creditors to recover defaulted loans through land sales. The Registration Department attributed the rise in the number of new land registrations in Coimbatore district after the MARA to the 'disposal of immovable properties by sale for discharging the debts'.[48]

In discharge settlements, courts favoured creditors as long as the value of the sale matched the value of the unpaid loan. In the court dispute *Kruttiventi Mallikharjuna Rao and ors. v. Vemuri Pardhasaradhirao and anr.*, adjudicated in 1943, the lender provided the borrower with a mortgage loan of 1,500 rupees at 12 per cent interest per annum in 1927. The borrower repeatedly defaulted on the loan until it compounded to 3,400 rupees in 1934. Both parties then agreed to an oral contract, in which the borrower would sell the mortgaged land to the creditor for the value of the defaulted loan. A written contract was not drawn up. The creditor took possession of the property in 1935, leased a part of it and cultivated the rest. In the early 1940s, the borrower petitioned the courts to reverse the sale. The appeal in the Madras High Court claimed that the creditor earned the value of the loan in the rents and cultivation profits made since the transfer. The borrower arrived at this conclusion after deducting the size of the loan to fit the parameters in the MARA. As written sale deeds did not accompany the original transfer, the borrower claimed the transaction was still a mortgage and since the debt was repaid, the property could return to the original owner. Judges in the High Court ruled in favour of the creditor, stating that the sale in 1934 was a settlement offer for the repayment of unpaid loans. A sale deed was drawn up, and the creditor took formal possession of the property.[49]

Problems occurred when creditors attempted to use the sale arrangement to inflate the value of the unpaid loan. When the courts were able to identify this, judges placed injunctions on the sale until they arrived at the appropriate figure, accounting for debt reductions from the MARA. In the 1938 case, *P. R. Govindaswami Naicker v. C. Javanmull Sowcar and*

---

[47] Courts determined the value of a plot of land by extrapolating from the net annual value of tax assessed on said plot.

[48] *Report on the Administration of the Registration Department* (1941), 2.

[49] Kruttiventi Mallikharjuna Rao and ors. v. Vemuri Pardhasaradhirao and anr. (1943 2 MLJ 584, Madras, 12 October 1943).

anr., for example, judges found that the creditor was 'about to recover by the sale of the debtor's property, mortgages to him the full amount of the debt, that is to say, without deducting the amount by which it has become reduced by the operation of the Agriculturists Relief Act'.[50] The judges placed a temporary injunction on the sale. The potential for moneylenders to disguise sales as inflated loan repayments and the rise in sales following intervention indicates an important difference between the impact of credit laws in Madras versus other Indian provinces. Indeed, Chaudhary and Swamy's study of land restrictions and credit in early 1900s Punjab suggests that the number of sales declined at a similar rate as the number of mortgages in the short term. In their view, land alienation policies in Punjab applied to sales as well as mortgages, therefore, explaining the immediate decline in both markets.[51] In this context, the government's encouragement of sales in Madras provides a unique outcome of intervention, in which creditors settled unpaid debts without committing to interest rate restrictions.

Creditors' ability to mask inflated loan repayments as land sales and borrowers' ability to injunct or reverse transfers and repayments caused confusion in the courts. Judges questioned whether to challenge the value of the sale on the borrower's behalf or protect the moneylender and allow the sale as a means of ensuring the repayment of loans. In one case, judges reduced the repayment amount but ruled in favour of the sale, suggesting the MARA did not apply to agreed debt settlements before 1 September 1937.[52] In another, the creditor and borrower agreed to the sale as a settlement of unpaid debts before 1937 but judges cited the MARA and stopped the sale to ensure the value of the sale matched the value of the loan with the imposed interest rate ceiling.[53] On the MARA causing confusion in courts, the judge in the latter case remarked,

I must remark that contentions like the one advanced are rendered possible by the language of the various provisions of the Act. The Act is one of the most ill-drafted enactments now existing on the statute book. Every section bristles with difficulties and it is no wonder that the Act has become a fruitful source of litigation.[54]

---

[50] P. R. Govindaswami Naicker v. C. Javanmull Sowcar and anr. (1938 2 MLJ 918, Madras, 21 May 1938).

[51] Chaudhary and Swamy, "A Policy of Credit Disruption," 4.

[52] B. K. Narayanaswami Chettiar v. Gurukkar Rudrappa and anr. (1943, Madras, 26 November 1943).

[53] V. Sreenivasachariar and anr. v. Krishniah Chetty and ors. (1939, 1 MLJ 860, Madras, 4 September 1939).

[54] V. Sreenivasachariar and anr. v. Krishniah Chetty and ors. (1939, 1 MLJ 860, Madras, 4 September 1939).

The next section of this chapter considers similar areas of confusion, focusing on legal disputes that highlighted contradictions between MARA and contract laws.

The rise in sales was not just because creditors opted for quick settlements of debts. The interest rate ceiling made land a more lucrative investment opportunity than moneylending. Peasants with disposable income preferred to invest in the land market, rather than in the credit market.[55] On the nature of land and credit substitution after intervention, Naidu and Vaidyanathan compared the moneylender to a 'burnt cat', suggesting that lenders did not 'lend easily to agriculturists' after the MARA. Instead, wealthy lenders preferred to invest their disposable income to buy land, rather than lend in the credit market.[56] Whether it is because creditors settled old debts or avoided the mortgage market, the rise in sales demonstrates that lending contracted following the MARA.

In short, this section shows that the mortgage market contracted after the MARA. Though sale instruments as court settlements for unpaid debts and the rise in commodity prices allowed creditors to recover overdue loans, evidence shows that intervention contracted the mortgage market in the short term. Debt settlements increased while creditors attempted to skirt the law by acquiring lands worth more than the size of the loan, while the provision of new mortgage loans declined. The previous chapter shows that new loans were commonly unsecured in the rural credit market. Lenders commonly executed debt instruments, including mortgages, only following initial defaults. The chapter now turns to transitions in the supply of unsecured and contracted loans to fully analyse the impact of intervention on the credit market.

Intervention and Promissory Notes

The interest rate ceiling enforced in the 1930s conflicted with nineteenth-century contract laws. Credit policies contradicted the 1872 India Contract Act and the 1881 Negotiable Instruments Act, and challenged the legitimacy of promissory notes. The MARA aimed to regulate the terms in contracted loans, thus possibly nullifying loans contracted before the government implemented the MARA. In doing so, the MARA also blurred the boundaries between the provincial assembly and the federal legislature. Though the federal government delegated

---

[55] This trend continued in the early 1940s as investors found land a safe investment in wartime. See *Report on the Administration of the Registration Department* (1947).

[56] Naidu and Vaidyanathan, *The Madras Agriculturists Relief Act*, 25.

some policymaking powers to the provinces, contract laws remained a federal concern.[57] Opposition to borrower protection claimed the MARA affected the use of contracts and was thus *ultra vires* of the provincial legislature. The law, as a result, cast a spotlight on courts to determine both the validity of contracts signed before the law was implemented and the scope of the law to regulate different types of credit contracts. The MARA, therefore, was not easily enforced and subject to judicial scrutiny in the short term.

Moneylenders challenged the legality of credit laws in lower courts, with appeals eventually leading to the Madras High Court. Following the enforcement of the MARA, one moneylender initiated a dispute against the provincial government in a lower district court, questioning the conflict between laws protecting the freedom of contract and laws protecting borrowers. The judge invalidated the MARA on grounds of its conflict with prior contract laws. The lower court's verdict criticised the design of the MARA for failing to explicitly distinguish its scope from the principles stated in the Negotiable Instruments Act. According to the district court's final judgement issued on 19 September 1938,

Considering the relevant sections of the Government of India Act 1935 together with the legislation in respect of promissory notes and bills of exchange under the Negotiable Instruments Act, it seems to me clear that the promissory note is a subject matter which is outside the province of the legislative powers of the provincial legislature and therefore as it is we do not find any mention of promissory notes or other documents representing notes while we find the word 'debt' alone in the Act IV of 1938. The question is whether 'debt' coming within that definition of the act will cover a debt under a promissory note or any negotiable instruments and upon this point there can be no doubt that all debts affected by the provisions of Act IV of 1938 of the Madras Provincial Legislature cannot comprise the debts due under a promissory note or other negotiable instrument coming under the provisions of the Negotiable Instruments Act.[58]

The district court judge restricted the policy scope of the MARA by ruling that changes to contract laws were outside the legislative scope of provincial government. Following the decentralisation of policymaking in 1919 and the Government of India Act in 1935, a Concurrent Legislative List determined the scope of law making for the central and provincial governments.[59] The provincial legislative list included agricultural credit, while central government was responsible for changes to

---

[57] Naidu and Vaidyanathan, *The Madras Agriculturists Relief Act*, 22–23.

[58] Naidu and Vaidyanathan, *The Madras Agriculturists Relief Act*, 22–23.

[59] Mada Nagaratnam v. Puvvada Seshayya and anr. (1939, IMLJ 272, Madras, 7 February 1939). Section 100 of the Government of India Act defined the areas of legislation devolved to federal and provincial legislatures.

contract laws. As such, the court ruling did not annul the MARA, but it did allow promissory notes to operate outside the scope of the law. According to the judge, the vague wording of provisions in the MARA left room for misinterpretation. The law did not explicitly mention 'promissory note' and instead broadly defined the scope of regulation as 'debt'. The judge interpreted this to include unsecured, non-contracted credit transactions. The court ruling declared that credit transactions ratified by contracts were regulated by nineteenth-century contract laws and not targeted policies in the 1930s. The lower court restricted the scope of the interest rate ceiling to loans without promissory notes. The judgement, therefore, reinforced the freedom of contract by stressing failure in the design of MARA in its lack of consideration for the frequent use of promissory notes in rural credit.[60]

Acting to prevent watered-down credit regulation, district court judges appealed the decision to remove promissory notes from the scope of the MARA in the Madras High Court. Judges from three regional courts, the District *Munsiff* in Guntur, the District *Munsiff* in Cuddalore, and a Subordinate Judge in Coconada collectively referred to a High Court Bench to revisit the legal capacity of the MARA. Writing in the six-month period between the lower court's verdict and the final decision in the High Court, Naidu and Vaidyanathan stated, 'if the Act is held not to apply to negotiable instruments the relief to agriculturists becomes so small as to make the Act practically a dead letter … Everything depends on the decision of the High Court which is keenly awaited by many debtors and creditors.'[61] Indeed, it was not just the anxiety of creditors and debtors that was tested in the interval between judgement and appeal. Members of the executive and judiciary awaited clear instruction on the scope and enforceability of borrower protection.

The High Court's decision, issued on 7 February 1939 in the landmark case *Mada Nagaratnam v. Puvvada Seshayya*, repealed the previous judgement on the scope of borrower protection. The case was heard by a bench of three judges and the final judgement was issued by the Chief Justice of the Madras High Court, Alfred Lionel Leach.[62] Leach

---

[60] An eventual reversal of this initial judicial response constrains our ability to accurately predict the counter-factual history of the role of promissory notes in the credit market. However, considering the incentives that justified its use prior to the MARA, the chapter postulates a continued use of contract in the event of its exclusion from usury laws.

[61] Naidu and Vaidyanathan, *The Madras Agriculturists Relief Act*, 22–23.

[62] Alfred Henry Lionel Leach qualified as a British barrister in 1907. Leach spent the majority of the 1930s and 1940s in South Asia, first as a judge in the Rangoon High Court in Burma, and then the Chief Justice of the Madras High Court from 1937 to 1947.

overturned the lower court's verdict by declaring the MARA as compatible with prior contract laws. The High Court upheld terms in contracts as long as they did not interfere with usury regulation. Invalidating the respondent's argument on the legal protection of contracted debts by the 1881 Negotiable Instruments Act, the High Court Bench declared,

Negotiation of a promissory note is not prohibited nor is it said that a maker or an endorser shall not be liable. The only effect of the Madras Agriculturists Relief Act so far as Negotiable Instruments are concerned is to reduce liability where the maker or endorser is an agriculturist.[63]

The High Court sought to maximise the scope of the MARA. Judges in Madras took a clear position on the role of contract relative to usury laws. In the conflict between contract laws and borrower protection, courts prioritised the latter. The High Court Bench predicted that the MARA would have an insignificant impact if contracts were excluded from its scope. According to Leach, excluding promissory notes would render the Act inconsequential given, 'the practice of lending money on promissory notes being so widespread'.[64] Leach enforced the Act with the recognition that the protection of borrowers would have little effect had promissory notes been excluded from intervention. In adopting this position, the Madras High Court legitimised the increased policy sphere of the provincial legislature. Judges disagreed with the respondent's petition that the MARA allowed the provincial government to interfere in a policy space outside its jurisdiction. The judiciary granted the provincial government powers to implement debt relief measures without concern for its impact on the role of contract.

Despite attempts to challenge the MARA, the judiciary sustained the decision made by the Madras High Court in 1939, until the Act was eventually amended in 1976. The case of *Subramaniam Chettiar v. Muthuswami Goundan* appealed against the 1939 verdict by questioning the validity of the MARA in reference to its conflict with legislative authority. The appellants approached the Federal Court in 1940 to question the validity of the MARA, given that the federal government, according to the Government of India Act in 1935, held the power to make amendments to contract laws. The Federal Court admitted the case, however, the provincial courts in Madras could enforce the interest rate ceiling while the case proceeded. Federal court judges dealt specifically with the scope of the provincial legislature and not the conflict with

---

[63] Mada Nagaratnam v. Puvvada Seshayya and anr. (1939, IMLJ 272, Madras, 7 February 1939).

[64] Mada Nagaratnam v. Puvvada Seshayya and anr. (1939, IMLJ 272, Madras, 7 February 1939).

promissory notes. The Chief Justice of the Federal Court, Maurice Gwyer, ruled in favour of Lionel Leach's High Court decision.[65] According to Gwyer, the Federal Court did not have sufficient mandate to interfere in the implementation of debt relief laws. The overlap between debt relief laws and the Negotiable Instruments Act was indirect. That the MARA might affect the negotiability of contract, in the Federal Court's view, was neither its intention nor a valid concern. Indeed, as mentioned by the High Court in 1939, the MARA did not dispute the use of contracts; instead, it regulated the terms contained in contracts. In his final judgement, Gwyer proclaimed,

> It must inevitably happen from time to time that legislation though purporting to deal with a subject in one list touches also on a subject in another list ... I am clear that the pith and substance of the Madras Act, whatever it may be, cannot at any rate be said to be legislation with respect to negotiable instruments or promissory notes, which are central subjects. And it seems to me quite immaterial that many or even most of the debts with which it deals are in practice evidenced by or based upon such instruments. I am of the opinion, therefore, that the Act cannot be challenged as invading the forbidden field of the Federal Legislative List.[66]

Eventually, the judiciary issued an ordinance in 1945, enforcing the interest rate ceiling prescribed in the MARA. Credit disputes in provincial courts were subject to judicial intervention after 1937. In the case of *N. S. Sreenivisa Rao v. G. M. Abdul Rahim Sahib*, for example, High Court judges amended interest rates. The creditor and borrower contractually, on signed promissory notes, agreed an interest rate of 12 per cent per annum in 1944. The creditor, in this case also the plaintiff, approached the courts to enforce repayment at the agreed terms. The lower court ruled in favour of the defendant, prompting the creditor to appeal this decision in the High Court. Citing section 13 of the MARA, judges in the High Court ruled in 1956 that the borrower repay the principal with an additional interest, set at a rate of 5.5 per cent per annum.[67] Did the inclusion of contracts into the scope of the MARA impact the supply of credit? Credit supply contracted following the enforcement of borrower protection laws in various provinces in the late 1930s. According

---

[65] Maurice Linford Gwyer was a judge and academic in late-colonial India. Gwyer was the Chief Justice of India's Federal Court between 1937 and 1943 as well as Vice Chancellor of Delhi University between 1938 and 1950.

[66] "Federal Court," *The Times of India*, 7 December 1940.

[67] N. S. Sreenivisa Rao v. G. M. Abdul Rahim Sahib (1956, 2 MLJ 189, Madras, 20 March 1956). In the time between the date of loan issue and the case hearing, the borrower repaid a part of the loan to the creditor. Judges took this into account and therefore enforced the interest rate of 5.5 per cent rather than 6.25 per cent on the remaining amount.

to one account, 'consequent on the legislation to abolish the system, the landlords (across India) have completely given up their practice of advancing loans to cultivators'.[68] Approximately three-quarters of the total number of licensed moneylenders operating in rural United Provinces exited the market between 1936 and 1949.[69]

Descriptive reports from policy officials and commentators suggested that credit supply in rural Madras declined after the MARA was enforced. The Madras Estates Land Act Committee, for example, wrote in 1939 that the MARA successfully 'scaled-down' debts. Just one year after the MARA was implemented, the Estates Land Act Committee reported that moneylenders, 'whose debts have been cut down under the Act (MARA) would not be enthusiastic and ready to lend moneys to the agriculturist to the extent to which they were doing before the Act was passed'.[70] The law both discouraged fresh lending and did not provide an adequate substitute for suppliers that exited the market. Commentators on credit argued in the 1940s that the lack of available credit pointed to a supply disruption as the demand for credit persisted.[71] The abrupt contraction in credit supplied by moneylenders resulted in an increase in the demand for *Takkavi* loans (a limited number of which were granted by district governments).[72] Yet, this was not supplied at a scale large enough to match the decline in private credit. Soon after the courts legitimised the MARA, the market for rural loans contracted, the moneylender was less active in villages and the government did not design a suitable plan to match the growing need for credit with alternative sources.

Economists and political administrators in the 1940s and 1950s concurred with the Estates Land Act Committee, reporting that debt relief disrupted credit supply in rural Madras. Economists including C. W. B. Zacharias, professor at the University of Madras, and G. D. Agarwal, an agricultural economist, claimed that the MARA 'made creditors less certain of their future position' and, as a result, 'had the baneful effect of drying up the sources of credit in village areas'.[73] Claude Francis Strickland, a civil servant in 1920s Punjab and later member of the

---

[68] S. Thirumalai, *Post-war Agricultural Problems and Policies in India* (Bombay: The Indian Society of Agricultural Economics, 1954), 190.

[69] G. D. Agarwal, *Reorganisation of Agricultural Credit* (Kanpur: Industrial Art Printery, 1952), 129.

[70] *Madras Estates Land Act Committee Report: Part I* (Madras, 1939), 223.

[71] Agarwal, *Reorganisation of Agricultural Credit*, 129.

[72] Naidu and Vaidyanathan, *The Madras Agriculturists Relief Act*, 23–24.

[73] Agarwal, *Reorganisation of Agricultural Credit*, 129; C. W. B. Zacharias, *Madras Agriculture* (Madras: University of Madras, 1950), 167.

Indian Village Welfare Association, drafted an especially strong criticism of credit intervention in Madras.[74] Strickland's position is intriguing as he was a promoter of strict credit regulations in the 1920s. In an article published in the *Quarterly Journal of Economics* in 1929, he argued that peasants needed protection from the state to avoid over-borrowing and defaulting on high-priced debts.[75] When it became clear that the MARA disrupted the supply of loans, Strickland wrote that intervention per se was not the wrong strategy but the design of intervention was the problem in Madras. Writing in a non-legislative role in the 1930s, Strickland believed that successful intervention could achieve a balance between protecting peasants and maintaining an active credit market, a balance that the MARA did not achieve. In an excerpt of a pamphlet published by the Indian Village Welfare Association in 1939, Strickland drew an analogy comparing borrower protection to medical surgery where excessive legislation did more harm than good for the rural economy. He suggested that the MARA, 'impaired the credit of an agriculturist', contrasting successful surgery in his analogy, where 'a good surgeon works quickly and leaves the patient thereafter to return to normal life'.[76] Criticising the design of the MARA was the only way Strickland could reconcile his call for stricter credit regulations in the 1920s with his criticism of regulations in the 1930s. He was not the only political administrator in search of such reconciliation.

Narayanaswamy Naidu, member of the Congress-controlled legislature that drafted and implemented the MARA, recorded the decline in credit supply using village-level data in the early 1940s. Commissioned by the provincial government, a team led by Naidu conducted a credit survey of 8,530 households in 160 villages across Madras. Naidu published results from the survey in a report published in 1946. The report explains that surveyors carefully selected villages that reflected differences in geographical and socio-economic features, surveying rich and poor households in wet and dry regions within the province. Naidu's team of investigators surveyed villages to estimate the extent of borrowing in two years,

---

[74] C. F. Strickland, *The Relief of Agricultural Debt* (London, 1939), 15. Claude Francis Strickland joined the Indian Civil Service soon after graduating from New College, University of Oxford. Similar to Darling, Strickland spent much of his service working on rural finance and development in Punjab. Strickland was also Registrar of Cooperatives in Punjab between 1920 and 1927. Strickland is most cited for works on cooperatives in India and Africa. In the Indian case, Strickland's paper in the *Quarterly Journal of Economics* is one of the first pieces of academic writing on credit cooperatives in India.

[75] Strickland, "Cooperation and the Rural Problem," 513.

[76] Strickland, *The Relief of Agricultural Debt*, 15.

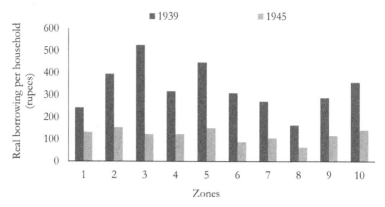

Figure 5.1 Real value borrowed per household in ten zones, 1939 and 1945 (1939 prices)
Sources: *Report of the Economist*, 43; McAlpin, "Price Movements."
Notes: The source aggregated individual observations of 8,530 families into anonymised regional zones. I divide the real value of credit by number of families in each zone. I deflate nominal credit data using McAlpin's agricultural price index. Total borrowing is inflation-adjusted to 1939 prices.

1939 and 1945. Surveyors grouped villages into ten zones and aggregated the household-level data zonally. The report anonymised the villages and the zones. The data does not specify type of loan instrument. However, as the team collected data from households across income classes, we can assume that the data is a representative sample of unsecured and different types of contracted loans. Figure 5.1 illustrates the data by zone, adjusting for commodity price inflation between the two years. The data shows that the value of credit borrowed per household declined by a significant margin. Zone 3 showed the largest decline where the real value borrowed per household was 76 per cent lower in 1946 relative to 1939.

The result seemed to have provoked concern among some policy groups and celebration in others. In some cases, the same policy official provided conflicting reports. Take Naidu, the author of the 1946 report, for instance. Naidu celebrated the reduction in credit supply in 1946. He believed that the reduction was evidence of diminishing exploitation as borrowers were no longer held in perpetual debt bondage, under the market power of monopolist lenders.[77] However, in a co-authored report in 1939, Naidu had previously commented negatively on the MARA,

---

[77] *Report of the Economist*, 43.

claiming, 'the first effect of the Act will be a drastic curtailment of credit and the seasonal agricultural operations will suffer through the drying up of credit'.[78] From a survey of villages in the Cuddalore municipality after the MARA was enforced, Naidu and Vaidyanathan found that 'a good number of agriculturists have left their land fallow on account of their inability to get credit'.[79] This contradicts Naidu's position in the 1946 report, which translates declining household debts to freedom from 'the disease of indebtedness' and rising prosperity.[80]

The MARA, in other words, stirred incoherent responses from policy officials in the years after 1938. Contemporary reports from government officials and economists agreed that the impact was a reduction in credit supplied, which in turn was not a demand-driven transition but instead reflected a supply-side shock where credit became less accessible after intervention. The policy officials that called for strict credit interventions in the 1920s and early 1930s either criticised the design of the MARA or supported the decline in credit supply as a solution to the problem of persistent indebtedness. It seems that praising debt reduction was the more popular response within policy circles as the law in its original form did not change despite reports of declining credit access.

As illustrated in Figures 5.1 and 5.2, household surveys show that the real value of credit borrowed contracted across income categories. When deflated by prices, the value of loans across borrowing categories declined between 1939 and 1945. However, the wealthier borrowers were more affected than the poor. Nominal borrowings declined for the top three income classes, with a substantial decline for the richest households. In contrast, nominal borrowings increased for households in the lowest income classes. Indeed, the average debt per capita among 1,130 small-holders in Class IV increased from 20.5 rupees to 21.3 rupees between 1939 and 1945. The debt per capita increased by a larger margin, prior to price adjustments, for tenants and labourers. In contrast, the average debt per capita decreased from 188.5 to 113.3 rupees for Class I borrowers and 91.7 to 64.1 rupees for Class II borrowers. While the surveyors suggest that rising wartime prices benefitted the rich more than the poor and this reflects in the distinctive amounts borrowed, a more plausible explanation seems to be in the type of loans provided. As the next section of the chapter will show, unsecured loans and crop-sharing arrangements operated outside the scope of the MARA. Mortgages, promissory notes and other loans

---

[78] Naidu and Vaidyanathan, *The Madras Agriculturists Relief Act*, 23.
[79] Naidu and Vaidyanathan, *The Madras Agriculturists Relief Act*, 23.
[80] *Report of the Economist*, 38.

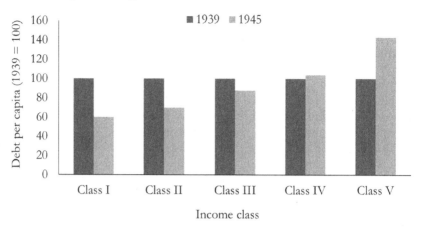

Figure 5.2 Growth rate in nominal debt per capita, 1939 and 1945
Source: *Report of the Economist*, 109.
Notes: The report aggregated individual observations of 8,530 families by
borrowing class. The report defined each borrowing class as follows. Class I was
defined as 'Big Landholders' where borrowers owned land above 25 acres. Class
II was defined as 'Medium Landholders' where borrowers owned between 5 and
25 acres. Class III was defined as 'Small Landholders' where borrowers owned
less than 5 acres. Class IV borrowers were tenants and Class V borrowers were
landless labourers. The number of families chosen in the survey differed by class.
Of the total 8,530 surveyed families, 240 belonged to Class I, 2,097 belonged to
Class II, 3,784 belonged to Class III, 1,130 belonged to Class IV and 1,279
belonged to Class V. I index the data for each class for ease of comparison
between the classes. The base year in the index is 1939.

that were sized high enough to warrant enforcement in courts were most
affected by the MARA. Therefore, small loans to the poor remained
informally enforced and untouched by government regulations.

In short, credit intervention led to a judicial conflict between the protection of free enterprise and more equitable markets. Judges prioritised
the latter, limiting the scope of contract laws and expanding the scope of
credit laws. This section has demonstrated that state intervention led to a
contraction in the supply of unsecured and contracted loans. The disruption in credit supply reinforced the contentious nature of the MARA. The
MARA triggered a loss in efficiency as borrowers had restricted access to
credit following the state-imposed artificial price ceiling. However, the
decline in lending differed by class of borrower. Credit to high-income
borrowers saw a larger decline than credit to low-income borrowers. The

next question to consider is whether moneylenders in the post-MARA period provided loans in accordance with regulation. We turn to whether the credit market operated more equitably after the MARA.

Intervention and Enforcement Costs

After intervention, the use of contracts declined and a black market for rural credit emerged. Creditors inflated the value of loans in contracts to account for higher interest rates than legally permitted. Creditors operated outside the legal structure where interest rates charged exceeded the imposed restriction. Indeed, from a survey of moneylenders in the early 1950s, half of all loans in the Coimbatore district reported interest rates of between 10 and 12.5 per cent in 1954 while only a quarter reported rates below 7 per cent.[81] Puzzlingly, the Indian government commissioned the survey to collect this data. Despite the official status of the report, lenders testified to charging higher interest rates than legally permitted.

Evidence suggests that lenders resorted to fraud and law evasion after the MARA. The Rural Banking Enquiry Committee reported in 1950 that credit legislation 'had the effect of driving a large number of moneylenders out of business or encouraging them to resort to evasive practices resulting in restricted and costlier credit, particularly to the small agriculturist'.[82] Other contemporary commentators argued that debt relief laws had an insignificant effect on equity in rural credit markets. Writing in 1952, Dantwala, an agricultural economist, believed that 'honest moneylenders' opted out of the market as they were not prepared to lend with new interest rate restrictions.[83] The 'dishonest moneylender' then dominated the market by endorsing methods of law evasion.[84] This is supported by a report in the same year which stated that 'their (the cultivator's) dire need for credit has given encouragement

---

[81] *Rural Credit Survey District Monograph: Coimbatore* (Bombay, 1957), 16.

[82] *Report of the Rural Banking Enquiry Committee* (Delhi, 1950), 52.

[83] M. L. Dantwala was a well-published economist and political activist. Politically, Dantwala was a fervent supporter of Gandhi and joined other activists in the movement for Indian independence. Academically, Dantwala, while imprisoned in Bombay for his political activism, completed a doctorate in economics from Wilson College in 1937. He published on agriculture in the 1940s and 1950s. Dantwala was known as 'the founding father of modern agricultural economics in India'. See Anonymous, "Obituary: Professor M. L. Dantwala." *Indian Journal of Agricultural Economics* 53, no. 4 (1998): 567.

[84] M. L. Dantwala, "Agricultural Credit in India – The Missing Link." *Pacific Affairs* 25, no. 4 (1952): 351–52.

to a class of unscrupulous moneylenders who can effectively evade the provisions of the debt legislation by practicing dishonest means'.[85]

How did creditors manage to continue lending and ignore the law? The practice of contract manipulation became more widespread in the 1940s. Lenders inflated loan principals on promissory notes to include higher rates of interest. In cases of default, creditors renewed promissory notes, adding previously unpaid interest to the loan principal.[86] Interest rates compounded, through inflated contracts, ultimately matching those charged prior to the enforcement of MARA.[87] Legal records provide evidence of this contract falsification. In *Garimella Mallikharjuna Rao v. Mangipudi Tripura Sundari*, for example, a credit contract in 1936 contained a rate of interest higher than the legal ceiling. Following a series of defaults, the creditor renewed the promissory note in 1939, 1942 and 1945. In each renewal, the promissory note recorded interest rates lower than the ceiling, though inflated loan principals to recover additional interest payments. The creditor refused to renew the promissory note beyond 6 April 1945 and expected the repayment of overdues, valued at 1,072 rupees and 5 annas. The borrower sued the creditor in the District Court in Amalapuram for attempting to recover unpaid loans with interest rates exceeding the legal limit. The court ruled in favour of the creditor. Judges claimed there was no evidence of contract falsification or unwillingness to conform to the law. The decision was appealed in the High Court where judges ruled in favour of the borrower. The court reduced the repayment value to 650 rupees and 2 annas, and attached an interest rate of 5.5 per cent per annum to the loan from the date of the District Court's decision in 1947 to the final High Court verdict in 1953.[88]

After the MARA was implemented, judges ordered some moneylenders to present account books and ledgers in court disputes.[89] Ledgers, however, were also frequently manipulated. Lenders fraudulently inflated the value of loan principals in their account books.[90] In one dispute, *A. L. Vr. St. Veerappa v. Chinnasamy Alias Samba Goundan and ors.*, the creditor inflated three promissory notes attached to loans

---

[85] Agarwal, *Reorganisation of Agricultural Credit*, 129.   [86] *Rural Problems in Madras*, 351.
[87] Zacharias, *Madras Agriculture*, 179.
[88] Garimella Mallikharjuna Rao v. Mangipudi Tripura Sundari (1953, 2 MLJ 313, Madras, 27 March 1953).
[89] The case A. L. Vr. St. Veerappa v. Chinnasamy Alias Samba Goundan and ors. (1950, 2 MLJ 328, Madras, 5 April 1950), provides an example where principals were not recorded on contracts prior to the borrower's signature. The creditor inflated the principal without the borrower's consent following default.
[90] *Rural Problems in Madras*, 351.

provided to the same borrower in the 1920s. The lender recorded inflated principals in ledgers. The borrower signed and thumb-printed the ledgers. Both parties signed the first promissory note in 1922, the second in 1923 and the third in 1925. The third recorded an unpaid value of 2,500 rupees. The creditor attempted to enforce the repayment of this loan in the District Court in Coimbatore in 1944. The borrower accepted that loans in 1922 and 1923 were unpaid and the 1925 promissory note was a loan extension. However, the borrower argued that the loan extension violated the MARA as it allowed the creditor to recover more than double the initial principal provided. Indeed, as previously discussed, repayments that exceeded double the original principal violated the *Damdupat* rule in the MARA. The borrower claimed that the lender deliberately 'suppressed all the account books' which would indicate the inflation of the loan beyond the legal value.[91] District court judges ruled in favour of the borrower and wrote off the majority of the unpaid loan for exceeding double the initial principal. When the creditor appealed this decision in the High Court, judges subpoenaed the ledgers to estimate the value of loans unpaid, adjusting for regulatory deductions. The creditor presented three ledgers that did not record the loan in dispute. High court judges sustained the lower court's decision.

In the longer term, the MARA discouraged the use of contracts altogether. Government reports in the 1930s commonly describe the use of pro-notes as 'widespread'.[92] As shown in the previous chapter, co-applicant guarantees were a universal requirement for peasants borrowing against pro-notes. However, similar reports in the 1940s and 1950s sparsely mention the use of this instrument or borrowing condition.[93] Surveying loans owed to agriculturist moneylenders in six districts, the Rural Credit Survey classified borrowing by security provided. Creditors secured some loans with mortgage instruments, but none by promissory notes. Indeed, the survey reported in 1954 that co-applicant guarantors were not a requirement for borrowing in any of the selected districts.[94] Loans secured by immovable property, mortgage loans in

---

[91] A. L. Vr. St. Veerappa v. Chinnasamy Alias Samba Goundan and ors.

[92] This is especially apparent in the *Provincial Banking Enquiry* in 1930 (*Madras Provincial Banking Enquiry Committee Report*, Vols. I–V (Madras, 1930)) and *Report on Indebtedness* in 1935.

[93] The instrument is sparsely mentioned in *Report of the Economist* in 1946 and *Rural Credit Survey* in 1954.

[94] The survey categorises the requirement for a co-applicant as 'Guarenteed by Third Party', reflective of the use of promissory notes. The survey listed the number of loans guaranteed by a third party as 0 for all districts and hence of no value. See *Rural Credit Survey*, 553.

other words, made up 24 per cent, 27 per cent and 50 per cent in Chingleput, Coimbatore and Ramnathapuram, respectively. The same ratio was much lower, 0, 0 and 2 per cent in Cuddapah, Kurnool and West Godavari. The majority of rural lending in Madras was unsecured by 1954.[95]

The decline in the use of contracts reflected the moneylender's aversion to courts. Disputes resolved outside the formal legal structure were excluded from the purview of borrower protection laws. The provincial government delegated the enforcement of the MARA to the courts. Judges had discretionary powers to decide if credit arrangements violated the terms of debt relief laws, and then amend such arrangements to bring them in line with the new law. As such, the scope and impact of the MARA, or potential for the act to enforce more equitable outcomes for borrowers, were conditional on lenders and borrowers resolving credit disputes in courts. As shown in the previous chapter, creditors were reluctant to approach courts and formal procedures for small loan disputes in the unregulated market. The enforcement of the MARA only accentuated this pattern, extending the practice of informal dispute resolution for a larger spread of debt recovery disputes.

Figure 5.3 highlights key transitions in the number of credit disputes between 1925 and 1960. The Depression period saw an increase in the volume of credit-related litigation. This process corrected as the number of cases in 1933 returned to its previous position in the late 1920s. Coinciding with the onset of legislative measures (the 1935 Madras Debtors Protection Act), there was an initial decline in the number of credit proceedings in the late 1930s. The largest shift occurred between 1939 and 1946.[96] The number of credit disputes in courts more than halved in this period. This trend continued throughout the 1950s. According to the Rural Credit Survey, twenty-nine out of thirty-one surveyed moneylenders in select rural districts near the eastern coast recorded unrecovered loans in the early 1950s. However, fewer than 10 per cent of lenders reported accessing courts to recover disputed loans in the same region.[97]

Provincial courts counted the number of credit disputes tried under the MARA, referring to cases where lenders charged borrowers interest rates higher than the ceiling and judges intervened, amending prices to fit

---

[95] *Rural Credit Survey*, 553.
[96] With the unavailability of data between 1940 and 1945, it is difficult to determine the exact date of this transition.
[97] *Rural Credit Survey*, Part I, 474. The data represents 'East Coast' districts from Madras, Mysore and Hyderabad. The survey included the following districts: Nizamabad, West Godavari, Chingleput and Ramnathapuram.

Figure 5.3 Number of credit disputes in civil courts, 1925–57
Source: *Statistics of Civil Courts in the Madras Presidency* (1925–58).
Notes: The data estimates the total number of registered disputes involving money in all civil courts across the province. Data is unavailable for the following periods: 1940–45 and 1948–52.

the law. Courts catalogued such disputes as 'cases under the Madras Agriculturists Relief Act'.[98] The number of cases registered under the MARA as a ratio of total loans provides an estimate of the scope and impact of credit intervention. As shown in Table 5.2, the number of MARA cases between 1938 and 1945 was 10 per cent of the number of mortgage loans provided between 1938 and 1941 alone. The value of credit under dispute between 1938 and 1945 was 20 per cent of the value of mortgage loans between 1938 and 1941, a small number considering default rates were high in Madras.

We can use patterns identified in the unregulated market to speculate the ratio of MARA cases to total loan defaults (mortgages plus unsecured). Pre-MARA provincial reports suggest that mortgage lending accounted for half of total rural lending.[99] The Provincial Banking Enquiry also suggests that default rates above 30 per cent were common in rural credit markets across districts in 1929.[100] Assuming these trends continued into the early 1940s, and the total number of credit transactions was double the number of mortgage loans while approximately one in every three loans went unrecovered, I can speculate that the number of MARA disputes in courts between 1938 and 1945 was only about 20 per

---

[98] *Report of the Economist*, 53. Hereafter referred to as 'MARA cases'.
[99] See Chapter 3.   [100] See Chapter 2.

Table 5.2 *MARA cases relative to mortgage loans, 1938–1945*

Cases 1938–45 (1)	Case value 1938–45 (2)	Mortgages 1938–41 (3)	Mortgages value 1938–41 (4)	Ratio 1–3	Ratio 2–4
204,528	95,466,104	1,479,302	433,147,259	0.1	0.2

Sources: Report of the Economist, 53; Report on the Administration of the Registration Department (1939–41).
Notes: The data on legal cases runs from March 1938 to September 1945. The first column measures the total number of registered disputes under the MARA. By September 1945, courts disposed of 203,874 cases while 654 disputes were still pending. The second column measures the value of credit transactions (rupees) involved in the registered cases. The third and fourth columns measure the number and value (rupees) of mortgage loans between 1938 and 1941. We do not have access to mortgage data for the 1941–1945 period. Ratios calculated by the author.

cent of *defaulted* credit transactions between 1938 and 1941 alone.[101] In practice, the ratio of MARA cases to total lending was likely to have been even lower than speculated here. As discussed in the previous chapter, civil court reports in the 1920s estimate a much lower ratio of mortgage to unsecured loans. Further, this figure declined in the 1940s because lenders were reluctant to attach mortgage contracts to loans after intervention. Including a larger number of unsecured loans in my speculation would show that MARA cases made up an even smaller share of total disputes. Judges, in other words, intervened in a fractional number of credit disputes in the early 1940s, restricting the scope of regulation.

Loan sizes were high in MARA cases. As shown in previous chapters, the average size of mortgage loans was higher than unsecured loans. The size of loans in MARA cases was even higher. From the data presented in Table 5.2, the average size of disputed loan tried under the MARA was 467 rupees. The average size of mortgage loan was about 293 rupees. In other words, the size of loans under judicial review far exceeded the size of small, unsecured loans in the same period. Following the MARA, creditors either avoided courts or seemed to approach courts when the size of loans far exceeded the average.

---

[101] 1,479,302 mortgage cases were registered between 1938 and 1941. Assuming this was half of total rural lending, the total number of credit transactions in the period was 2,958,604. If one in three loans went unrecovered, we can estimate the total number of transactions in dispute as 976,339. Dividing the number of MARA cases, 204,528, by the speculated number of debt disputes, 976,339, gives us a figure of about 21 per cent.

The decline in courts and contracts was driven by rising enforcement costs. The obligation to report lower interest rates on signed contracts increased the costs of formal enforcement. Put differently, dispute costs could no longer be transmitted to reported interest rates on promissory notes, which in turn raised the minimum loan size required to justify the use of this instrument. More generally, creditors responded to intervention by operating outside the limits of legal procedure. The MARA imposed a conflict between formal and informal enforcement arrangements where moneylenders were incentivised to adopt the most cost-efficient procedure. In this context, lenders evaded the artificial price control by avoiding courts and adopting alternate enforcement arrangements instead. Informal dispute resolution substituted for this decline in the role of formal procedure as an enforcement mechanism. Creditors relied on alternate forms of loan securities to evade legal procedures. From a cast study of villages in 1939, for example, Naidu and Vaidyanathan claim that creditors demanded jewellery or household furniture as forms of credit security.[102] The MARA did not regulate these methods of lending.

Crop was a common substitute for contract or land as a form of collateral in the regulated market. The ease of this substitution was driven by the distinctive features of the credit market in Madras. Homogeneity in the occupations of lenders and borrowers, and increasing commodity prices in the 1940s, lowered the costs of interlinked transactions. In the absence of formal contracts, crop was a viable article of collateral for lenders that were also cultivators.

Sources suggest that sharecropping arrangements between landlords and tenants were common in non-commercialised regions, though do not indicate that there was a rise in this particular credit arrangement after the MARA was implemented. Under sharecropping contracts, landlords advanced loans exclusively to tenants. Borrowers repaid loans by sharing produce at the end of the harvest, interlinking the transactions of rent and credit.[103] In each structure, the value of crop obtained by the moneylender included repayment of the principal and interest on the loan provided.[104] There were two reported structures of sharecropping in

---

[102] Naidu and Vaidyanathan, *The Madras Agriculturists Relief Act*, 23.

[103] Anthropological studies by Kathleen Gough and Joan Mencher discuss sharecropping arrangements in the Tanjore and Chengleput districts in Madras. See Kathleen E. Gough, "Brahman Kinship in a Tamil Village 1." *American Anthropologist* 58, no. 5 (1956): 826–53; Joan P. Mencher, *Agriculture and Social Structure in Tamil Nadu : Past Origins, Present Transformations and Future Prospects* (Durham, NC: Carolina Academic Press, 1978).

[104] Zacharias, *Madras Agriculture*, 152–54.

Madras during this period. The *Kuthugai* arrangement relied on fixed rent transactions. The *Varam* arrangement functioned as a joint venture with a pre-determined crop allocation to both agents. In both arrangements, tenant-borrowers paid landlord-lenders an amount at the end of the production cycle, which included rent and credit. However, the fixed rental structure relied on cash.[105] In order to purchase the inputs required, landlords provided cash loans at the start of the production cycle. Creditors pre-determined a fixed rent which borrowers paid at the end of the production cycle.[106] Under the crop allocation arrangement, landlords and tenants shared the final produce in kind at a pre-determined ratio by both parties. The sharing ratio at the end of the production cycle depended on the ratio of inputs supplied by landlord and tenant.[107] According to the 1918 District Gazetteer, landlord-creditors provided tenant-borrowers '30 or 33 per cent' of the total produce through the *varam* system in the Tanjore district.[108] This finding demonstrates the second difference between both arrangements – the role of the tenant. Cultivation was pursued as a joint venture by both landlord and tenant under the crop distribution arrangement.[109]

As shown in Table 5.3, creditors were more likely to rely on informal sharecropping arrangements in districts where farmers commonly transacted in kind. Sharing, between landlords and tenants, in cash was a negligible share of total cash expenditure in villages. The proportion of produce tenants shared with landlords was high relative to total expenditure in kind, suggesting that sharecropping was increasingly common in non-monetised settings. Sharecropping, as a contractual arrangement, was only operational when the transacting agents were previously linked by tenancy contracts. As such, sharecropping contracts did exist before the MARA. An official report of the unregulated market in 1935 found that landless labourers and tenants did occasionally borrow on sharecropping arrangements.[110] When the conditions allowed for its use,

---

[105] Zacharias, *Madras Agriculture*, 148.

[106] It was common for transactions at the end of the production cycle to have been in kind under sharecropping contracts. Creditors pre-decided the amount of produce shared at the end of the harvest at the start of the cultivating season according to a predicted market price of the final commodity. Lenders determined the volume shared according to the market price of the commodity.

[107] Landlords provided inputs into cultivation as loans in kind. Landlords filtered the principal and interest of the loan into the amount of produce owed to the landlord creditor at the end of the cycle.

[108] *Madras District Gazetteers: Tanjore*, 111.

[109] P. J. Thomas and K. C. Ramakrishnan, *Some South Indian Villages: A Resurvey* (Madras: University of Madras, 1940), 346.

[110] *Report on Agricultural Indebtedness*, 18.

Table 5.3 *Landlord–tenant cash and kind expenditure, 1954*

Region	Cash expenditure (%)	Cash contributions (%)	Kind expenditure (%)	Kind sharing (%)
South Deccan	69.2	1.4	30.8	33.6
East Coast	62.3	1	37.7	43.8

Source: *Rural Credit Survey*, Part II, 834–54.
Notes: Cash Expenditure estimates the proportion of cultivation expenditure paid in cash. Cash Contributions then sub-divides this cash expenditure by the amount spent by landlords on cash contributions to tenants and co-sharers. Kind Expenditure estimates the proportion of expenditure in kind to total cultivation expenditure. Kind Sharing estimates the share of produce shared with the landlord or co-sharer as a proportion of the total expenditure in kind. Payments solely for rent are excluded from this table. The table documents the amount of produce shared between landlords and tenants apart from rents. South Deccan districts include Hassan, Bangalore, Coimbatore and Cuddapah. East Coast includes Nizamabad, West Godavari, Chingleput and Ramnathapuram.

sharecropping was a supplement to, rather than substitute of, formal procedure as an enforcement mechanism. Because the contract was exclusively made between landlords and their tenants, and informally enforced, the arrangement was unaffected by the MARA. This could explain the rise in the nominal value of loans to tenants and labourers between 1938 and 1945, as depicted earlier in Figure 5.2.

Contemporary studies in the 1940s suggest that forward contract crop-sharing arrangements became more common for lenders and borrowers who were not tied to tenancy agreements. When executing forward contracts, creditors and debtors agreed on a predicted value of crop prior to the harvest. Borrowers promised the repayment of loans in cash or a volume of crop. Creditors determined the repayment amount according to predicted commodity prices. Through this structure, the moneylender benefitted from the price differential of the commodity at sale and the commodity at attachment. Lending through forward contracts was common for trade but not agriculture in the unregulated credit market. Different markets serviced loans for cultivation and loans for trade in the 1920s and 1930s. Borrowers used agricultural credit to finance cultivation expenses and borrowed at the start of the production cycle. Borrowers used trade credit to finance the costs of storage, transport and marketing.[111] The Provincial Banking Enquiry distinguished between the suppliers of trade credit and the suppliers of agricultural

---

[111] *Rural Problems in Madras*, 314.

credit in 1929.[112] Trade creditors were commonly 'traders and commis-sion agents', or 'petty merchants' including shopkeepers and local retail-ers. Merchants with storage facilities, who benefitted from the price differential of commodities, tended to provide trade credit.[113] In other words, suppliers of trade and marketing loans differed from those pro-vided credit for cultivation expenses in the unregulated market. However, crop-sharing arrangements increased in popularity in the 1940s. Writing on credit systems in the late 1940s, Thirumalai observed that moneylending was moving away from formal contracting and towards informal arrangements, noting that 'in the present unorganised set up, the finance for marketing is unwittingly merged in the ordinary loans extended to cultivators at the time of sowing'.[114]

Creditors designed crop-sharing contracts to be profitable in the 1940s. Lenders charged an interest rate calculated by the difference between the predicted price and market price. The magnitude of com-modity price volatility determined the scale of downside risk in this method of lending. Decline in market price automatically diminished the value of collateral held by the lender. Moneylenders managed the risk of price shocks, to some extent, by pre-negotiating the value of crop at a much lower rate than the predicted market price. Forward contracts allowed lenders to not just negotiate the price of collateral, but also the volume of attached commodity. Indeed, one survey of rural credit arrangements in the late 1940s found that some creditors provided loans against the borrower's entire produce as collateral.[115] The flexibility available to lenders to claim the borrower's entire produce acted as an insurance against deflationary shocks.

The rise in commodity prices in the early 1940s made the use of forward contract crop arrangements lucrative. According to one report, the price of rice and cotton increased by three times between 1938 and 1945.[116] Groundnut prices increased by four times in the same period. According to a government report in 1946, the price hike prompted farmers to colloquially refer to groundnut as the *Chitukilichan nut*.[117] Literally translating to 'tearing to pieces contracts nut', language used in the report reflects the impact of rising prices on the changing attitudes towards commodity as a valuable unit of collateral in rural credit.

[112] *Provincial Banking Enquiry*, 30.   [113] *Provincial Banking Enquiry*, 30.
[114] Thirumalai, "Post-war Agricultural Problems," 197.
[115] Zacharias, *Madras Agriculture*, 152–54.   [116] *Report of the Economist*, 47.
[117] *Report of the Economist*, 22.

The structure of village administration lowered enforcement costs in crop-sharing arrangements. Avoiding courts and legal procedures, creditors resorted to enforcing social sanctions on defaulters. Creditors and borrowers transacted in the same village, allowing the former to easily identify the creditworthiness of the latter. Lenders excluded risky borrowers, in this case previous defaulters, from participating in the local credit market.[118] The debtor's fear of credit being withheld in the future enforced the timely repayment of loans.

Ethnographic studies conducted in the 1950s and 1960s found that elite networks colluded to enforce social sanctions in South Indian villages. Collectives of 'headmen' arbitrated small credit disputes in villages.[119] Elite networks enforced harsh punishments for repeated defaulters. Kathleen Gough studied villages in the Tanjore district in the mid-1950s and observed that a network of village elites belonging to the same caste often formed courts that adjudicated small credit disputes, relying on social sanctions to punish defaulters. Gough observed that landowners, shopkeepers, moneylenders and panchayat committees typically belonged to the same caste within villages in the Tanjore district. Lenders used caste networks to ensure defaulters could not access fresh loans, rent land or find employment in the village.[120] When credit disputes were for small sums and contracts were enforced informally, outside of courts, caste and elite networks sanctioned defaulters in the 1950s.

In short, the MARA incentivised lenders to operate outside formal procedures. It increased the costs of enforcing credit contracts in courts. Judges invalidated contracts that declared rates higher than 6.25 per cent. Lenders, unable to compensate for enforcement costs through credit prices on contracted loans, sought alternative contractual arrangements to manage risks and adjust lending costs. Creditors recovered a higher interest rate on forward contract loans, benefitting from the difference between the market price of crops and the predicted prices at the time of lending. These lending arrangements were enforced informally and outside courts. Interest rates were unregulated as loans were not subjected to judicial review, priced as high or higher than prices in the unregulated market. Intervention did not do much to make the credit market more equitable.

State officials did acknowledge that moneylenders found ways to evade the law, and tried amending the law in the 1970s to curb evasion. The amended Madras Agriculturists Relief Act (The Tamil Nadu Debt Relief

---

[118] *Rural Credit Survey*, Vol. II, 172.   [119] *Rural Credit Survey*, Vol. II, 56.
[120] *Rural Credit Survey*, Vol. II, 56; Gough, "Brahman Kinship."

Act) in 1976 contained a specific provision for loans paid in cash but repaid in kind.[121] Lawmakers tried to include crop-sharing arrangements within the regulatory scope of courts and debtor protection laws. However, this amendment did not solve previous issues in design. Lending regulation continued to be administered through courts. As a result, the amended law expanded the scope of judicial discretion and not the sphere of the regulation itself.

Conclusion

Credit intervention in the 1930s aimed to bring moneylenders within the sphere of formal administration in Madras. The government attempted to control credit exploitation through laws enforced by courts. The design of intervention seemed to misunderstand the previously formal nature of the unregulated credit market. A market left to its own devices for much of the colonial period, evidence shows a symbiotic relationship between informal exchange and formal institutions. As the previous chapter suggests, creditors relied on contracts and courts, pricing the costs of accessing these formal institutions to the borrower. Targeted credit intervention in the late 1930s caused a reversal in this form of exchange. Paradoxically, state intervention disassociated the market from the regulatory capacity of the state. Whereas most historians think that the credit market was always informal and that was the source of its problem, this account suggests that the informal was, if not created, recreated and strengthened by regulation. Regulation was part of the problem of market failure.

The provincial government interpreted high interest rates as a sign of exploitation, elite capture and peasant distress. The policy response was direct interest rate regulation supplemented with a strengthening of property rights. The aim was an undisrupted supply of credit on more equitable terms for the borrower. In practice, laws not only failed to make equity gains but also triggered losses in efficiency. The credit market contracted and unsecured loans were provided at illegal rates of interest.

Policy lessons from the chapter suggest that intervention was a superficial attempt at targeting inequities in rural credit. The interest rate ceiling tightened credit constraints, affecting peasants' access to loans while also increasing enforcement costs and placing an upward pressure on credit prices. State intervention increased the costs of recovering formally contracted loans in courts, though had little impact on crop-

---

[121] Section 8, Tamil Nadu Debt Relief Act 1976.

sharing arrangements. Accordingly, credit supply declined and money-lenders that continued lending changed their preferred enforcement arrangement. Peasants accessed credit through illegal black markets where prices were non-transparent and crop-substituted land as a form of collateral. Increasing commodity prices in the early 1940s made this shift lucrative for creditors.

If the price ceiling did not work, then did the government's attempt to increase competition in the credit market bring more successful results? Indeed, enforcing the interest rate ceiling was one approach to bring down high credit prices while establishing credit cooperatives to compete with private moneylenders was another. Cooperatives had the potential to lend in larger sums to poor peasants as they offered a combined solution to enforcement and liquidity constraints. However, as the next chapter demonstrates, cooperatives did not produce the desired results in rural Madras.

6   Regulating Cooperatives[*]

As discussed in previous chapters, the colonial government acted on a belief that investment rates were low and the price of credit was high because markets were supply-constrained and non-competitive in rural India. One aspect of state intervention was the regulation of moneylenders in the 1930s. The other aspect was the initiative to generate competition in the market. Policy initiatives from the early twentieth century established competing creditors to rival private moneylenders. Officials in the colonial government expected greater market competition to increase the supply of low-cost rural credit.

The high risk of lending in the Indian countryside was a barrier to entry for commercial banks. Cooperative banking offered a potential solution to the problem.[1] Contemporary studies on Raiffeisen cooperatives in Western Europe referred to these as models to follow.[2] Present-day scholarship endorses that view. Cooperatives in Germany and the Netherlands provided credit to the poor and reported profits in the nineteenth and early twentieth centuries.[3] Scholars explain their success by highlighting two

---

[*] A shorter version of this chapter is published in the *Business History Review*. See Maanik Nath, "Do Institutional Transplants Succeed? Regulating Raiffeisen Cooperatives in South India, 1930–1960." *Business History Review* 95, no. 1 (2021): 59–85.
[1] Joseph E. Stiglitz, "Peer Monitoring and Credit Markets." *The World Bank Economic Review* 4, no. 3 (1990): 351–66; Timothy Besley and Stephen Coate, "Group Lending, Repayment Incentives and Social Collateral." *Journal of Development Economics* 46, no. 1 (1995): 1–18; Maitreesh Ghatak, "Screening by the Company You Keep: Joint Liability Lending and the Peer Selection Effect." *Economic Journal* 110, no. 465 (2000): 601–31; Jonathan DeQuidt, Thiemo Fetzer, and Maitreesh Ghatak, "Group Lending without Joint Liability." *Journal of Development Economics* 121 (2016): 217–36. Each article broadly agrees that group lending arrangements can, under certain conditions, deliver a structure of risk sharing that reduce information and enforcement costs.
[2] Malcolm Darling, *Some Aspects of Co-operation in Germany, Italy and Ireland* (Lahore: Government Printing, 1922).
[3] Abhijit Banerjee, Timothy Besley, and Timothy Guinnane, "Thy Neighbor's Keeper: The Design of a Credit Cooperative with Theory and a Test." *The Quarterly Journal of Economics* 109, no. 2 (1994): 491–515; Maitreesh Ghatak and Timothy W. Guinnane, "The Economics of Lending with Joint Liability: Theory and Practice." *Journal of Development Economics* 60, no. 1 (1999): 195–228. This scholarship shows that the

Table 6.1 *Principles of a Raiffeisen cooperative*

Feature	Outcome
Self-funded	Rich and poor save in banks. Defaults diminish savings.
Self-supervised	To prevent losing savings to bad loans, members identify creditworthy borrowers and enforce the repayment of loans through social sanctions.
Externally Regulated	Regulators hold managers accountable.

Sources: Banerjee et al., "Thy Neighbor's Keeper"; Ghatak and Guinnane, "The Economics of Lending with Joint Liability."
Notes: Adapted from the framework of Raiffeisen cooperatives presented in the sources.

key pre-conditions for successful cooperative banking.[4] First, cooperatives were self-funded within small membership groups. Rich and poor peasants saved in local cooperatives, while a high ratio of savings to external borrowing ensured banks were not over-leveraged. Second, governments in Western Europe implemented regulatory and supervision structures that ensured cooperatives were well managed. In the context of high savings and strong regulation, members absorbed the risk of lending which not only allowed German and Dutch cooperatives to form a source of low-cost credit for peasants but also guaranteed their profitability and resilience to crisis.[5] Table 6.1 summarises key principles underlying inclusive and profitable cooperative lending.

structure of Raiffeisen banks in nineteenth-century rural Germany contained the fundamental principles for profitable group lending.

[4] Timothy W. Guinnane, "A Failed Institutional Transplant: Raiffeisen's Credit Cooperatives in Ireland, 1894–1914." *Explorations in Economic History* 31, no. 1 (1994): 38–61; Timothy W. Guinnane, "Cooperatives as Information Machines: German Rural Credit Cooperatives, 1883–1914." *The Journal of Economic History* 61, no. 2 (2001): 366–89; Timothy W. Guinnane, "A 'Friend and Advisor': External Auditing and Confidence in Germany's Credit Cooperatives, 1889–1914." *Business History Review* 77, no. 2 (2003): 235–64; Christopher L. Colvin and Eoin McLaughlin, "Raiffeisenism Abroad: Why Did German Cooperative Banking Fail in Ireland but Prosper in the Netherlands?." *Economic History Review* 67, no. 2 (2014): 492–516; Christopher L. Colvin, "Banking on a Religious Divide: Accounting for the Success of the Netherlands' Raiffeisen Cooperatives in the Crisis of the 1920s." *The Journal of Economic History* 77, no. 3 (2017): 866–919. This scholarship demonstrates the benefits of localised membership, savings and supervision as the drivers of success in German and Dutch banks but failure in Irish cooperatives.

[5] Colvin, "Banking on a Religious Divide," emphasises the importance of religious institutions in supervising the allocation of loans, thus protecting Dutch cooperatives from a banking crisis in the 1920s.

Early- to mid-twentieth-century India presents a useful case study of cooperatives. Cooperatives were a state-driven initiative in India, and the colonial government set up the first Indian cooperative in the Madras province in 1904. The success of rural cooperatives in Europe inspired this initiative. According to an Indian economist in the 1930s, 'the study of the small village banks in Germany towards the close of the last century attracted the attention of those who were eager to solve the problem of rural poverty.'[6] Policymakers in colonial and post-colonial India continued to invest their confidence in the cooperative movement as a solution to the credit problem. They believed that 'great things were expected of the cooperative movement in India, on the analogy of its phenomenal success in Europe.'[7]

The chapter shows that the transplanted cooperative banking model did not perform well in South India. The cooperative sector grew exponentially in the early- to mid-twentieth century. The size of the cooperative sector in 1950s Madras mirrored that of Germany at the turn of the century.[8] However, cooperatives failed to displace the village moneylender. Managers of cooperatives selectively allocated loans and despite this selective allocation, the cooperative sector was unprofitable.

Why did the experiment fail to achieve its main aims? The chapter answers that administrators in late-colonial and early post-colonial India designed a cooperative model that differed from the European model in important ways. Prevailing political objectives prioritising equity over efficiency led to a cooperative structure operating with low savings and weak regulation. The regulatory problem ultimately led to exclusion of poorer peasants from accessing credit and over-leveraged cooperative banks.

What was the problem with regulation? The stylised model of Raiffeisen banking in Europe suggests that cooperatives could succeed because savings rates were high. In Madras, however, poor peasants did not raise enough capital while rich peasants refused to save in village cooperatives. Depositors were few and members cum borrowers were plenty, restricting the role of social capital and self-supervision as regulatory mechanisms. Contrary to the European model where poorly resourced banks could succeed if they were well regulated, cooperatives in rural Madras were regulated by administrative bodies which did not enforce competent banking regulation. The Indian government created the first Banking

---

[6] Krishna Kumar Sharma, *The Indian Money Market* (Bangalore: Bangalore Print & Pub., 1934), 63.
[7] W. R. S. Sathyanathan, *Report on Agricultural Indebtedness* (Madras, 1935), 58.
[8] Guinnane, "A 'Friend and Advisor'"; 237, estimates that 19,000 cooperative banks operated in Germany in 1914. Over 17,000 banks operated in Madras in 1952.

Regulation Act in 1949 and it did not cover cooperatives. Specific laws passed by the governments in the provinces regulated cooperatives in the colonial and early post-colonial period. Political and organisational interests overlapped, leading to the mismanagement of cooperative banks. Post-colonial Indian governments injected public money into the cooperative sector in the belief that this would increase credit access for poor borrowers. However, flaws in regulatory design persisted, allowing managers to falsify accounts, embezzle and insider-lend.

The chapter is divided into four sections. The first summarises the evolution and key features of the state-designed cooperative model in the province. The second traces the expansion of the cooperative sector and its lack of profitability in the early to mid-twentieth century. The third demonstrates that cooperatives were mismanaged because of low savings and weak regulation. The fourth shows that state financing in the 1940s sustained failing cooperatives but prolonged flaws in the sector's regulatory structure.

Designing the Cooperative Model

The colonial government established credit cooperatives in 1904; however, these were not the first type of group lending arrangements in Madras. Mutual credit associations operated prior to the cooperative movement. Rotating credit and savings organisations were common in the Malabar district of western Madras in the nineteenth century.[9] Groups of peasants within villages collected their savings into Chit Funds. These funds were informal, organised and managed within groups of friends or relatives. One member of the group managed the fund and collected a minimum deposit from the other members. Once collected, the manager issued a chit, a form of negotiated instrument, that defined the contents of the fund. The manager provided loans, by discounting the chit, to one borrower at a time. This was done by auction or lottery. When auctioned, the fund provided loans to members that offered the highest discount rate. Alternatively, in the prize chit format, each member of the group discounted the chit, the order of which was random and defined by drawing from a lot.[10]

Mutual saving and credit associations were also common among colonial officers. British officials in Madras city and some town centres in the districts operated *nidhi* funds from the mid-nineteenth century.[11] These funds functioned similar to English Building Societies in the nineteenth

---

[9] *Madras Provincial Banking Enquiry Committee Report*, Vols. I–V (Madras, 1930), 34–35.
[10] *Provincial Banking Enquiry*, 34–35.   [11] *Provincial Banking Enquiry*, 33.

century. Groups of friends or colleagues formed an informal association, and each member contributed a portion of their savings each month to a fund. Managers of the fund allocated loans to members of the group at interest rates that were lower than the rates charged by moneylenders. The fund remained intact for a set number of months, after which it was liquidated, and each member received a contribution larger than their investment. The share of the fund received depended on the size of the initial investment. *Nidhi* funds in Madras were started and operated by the British officers. Officials restricted participation in the *nidhis* to members of the government with fixed monthly incomes.[12]

The colonial government believed that chit and *nidhi* funds had problems as they were unregulated and serviced a small portion of the wealthy population. These were informal associations and operated outside the sphere of government regulation. Government reports suggested that managers of these funds typically embezzled from them. The other members did not have laws or legal support to enforce repayments and punishments on the embezzling managers.[13] Furthermore, these funds catered to a small section of the rural population. Poor peasants continued to rely on moneylenders for credit. As a result, serious discussions on establishing regulated competitors to moneylenders began in the late nineteenth century.

Colonial administrators began highlighting the cooperative banking structure, mirroring the one that operated in central Europe, as a solution to rural credit problems in late nineteenth-century India. Following the Deccan Riots in 1874, William Wedderburn, a District Judge in the Sind province, circulated a proposal in 1882 for the creation of cooperative banks in India.[14] The British-ruled government rejected Wedderburn's proposal.[15] Instead, the government implemented the 1884 Agriculturists Loans Act, which allowed provincial governments to provide *Takkavi*, or short-term working capital loans, to rural cultivators. However, this was

---

[12] *Provincial Banking Enquiry*, 33.

[13] Eleanor Margaret Hough, *The Co-operative Movement in India: Its Relation to a Sound National Economy* (London: P. S. King & Son, 1932), 50–52. Eleanor Hough was a doctoral candidate in George Washington University in the early 1930s. Hough wrote a thesis, involving a large amount of field work, on the failures of the cooperative movement in India.

[14] William Wedderburn joined the Indian Civil Service in 1860. Wedderburn served in the judiciary until retirement in 1887. Wedderburn was a District Judge until 1885, and a judge in the Bombay High Court for two years thereafter. Following retirement, Wedderburn was a prominent political figure. Wedderburn and Allan Octavian Hume were founding members of the Indian National Congress. Wedderburn served as president of the party in 1889 and 1910.

[15] Hough, *The Co-operative Movement in India*, 52.

not at a large enough scale to make an impact.[16] Lawmakers sought alternative solutions to the problem of imperfect competition in credit markets. From the early 1890s, the government began re-considering cooperative banks as a potential solution. The provincial government in Madras commissioned Frederick Nicholson to compile a report on successful cooperative models in Europe.[17] Orchestrating a path for regulated finance to replace moneylenders was the central purpose of the report. According to Nicholson, 'the substitution of organized credit for that of the money-lender is a necessary development of civilisation.'[18] While Nicholson travelled to Europe to write on the cooperative banking model in the early 1890s, cooperative credit organisations emerged in select Indian villages. In 1894, groups of villagers pooled savings and provided loans at low interest rates in sixty-four villages in Mysore.[19] Similar banks operated in Punjab and the United Provinces in the 1890s and early 1900s. From the turn of the twentieth century, the government undertook the responsibility of establishing and regulating credit cooperatives. This was not a bottom-up initiative. The government managed the size and scope of the cooperative movement in twentieth-century India.

Nicholson eventually circulated the finished report to the Madras Legislative Council in 1895. In the report titled 'Report on the Possibility of Introducing Land and Agricultural Banks into the Madras Presidency', Nicholson used the survey of cooperatives in Europe to suggest the conditions required for the transplant of a similar banking experiment in India. Nicholson identified three essential principles of Raiffeisen cooperation in Europe. First, the membership of each cooperative bank remained small and localised. Second, cooperative banks were self-funded through members' savings deposits. Third, cooperative banks determined the creditworthiness of borrowers by 'personal character' rather than land or physical collateral.[20] Nicholson asserted support for rural cooperatives and concluded the report with

---

[16] Hough, *The Co-operative Movement in India*, 52.
[17] Frederick Augustus Nicholson, educated in the Royal Medical College and Lincoln College, Oxford, joined the Indian Civil Service in 1869. He was stationed in the Madras Presidency throughout his career and was promoted from the lower ranks of district administrator to member of the Legislative Council in 1897. Nicholson is credited for his reports on rural development, including works on famine and banking. Colonial and post-colonial administrators refer to Nicholson as the 'father of the cooperative movement in India'.
[18] *Report Regarding the Possibility of Introducing Land and Agricultural Banks into the Madras Presidency* (Madras, 1897), 3.
[19] Hough, *The Co-operative Movement in India*, 52.
[20] *Report Regarding the Possibility of Introducing Land.*

the phrase 'Find Raiffeisen.'[21] His report convinced the government of the benefits of cooperative banking.

The British-ruled government in India set up one more committee, under the leadership of Edward Law in 1903, to advise them on the ideal legal structure to support the development of cooperative banking.[22] Nicholson was part of the committee but retired from government service the year after, the same year that the British-ruled government designed laws that defined the conditions for the establishment of new cooperative banks. Following the recommendations of Edward Law's committee, the colonial government in India implemented the first Cooperative Societies Act in 1904, which it later amended in 1912. With the responsibilities of designing and enforcing laws came an expansion in the administrative machinery to support cooperatives. The government formed Cooperative Departments at the federal level and in each of the provinces. The Registrar, typically a senior member of the Indian Civil Service, chaired the Cooperative Department in the provinces.

In India, cooperatives could not be formed without legal authorisation. This authorisation did not come from banking or company law. Laws executed by the Cooperative Department determined the guidelines for credit cooperatives to operate. Credit outfits operating within these guidelines could register, with the Cooperative Department, as credit cooperatives. Government and laws, therefore, were significant drivers of the growth of the cooperative movement in India. Indeed, section 47 of the 1912 Cooperative Societies Act prohibited organisations other than those registered by the Cooperative Department from using the name 'cooperative'. The government framed the cooperative structure such that it could only develop under the control of the state.

In this context, the 1904 and 1912 Cooperative Societies Acts identified key principles for the registration of individual cooperatives. These did not change during the period.[23] The law differentiated between urban and rural cooperatives. Cooperatives were rural if 80 per cent of the members were employed in agriculture. To register a rural cooperative, the establishment needed a minimum membership of ten people in the same village

---

[21] *Report Regarding the Possibility of Introducing Land*, 185.

[22] Edward FitzGerald Law was a British diplomat in the late nineteenth and early twentieth centuries. The British government in India appointed Law as a financial advisor in 1900. Law advised the government on currency reforms and tax policies. In 1903, Law led a committee to determine the framing of laws that would ultimately govern cooperative banks in the early 1900s.

[23] In India, laws referred to cooperatives as 'banks' and 'societies.' The chapter follows this terminology and uses the terms interchangeably. Commercial banks did not lend in rural Madras before 1960.

or town. If these requirements were satisfied, prospective cooperatives applied to the Registrar of the Cooperative Societies Department in the provincial government to register. Cooperatives could not form without the Registrar's approval.[24] If approved, the Registrar provided the new cooperatives with a registration certificate. The new cooperative registered an official building address with the Cooperatives Department.[25] With the expansion in the number of cooperative banks in the early twentieth century came an increase in the number of employees in the Cooperatives Department. The Registrar appointed Assistant Registrars, who also had the power to register new cooperatives. By 1920, there were nine Assistant Registrars in the Cooperatives Department in Madras.[26]

When federal laws were vague in instruction, they extended the legislative capacity of provincial government. On capital structure, for example, the 1912 Cooperative Societies Act defined the process for registration and requirements for share subscriptions but did not specify financial linkages between cooperatives. Similarly, the Act did not contain details on the regulation of the cooperative banks. The Act provided vague instructions on the rights of members, using phrases such as 'mutual watch' to define management accountability. Sections 35 and 36 of the Act provided Registrars with the powers to inspect and supervise the affairs of each cooperative and instructed managers to comply with the Registrar's enquiries. The provincial governments, under the Registrar's leadership, had the flexibility to mould the cooperative structure. Each cooperative had its own set of by-laws. Prospective cooperatives could not register unless the Registrar approved its by-laws.[27] The managers of cooperatives drafted these laws in accordance with guidelines provided by the Cooperatives Department. In other words, federal laws did not always design the cooperative structure. Provincial policymakers played a significant role.

Eventually, the federal government delegated the power to legislate in the cooperative sector to the governments in the provinces. Following the 1912 Cooperative Societies Act, the colonial government set up a committee under the leadership of Edward Maclagan to make recommendations for the ideal policy structure to support expansion of cooperatives.[28] The committee suggested that the provincial governments take control of legislating in the cooperative sector. Five years

---

[24] *A Short Introduction to Cooperation in the Madras Presidency* (Madras, 1920), 11–12.
[25] Section 15, 1912 Cooperative Societies Act.
[26] *A Short Introduction to Cooperation*, 11.   [27] *A Short Introduction to Cooperation*, 11–12.
[28] Edward Douglas Maclagan joined the Indian Civil Service in 1883. Maclagan was stationed in Punjab as Chief Secretary to the Government of Punjab, Secretary to the Revenue Department, Secretary to the Education Department, Lieutenant Governor

Table 6.2 *Structure of cooperative banking in Madras*

Organisation c. 1930	Role
Government	Enforced laws and regulated cooperative banks.
Provincial Bank	Savings bank in the city. Provided a small amount of credit to district and primary banks.
District Bank	A savings bank for members, non-members, primary banks and local government. Provided credit to primary banks.
Primary Bank	A savings bank for members and non-members. Lending bank for members in rural villages.

Source: The Madras Co-operative Manual (Madras, 1921).

later, and as part of the 1919 political reforms, the federal government officially delegated power to the provincial governments. The provincial governments enforced laws that regulated the cooperative movement. The government in Bombay enforced laws in 1925. The government in Madras, using the recommendations of the 1928 Townsend Committee report, implemented the Madras Cooperative Societies Act in 1932. Using examples of the initiatives taken in the provinces, the Maclagan Committee made recommendations for capital and management structure in the rural cooperatives. These were later included in the laws enforced by provincial governments. Did this model facilitate rural cooperation in Madras?

If the aim was to expand the supply of credit in villages, that aim was initially met to a small extent. Cooperatives accepted deposits from members and non-members, hoping these deposits would finance the expansion in credit supply.[29] By 1905, it became clear to policymakers that cooperatives struggled to raise savings from villages alone.[30] The government, still focused on expanding credit supply, created a three-tier banking structure to compensate for the low level of savings in villages. Table 6.2 summarises the responsibilities allocated to each tier. The provincial government established the Madras Central Urban Bank (MCUB), which accepted deposits from members and non-members in metropolitan Madras. The MCUB provided credit to primary banks.[31] The number of primary banks increased in the early twentieth

and finally Governor of the province. Maclagan compiled the report on cooperatives while being the Secretary to the Revenue Department in 1914.

[29] Cooperatives, as per law, could only provide loans to members.

[30] *The Madras Co-operative Manual* (Madras, 1921), 7.

[31] The MCUB later changed its name to the Madras Provincial Cooperative Bank.

century, exceeding the financial scope of the MCUB. The government created district banks to provide loans to primary banks in 1909. District banks were funded by three groups. First, members and non-members saved and owned shares in district banks. Second, primary banks deposited reserves into district banks. Third, municipal and district-level government departments saved public money in district banks. District banks did not lend to individual borrowers but exclusively to primary banks. As such, the cooperative three-tier structure included primary banks as creditors to cultivators in villages, apex district banks and an apex provincial bank as feeders to primary banks. The provincial bank played a comparatively insignificant role as the majority of lending from primary banks was funded by loans from district banks. Though operating beforehand, the Maclagan Committee recommended the three-tier structure to expand lending in rural areas. The 1932 Madras Cooperative Societies Act entrenched the three-tier structure. In developing this cooperative model, the government succeeded in expanding the supply of credit but made internal supervision challenging, as a later section will show.

The government supplemented the expansion in credit supply with rules that stipulated the participation of poor peasants in the management of primary banks. The government needed rich peasants to participate in order to keep savings high and cooperatives self-funded. Yet, it also needed to ensure that banks were not hijacked by richer cultivators that wielded greater social and political power in the countryside. The Cooperatives Societies Acts in 1904 and 1912 did not specify management structure.[32] The Registrar in Madras enforced rules on the election and supervision of cooperative bank managers. When prospective cooperatives fulfilled the guidelines to register, the Registrar or Assistant Registrar scheduled a meeting for the ten applicant members. The members voted in a governing board of five managers, or a *panchayat*, to manage the cooperative. The managers drafted by-laws and approved applications for new membership and loans.[33] Each *panchayat* included one president and one secretary. Once elected, managers were either honorary or professionally employed and paid an annual remuneration by the bank itself.[34] In the colonial period, primary banks held annual general meetings where members elected managers. Laws

---

[32] Hough, *The Co-operative Movement in India*, 86–87.
[33] *A Short Introduction to Cooperation*, 11–12.
[34] *Rural Credit Follow-up Survey* (Bombay, 1960), 441.

in the post-colonial period stipulated elections every three years. Though already operational for almost three decades, the 1932 Madras Cooperatives Societies Act entrenched these rules for the election of cooperative managers.

The provincial government in madras established Supervising Unions in 1910 to ensure transparency in the management of primary banks. The provincial government grouped primary banks, that were in close proximity to each other, in Unions. The aim was for managers from one primary bank to supervise and advise managers from another. The government implemented this policy to avoid the additional expenses of appointing external supervisors.[35] Unions did not audit primary banks. The government undertook this responsibility in the 1920s, as discussed in a later section. Supervising Unions performed two tasks. First, Unions reviewed the lending operations of primary banks and reported on the profile of borrowers. Second, Unions judged applications made by primary banks for loans from district banks.[36] Unions submitted annual reports of primary banks to their district bank creditors. In theory, reports from Supervising Unions identified management problems, including banks where rich managers discriminated against poor peasants.

The caste system was one potential barrier to cooperation in the Indian countryside. The government considered the diversity of membership a vital determinant of the success of the cooperative movement. Official reports classified members of primary banks by religion and caste. Surveyors recorded six categories including, 'Non-Brahmins, Brahmins, Adi-Dravidas, Christians, Muhammadans and other classes'.[37] Reports that classified members by groups of 'Brahmin' and 'Non-Brahmin' attempted to create a clear distinction between socio-economic classes. Government officials considered Brahmins as richer landowners and lower castes as smallholders and tenants. According to one provincial report in 1929, 12 per cent of members were Brahmins, 63 per cent were 'Non-Brahmin' and 25 per cent were from other religions and castes.[38] The provincial government celebrated this outcome. From these numbers, there was diversity in the voting membership group of each primary bank. However, contrary to the government's view, the presence of diversity alone was not enough to suggest cooperation. External supervision was needed to ensure one group did not discriminate against another. As subsequent sections will show, the Supervising Unions did not perform this role successfully.

[35] The Madras Co-operative Manual, 36.
[36] Annual Report on the Working of the Co-operative Credit Societies Act 1929 (Madras, 1928–39), 25–26.
[37] Annual Report (1929), 10.   [38] Annual Report (1929), 10.

We now turn to how the cooperative model performed.

Performance Puzzle: Expansion but Unprofitable

By all measures, the size of the cooperative banking sector increased by a significant margin during the first half of the twentieth century. Between 1907 and 1929, the number of cooperative banks increased from 63 to 15,238.[39] By 1952, there were 17,201 primary banks where 16,616 banks operated with unlimited liability and 88 banks operated with limited liability.[40] Membership, total working capital and the value of loans provided by primary banks more than doubled between 1928 and 1953. Total membership in primary banks increased from 652,285 in 1929 to 1,537,000 in 1953.[41] The number of district banks remained stagnant at between fourteen and sixteen throughout the period, whereas the number of primary banks linked to each apex bank doubled between 1940 and 1955.[42] There was also a rise in the average number of members per primary bank between 1928 and 1955.[43] The Rural Credit Survey estimated that primary banks had an average membership of 88 in the 1950s.[44] This was lower than similar estimations in nineteenth-century Germany.[45] The rise in the number of village banks was supplemented by a rise in membership, implying that there was an increase in the number of cultivators with access to cooperatives.

The price of credit from cooperatives was an added success. Cooperatives charged lower interest rates than moneylenders. The government enforced a ceiling on the interest rates charged by primary banks. Rates fluctuated between 7.5 and 9.5 per cent per annum in the early 1930s. As discussed, moneylenders in the same period charged rates of 2 per cent per month. Under these conditions, the data suggests that there was an expansion in the supply of low-cost credit during the early to mid-twentieth century.

It is surprising then that cooperatives failed to capture a sizeable share of the credit market. A survey in 1935 estimated that credit from cooperatives accounted for just 6 per cent of all loans to cultivators.[46] A similar

---

[39] B. V. Narayanaswami Naidu, "The Co-operative Movement in the Madras Presidency." *Indian Journal of Economics* 14 (1934): 426.

[40] *Rural Credit Survey District Monograph: Coimbatore* (Bombay, 1957), 220; *Report of the Committee on Co-operation in Madras* (Madras, 1956), 425.

[41] *Annual Report* (1928–39); *Report of the Committee* (1956).

[42] *Report of the Committee* (1956), 425.

[43] *Annual Report* (1928–39); *Report of the Committee* (1956).

[44] *Rural Credit Survey*, Vol. II (1954), 216.

[45] Guinnane, "A Failed Institutional Transplant," shows that the average membership size of Raiffeisen cooperatives in Germany fluctuated between 75 and 200.

[46] *Report on Agricultural Indebtedness*, 40.

report in 1956 provides a figure of just 3 per cent across India while confirming similar results for the market in Madras.[47] Narayanaswamy Naidu, a provincial legislator in the Madras government, suggested that 7.9 per cent of rural households were members of credit cooperatives in the mid-1930s.[48] Similarly, 23.5 per cent of the provincial rural population were 'within the fold of rural credit cooperatives', with a small share of this group actually borrowing from cooperative banks in 1956, demonstrating that the lack of market penetration persisted throughout the period.[49]

Cultivators did not benefit equally from the expansion of cooperative credit. Borrowers were concentrated in a small sub-section of the rural population. Primary banks selectively allocated loans to richer peasants. Government reports in the 1950s recognised this problem. According to the Rural Credit Survey, 'small owners, tenants-at-will and labourers, the cultivators of areas with poor rainfall and the backward agricultural communities are hardly members of societies.'[50] Data on loan sizes and collateral requirements on those loans signal the income profile of borrowers. Loans exceeding 250 rupees accounted for nearly half of all cooperative credit provided in 1929 and 1956.[51] Loans from moneylenders were significantly smaller, suggesting that moneylenders rather than cooperatives were servicing the credit needs of the poor. Indeed, from a survey of moneylender-serviced credit markets in six villages in the Bellary district, the average debt per acre was 17 rupees in 1930.[52] Assuming the size of loans increased proportionally to the size of land ownership, these numbers suggest that cooperatives showed a preference for high-income borrowers.

Furthermore, cooperatives shifted from non-asset-based to mortgage lending from the 1920s. In the mid-1920s, mortgages accounted for 40 per cent of loans while borrowers accessed the majority of cooperative credit by attaching a co-signer to their loan applications. By 1938, as shown in Figure 6.1, 60 per cent of loans were secured by mortgage instruments. The government recognised that this was a departure from the original aims of the cooperative movement. Commenting on foreclosures in 1936, the Cooperative Department in Madras stated, 'these properties are undoubtedly a source of embarrassment to societies and it must be their anxious concern to dispose of them in consultation with their financing banks at the earliest opportunity.'[53] Cooperatives that

[47] *Report of the Committee* (1956), 41.   [48] Naidu, "The Co-operative Movement," 420.
[49] *Report of the Committee* (1956), 40.   [50] *Rural Credit Survey*, 223.
[51] *Provincial Banking Enquiry*, 152; *Report of the Committee* (1956), 29.
[52] *Provincial Banking Enquiry*, 62–63.   [53] *Annual Report* (1936), 12.

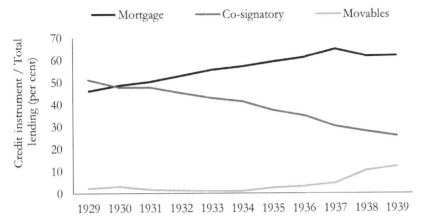

Figure 6.1 Security on loans, 1928–39
Source: *Annual Report* (1928–39).
Notes: Figure shows the value of loans attached to three credit instruments.
Mortgage refers to loans secured by land. Co-signatory refers to loans
contractually secured by third-party guarantors. Movables refer to loans secured
by crop. The source provides the total volume of lending by primary banks in a
given year, disaggregated to the volume of loans under the three types of credit
instruments in a given year. Ratios are calculated and converted to percentage in
the source.

acquired land from their members contradicted Nicholson's principles of
Raiffeisen banking. Collateral requirements excluded poor peasants from
accessing cooperative credit.

The Great Depression explains the shift from co-signatory lending to
mortgages.[54] The co-signatory method proved unsustainable during the
1930s crisis. Repayment rates were generally low in cooperatives. From
loans issued in the late 1920s, primary banks declared 30 per cent of
expected interest inflows as overdue. As illustrated in Figure 6.2, recovery rates continued to decline as overdue interest increased by a further
30 per cent between 1930 and 1934. Primary banks shifted to mortgage
lending in the hope that auctioning the land acquired from defaulters
would help mitigate losses. The colonial government enforced rules that
ensured each cooperative limited the total value of loans to the net value
of properties held in the cooperative's possession.[55] Cooperatives

---

[54] Homogeneity in the occupation of borrower members spread the impact of the crisis.
Cultivators constituted 89.1 per cent of the total membership of primary banks (*Annual
Report* (1929), 9). The commodity price crash in the early 1930s led to a rapid short-term
decline in the membership of primary banks (*Annual Report* (1929–34)).
[55] *Provincial Banking Enquiry*, 151.

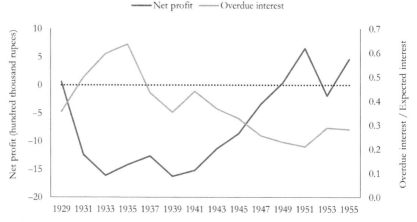

Figure 6.2 Profitability of primary banks, 1929–55
Sources: *Annual Report* (1928–39); *Report of the Committee* (1956), 425–35.
Notes: Figure shows that primary banks made losses throughout the period. The government collected data from each primary bank and aggregated this to the provincial level in the source. Profit and loss calculations made by the author. 'Net Profit' takes the difference between divisible profit and non-recouped loss in a given year. Net Profit plotted on the left *y*-axis. The dotted line indicates when primary banks break-even. 'Overdue Interest' is calculated in the source and plotted on the right *y*-axis. It measures default rates in a given year by estimating the ratio of unpaid interest to total interest obligations. For example, in 1934 the ratio of overdue interest to interest due was 0.64, which means that primary banks only recovered 36 per cent of their expected interest inflows that year.

enforced this parameter to moderate the difference between the value of the properties securitised and the value of overdue loans. The rules entitled cooperatives to liquidate properties in times of default. The provincial government expected cooperatives to generate positive net balances by auctioning land they acquired from defaulters.

The recovery from the Depression started in 1937. Membership in primary banks increased by 2.6 per cent between 1937 and 1938, with a larger increase of 8.3 per cent in the following year. Primary banks expanded lending operations in the same period. The value of loans provided by primary banks in 1939 was 1 per cent shy of the same measure in 1929. This was supported by rising commodity prices in the early 1940s.[56] However, cooperatives did not fully recover from the

---

[56] Michelle McAlpin, "Price Movements and Fluctuations in Economic Activity (1860–1947)." In *The Cambridge Economic History of India*, edited by Dharma Kumar

crisis. As demonstrated in Figure 6.2, primary banks reported net losses until 1950. The upward swing in commodity prices and the shift to mortgage lending had limited impact on the profitability of cooperative banks. Why did cooperatives endure losses despite the move to more selective lending?

One potential answer is that cooperatives were constrained by enforcement costs. Institutional barriers prevented banks from acquiring land in a timely and cost-efficient manner. Land transfer required the ratification of legal authority while court disputes were lengthy and expensive.[57] The colonial government created a legal structure, for cooperative banks, that functioned outside the scope of civil courts. The 1932 Madras Cooperative Societies Act specified that cooperative disputes were to be resolved by representatives of the Registrar, as chair, of the cooperative department in the provincial government.[58] The government created special arbitration courts within districts to enforce land transfers following defaults.[59] These forums failed to solve the problem. The rising number of pending disputes in the early 1930s triggered concerns among policymakers that arbitration courts were also a costly and inefficient method of enforcing repayments.[60] As such, moneylenders benefitted from lower costs of information, monitoring and enforcement. Cooperatives disbursed loans, monitored the use of loans and enforced repayments through formal procedures. Prospective borrowers submitted loan applications prior to disbursement and primary banks approached arbitration forums to recover unpaid bills. Formal procedure, however, was just one of other enforcement options for private moneylenders. Reporting to the Provincial Banking Enquiry Committee on the inability of cooperatives to displace moneylenders in the district, the Sub-registrar of Ganjam noted that moneylenders had variety of options to enforce the repayment of loans, whereas 'a cooperative society which is a corporate body' had little flexibility outside of formal procedure. Cooperatives, according to the sub-registrar, could not, 'exhibit such a close watch' of borrowers, 'as the person of the lender does'.[61]

The parallel functioning of courts and special arbitration forums, chaired by the Registrar of the Cooperatives Department in government,

and Meghnad Desai, 2: 878–904 (Cambridge: Cambridge University Press, 1983), appendix table 11A.1.

[57] Tirthankar Roy and Anand V. Swamy, *Law and the Economy in a Young Democracy* (Chicago: The University of Chicago Press, 2022).

[58] Section 51 of the Madras Cooperative Societies Act (VI of 1932).

[59] Arbitration forums were the preferred formal forums of appeal for banks and defaulters. The number of cooperative disputes in arbitration forums exceeded appeals in Civil Courts by a significant margin in the 1930s.

[60] *Annual Report* (1937), 10.   [61] *Provincial Banking Enquiry*, Vol. III, 1088.

led to conflicts between the judiciary and executive, ultimately causing enforcement inefficiencies. Borrowers that defaulted on loans to cooperatives commonly also defaulted on tax bills and loans to money-lenders. Different courts adjudicated each of the cases, leading to confusion on how best to enforce repayments. In *Govada Balabharathi Co-operative Credit Society v. Alapati Venkatakrishnayya*, for example, a borrower defaulted simultaneously on loans to a cooperative and a money-lender. The arbitration forum ordered for the borrower to transfer land to the cooperative while the civil court independently ordered for the transfer of the debtor's land to the moneylender. This motivated debates on whether 'the Registrar deciding cases under sections 51 of the Act is a court'.[62] Borrowers regularly questioned the decisions made by the special arbitration forums in civil courts. The outcome was a complicated enforcement structure that was a barrier to the efficient execution of mortgages. According to one report, 'the Government do not tend to lessen the difficulties of societies which have obtained decrees against defaulters and are executing them through the department.'[63] This conflict contributed to the inefficiency of arbitrations between cooperatives and defaulters. Land transfers were difficult to execute in the informal and cooperative credit markets.[64]

Some primary banks responded to the enforcement problem by collat-eralising commodities instead of land. Though capturing a small share of lending operations, Figure 5.1 shows that the number of loans against crop security increased six-fold between 1936 and 1939. The 1930s saw a rise in the registration of Loan and Sale Societies. These primary banks provided loans collateralised by commodities. When borrowers defaulted, the primary banks stored the commodities and traded them on the market. To mitigate the risk of price fluctuations, the primary banks provided working capital loans valued at 60 per cent of the bor-rower's produce prior to the harvest.[65] Primary banks collateralised the storage receipts of the warehoused commodities to obtain loans from district banks.[66] This arrangement became more popular in the late

---

[62] *Madras Journal of Co-operation* (Madras, 1935), 560.

[63] *Madras Journal of Co-operation* (1935), 562.

[64] Cooperatives struggled to auction the land they did acquire during the Depression period. Land markets were sluggish in the crisis years as cultivators did not invest in buying land. The acquired lands typically went idle under the ownership of the cooperatives. Primary banks were forced to bear the costs of maintaining the lands they acquired. See *Annual Report* (1937), 10–11.

[65] *Report of the Committee on Co-operation in Madras* (Madras, 1928), 14.

[66] *Report of the Committee* (1956), 8–9.

1950s. Credit and marketing primary banks were more rigorously differentiated from each other in this latter period.

However, enforcement barriers do not fully explain losses in the cooperative sector. According to Nicholson's prototype, self-help should have substituted external enforcement in the first instance. The requirement for courts in itself represents a failure in cooperation among members. The next section of the chapter shows that cooperatives shifted to mortgage lending and incurred persistent losses because of flaws in capital structure and regulatory design.

Low Savings and Weak Regulation

Primary banks, as illustrated in Figure 6.3, were not self-funded. They borrowed from district banks to fund their lending operations in Madras. High savings in district banks and low savings in primary banks entrenched a banking structure of debt dependence. As a result, primary banks were poorly regulated. Low savings restricted the capacity for mutual supervision in primary banks. Top-down regulation did not substitute for the absence of this bottom-up supervision. As mentioned before, the entire banking system in India did not have a formal regulator until the 1949 Banking Regulation Act, and even that act did not cover cooperatives.[67] The outcome of the flawed design, this section demonstrates, was weak regulation and mismanagement.

Figure 6.4 sketches the multi-layered banking structure of cooperatives in Madras. This banking structure operated throughout the period. However, the volume of capital flows between the layers changed in the late 1940s. Capital flowed in a two-tiered structure, between district banks and primary banks. As previously discussed, the provincial apex bank did not play a significant financial role in the cooperative movement. Primary banks were funded by savings deposits, investments in share capital and loans from district banks. District banks were funded by savings deposits and investments in share capital. Loans from government constituted a small share of cooperative operations. Governments financially participated by saving in district banks in the 1930s and early 1940s. As the next section will show, the role of government changed in the late 1940s. Government loans to district banks increased exponentially from 1947

---

[67] The 1949 Banking Regulation Act was modified to include cooperatives only in 1965. For laws and private banking in the colonial period, see Roy and Swamy, *Law and the Economy*. For a discussion on the Banking Regulation Act, see Autar Krishen Koul and Mihir Chatterjee, "International Financial Institutions and Indian Banking: A Legal Profile." In *India and International Law*, edited by Bimal N. Patel, 2: 207–30 (Leiden: Brill, 2008).

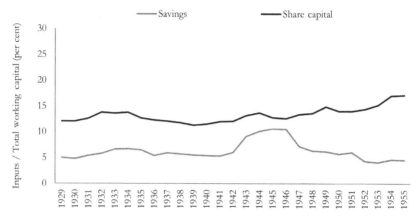

Figure 6.3 Ratio of savings and share capital to working capital in primary banks

Sources: *Annual Report* (1928–39); *Report of the Committee* (1956).

Notes: Figure shows savings and share capital constituted a small share of the working capital in primary banks. The sources provide data on the total working capital of primary banks with the value of savings, investment and debt. For ease of comparison, the author rounds all numbers to the nearest ten-thousand. The reports exclude data from the Ganjam district in 1936–37. Data scope shifts from 'composite' to 'residuary' state in 1953 to reflect the changing of state borders after independence. These two factors do not bias the results in any way.

onwards. While the three-tier capital structure did not change much, the top-tier played a more significant role in the post-colonial period.

As illustrated in Figure 6.3, primary banks in Madras raised most of their working capital through external borrowing.[68] Loans from district banks financed between 70 and 80 per cent of the required working capital in primary banks. Members' and non-members' deposits accounted for between 5 and 11 per cent of total working capital. The ratio of savings to loans presented similar results. The volume of savings in primary banks was between 4 and 11 per cent of the volume of lending throughout the period. Share capital played a marginally more important role than savings in primary banks. However, share capital included

---

[68] There was a decline in this ratio during the 1930s, which is explained by the rise in the reserve funds of each society. The ratio of external borrowings declined from 74 to 60 per cent between 1928 and 1935, coinciding with a rise in the ratio of the reserve fund from 6 to 16 per cent in the same period. Banks were either liquidated or more risk-averse during the Depression. The temporary decline in the ratio of external borrowings in the 1930s does not infer greater self-sufficiency.

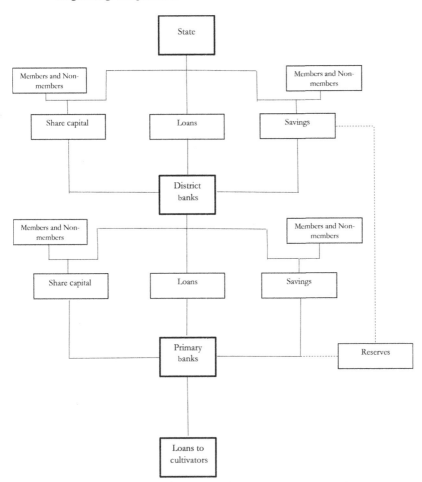

Figure 6.4 Capital structure of the cooperative sector, 1930–60
Source: Author.

investments from members and district banks. The majority of this investment was from district banks in the 1930s, accentuating the external funding problem.[69]

Why were savings low in primary banks? Colonial officials maintained that peasants were ill-informed about the benefits of saving such that disposable income was rarely saved and instead spent on extravagant

---

[69] *Annual Report* (1936), 30–31.

ceremonies.[70] In practice, savings rates were low because harvest failure was common and cultivation was unprofitable in bad years. An indirect confirmation of the claim that volatile seasonal incomes depressed rural savings is that the ratio of saving to working capital was higher in urban cooperatives during the same period.[71]

When the rich did have money to save, they did not deposit their savings in primary banks. Wealthy cultivators either allocated their disposable income in the credit market as moneylenders or to deposits in district banks. According to Panikar, '90 per cent of rural credit (in the 1950s) seems to come from the saving of rural families.'[72] Moneylending presented a more lucrative option to saving. As mentioned, there was a gap between the interest rates charged on loans from moneylenders and those offered by cooperative banks. Peasants earned a higher return from lending, rather than saving their disposable income. Depositors in primary banks commonly withdrew their deposits to lend in the informal market when prices were high. The possibility of a quick return on seasonal lending attracted new lenders to the informal market. Coinciding with a period of rising commodity prices, several depositors withdrew their savings from primary banks and provided short-term loans to peasants at higher interest rates between 1918 and 1920. The Cooperative Department tried resolving the problem with a short-term increase in interest rates. The department hoped that charging rates of 11 per cent would attract depositors.[73] Savings increased marginally after 1920, however, peasants continued to show a preference for lending, rather than saving in primary banks during the period. When designing the three-tier structure, the Maclagan Committee did acknowledge that peasants with disposable income preferred moneylending to saving. The Committee advised that primary banks should 'induce the moneylender to lend through the medium of the society by becoming himself a depositor or to convert a previous debt due from a member into a deposit with the society'. This advice did not translate into successful initiatives at attracting higher savings.

When money was being saved, cultivators chose to deposit in district rather than in primary banks. There was a marked increase in the number of individual depositors in district banks in the late 1920s.[74] The ratio of savings to loans in district banks was significantly higher than the same

[70] See Malcolm Darling, *The Punjab Peasant in Prosperity and Debt*. 4th ed. (Bombay: Oxford University Press, 1947).
[71] *Annual Report* (1928–39).
[72] P. G. K. Panikar, *Rural Savings in India* (Bombay: Somaiya Publications, 1970), 59.
[73] *Annual Report* (1920), 10–11.   [74] *Annual Report* (1936), 19.

ratio in primary banks. At the peak of the Depression in 1933–34, savings deposits accounted for 62 per cent of the total working capital of district banks. A combination of share capital and savings contributed 72 per cent of total working capital in the same year.[75]

Rich peasants chose to save in district banks because, based on the government's design, the deposits of members and non-members in district banks had a stronger guarantee than deposits in primary banks. Individual depositors were not the only savers in district banks. Local government departments saved as did groups of primary banks. The colonial government framed laws to ensure that primary banks maintained a reserve ratio, physically deposited in district banks. According to the laws, primary banks deposited this 'statutory contribution' in the district bank that they were indebted to.[76] This required reserve increased the value of deposits in district banks. When primary banks defaulted on loans to district banks, the reserve fund diminished before savings. Moreover, groups of primary banks borrowed from and deposited reserves in one district bank. District banks offset the defaults from one primary bank with the reserves of another.[77] District banks also restricted the volume of lending to failing primary banks. Indeed, district banks maintained higher reserves and reduced lending to primary banks in the 1930s.[78] Deposits from primary banks and risk-averse lending in crisis years, both enforced by government regulation, protected member and non-member deposits in district banks.

The Depression had a larger impact on primary than on district banks. Between 1929 and 1939, district banks reported a decline in net profits from 1.1 million rupees to just over 300,000 rupees. In the same decade, primary banks transitioned from earning a net profit of 60,000 rupees to reporting net losses of 1.62 million rupees.[79] Reserves and higher savings in district banks moderated the transmission of primary bank losses up the cooperative ladder. The combination of share capital, savings and reserve deposits constituted 77 per cent of the total working capital of district banks in 1933–34.[80] Deposits insured defaults, restricting losses incurred. In contrast, primary banks were funded by external borrowing. Defaults were high and deposits were small, leading to persistent losses.

Low savings posed a problem for supervision in primary banks. Members of cooperative *panchayats*, including presidents and secretaries,

---

[75] *Annual Report* (1934), 24.   [76] *Annual Report* (1930), 16–17.
[77] *Annual Report* (1936), 19.
[78] The volume of district bank to primary bank loans halved between 1929 and 1935 (*Annual Report* (1929–35)).
[79] *Annual Report* (1928–39).   [80] *Annual Report* (1934), 50–51.

were commonly neither savers nor shareholders. The incentive for self-contained supervision diminished as the burden of default was not borne by the deposits or share capital of governing members. According to Eleanor Hough's thesis on the management of Indian cooperatives in the early 1930s, 'the cooperative safeguards of mutual watchfulness and supervision are absent and everything depends on the committee's honesty and business ability'.[81] This problem persisted throughout the period. On the management of primary banks, the Rural Credit Survey in 1954 reported, 'there is a paucity of members who are actually cultivating lands themselves. The agricultural finance by the cooperatives would be more efficient and smooth if ways and means are devised to secure invariably the presence of some actual cultivators on the board of management'.[82] The employment of professional managers rather than shareholders resulted in a lack of monetary incentives to increase the profitability of primary banks. The provincial government reported the following in 1929,

Though the objects of co-operative banks and commercial banks may be different, the one seeking to increase the shareholders' profit being ruled by shareholders who have generally no other interest in the concern, while the other seeks to benefit the borrower shareholder, whose interest as borrower is far greater than his interest as shareholder.[83]

In other words, the governance structure in primary banks did not foster sound management through self-regulation.[84]

Supervising Unions did not solve the problem either. The number of Unions did not match the size of banking operations. An estimated 8,191 primary societies were affiliated with 262 supervision unions, at an average of 31 banks per union, in 1937.[85] The 262 Supervision Unions employed 432 supervisors in 1937. Furthermore, the ratio of banks to employees in unions amounted to 19 banks per individual supervisor in the same year. Each supervisor monitored the operations of 19 primary banks in the late 1930s, leading to inefficiencies in oversight. These inefficiencies increased transaction costs for members and primary banks. Primary banks underwent lengthy administrative processes before the disbursement of

---

[81] Hough, *The Co-operative Movement in India*, 60.   [82] *Rural Credit Survey*, 263.
[83] *Annual Report* (1929), 17.
[84] One barrier to self-regulation could have been illiteracy. Members needed a basic understanding of loan accounting and contracts to effectively supervise banks. However, certain institutional arrangements solved the problem in Madras. The Provincial Banking Enquiry reported in 1930 that cultivators approached local school teachers and clerks competent in simple accounting methods to assist in analysing loan documentation. Moreover, the provincial government established cooperative training institutes in districts. The institutes provided free assistance to illiterate members.
[85] *Annual Report* (1937), 25.

loans. The demand for credit, in turn, involved elaborate applications from participating members. Supervising Unions often vetted these. Similarly, loans from apex banks were conditional on applications from primary banks, which were again open to scrutiny from unions. The subsequent delays in the processing of loans conflicted with the seasonal demand for credit from cultivators.[86] According to the Provincial Banking Enquiry, 'So long as all this process is essential and it is essential for every loan that is applied for and sanctioned by the central bank it is useless to expect cooperative societies to meet the entire cash requirement for financing agriculture.'[87] The inefficiencies in supervision further restricted savings in primary banks. Unions monitored savings withdrawals to ensure primary banks remained liquid. Depositors needed to make applications, which were vetted by Supervision Unions, to withdraw their savings from primary banks. This was a time-consuming process. According to one government report, 'no one will put his money in a savings bank deposit if it takes a month or two to get the money back.'[88]

Moreover, there were conflicts of interest between the supervisors and primary bank managers. The government did not design Unions to hire external supervisors. Officials were concerned that external supervision would lead to the cooperative movement departing from its aims of being self-contained within villages. In his capacity as President of one primary cooperative in Madras, Deivasikhamani Mudaliar stated in 1937, 'for the efficient administration of village societies local knowledge and help is essential. The money lent to the villagers can be recovered easily only with their help. Nothing can be done in a village without the help of the villagers.'[89] Accordingly, the government implemented policies to ensure that supervision remained within the scope of the managers of primary banks. Members of Supervising Unions constituted representatives from the *panchayats* of primary banks. As a result, the governance structure of Supervising Unions extended, rather than corrected, the lack of management accountability in primary banks. Supervising Unions, as recorded in an official report in 1935,

cannot be independent and disinterested bodies, as they are run mostly by representatives of the very societies, which have to be supervised. Is it any wonder then that the supervisor is often forced, if he is to keep his job, to collude with the managements of credit societies in all their misdemeanours?[90]

---

[86] See Tirthankar Roy, "The Monsoon and the Market for Money in Late-colonial India." *Enterprise & Society* 17, no. 2 (2016): 324–57, for the seasonal reliance of the rural credit market in India.
[87] *Provincial Banking Enquiry*, 155.   [88] *Annual Report* (1928), 20.
[89] *Madras Journal of Co-operation* (1936), 510.   [90] *Report on Agricultural Indebtedness*, 60.

The reference to misdemeanour is significant. The government supplemented supervision with annual audits of primary banks. Audits were initially voluntary and paid for by the banks themselves.[91] This changed with the rising number of defaults in the late 1920s. From the early 1930s onwards, annual government audits were compulsory for all primary banks. Regular audits exposed the frequency of fraudulent lending practised by the managers of primary banks. The frequency of management fraud became more apparent during the Depression. According to one official report in 1931, 'in the prevailing tightness of the money market defaulting secretaries were no longer able to restore the stolen funds on the approach of an inspection.'[92]

Auditors provided certificates to all banks at the end of every audit. Certificates contained a grade, running from 'A' to 'D'. Government auditors branded Class A banks 'thoroughly good societies' while class D banks were 'bad societies which probably have to be liquidated'. In the financial year 1932–33, the government audited 13,425 banks, of which 1,735 banks were in the 'D' group.[93] Auditors carried out additional scrutiny on banks with the largest defaults to identify areas of mismanagement or, in severe cases, fraud. In the same year, seventy-seven cases of fraud were pending criminal prosecution. Arbitration forums charged eighty-seven individuals in total, of which seventy-seven were in management positions in primary banks.[94] There were consistent numbers of criminal prosecutions for the misappropriation of funds throughout the 1930s. As recorded in 1936, 'There are no signs of diminution in cases of defalcation; the department does its best to purge the movement of dishonest members but obviously can do little unless honest men come forward to run the societies.'[95]

On discovery of misconduct, employees from district banks or the provincial government superseded the management board of the mismanaged primary bank. In 1935, audit reports from the Krishna district exposed mismanagement in a regional cluster of primary banks. Employees from its financing district bank, the Krishna District Co-operative Bank, subsequently took control of the management of these banks.[96] The Krishna District Co-operative Bank placed a cap on new deposits and enforced more extensive application procedures for withdrawals of existing deposits from its member primary banks in 1936. In

---

[91] Section 17 of the 1912 Co-operative Societies Act allowed for *panchayats* to conduct the audit of banks.
[92] *Annual Report* (1931), 17.   [93] *Annual Report* (1933), 8.
[94] *Annual Report* (1933), 14.   [95] *Annual Report* (1936), 17.
[96] *Madras Journal of Co-operation* (1935), 324.

the absence of adequate reserves and increasing withdrawal applications, the district bank showed concern that 'the whole movement will lose credit'.[97] Following the supersession, the provincial government liquidated banks that failed to achieve a grade above 'D'.

Managers practised two types of misconduct, one more serious than the other. The first, and less serious of the two, was insider lending. Evidence shows managers provided loans to members of the same caste. The social composition of management boards in the cooperative sector in the North Arcot district in the early 1920s provides evidence of this form of discriminatory lending. There were 30,000 members of primary banks in the district, 2,700 or 9 per cent of which were Brahmin. According to one report, six out of seven directors of the district bank and twelve out of fourteen supervisors of primary banks were from the Brahmin caste.[98] The managers of primary banks in the district allocated the majority of loans to Brahmin members, while default rates saw a steady increase in the 1920s. By the early 1930s, the government liquidated eleven out of thirty Supervising Unions in the district for 'inefficient supervision and mismanagement of affairs'.[99]

The second type of management malpractice was embezzlement. Bank managers siphoned money for personal benefit. Legal records from the 1930s provide evidence of managers who issued loans either to themselves or to a network of their relatives. In the 1933 dispute *Re: Patri Venkata Hanumantha v. Unknown,* for example, the Secretary of a cooperative in the Guntur district was found to have issued large sums to either himself, his brother or his cousin in regular intervals in the late 1920s and early 1930s. Managers forged contracts, declaring fake names and mortgage securities. Borrowers did not repay loans, and managers declared these loans as unrecovered principal in the bank's account books. The prosecution argued that 'while the depletion in the resources of the bank was taking place on account of the series of misappropriations slyly committed by the 1st accused, the financial equilibrium of the bank became patently unstable and on account of the large overdues there was pressure from several quarters'.[100] Recipients of loans, including the

---

[97] *Madras Journal of Co-operation* (1935), 272.
[98] Directors of Supervising Unions were appointed from directors of primary banks in the district.
[99] *Madras Journal of Co-operation* (1936), 88.
[100] Re: Patri Venkata Hanumantha v. Unknown (1934 66 MLJ 193, Madras, 6 October 1933). Case records report similar methods of misappropriation throughout the period. In the case, Most Revd. Dr. L. Mathias, S.C., the Archbishop of Madras and the President of the Catholic Indian Association and anr. v. Kilacheri Agricultural Co-operative Bank (1938 1 MLJ 241, Madras, 5 October 1937), the secretary of the

Secretary of the bank, were indicted with prison sentences of ten years while those convicted of abetting the crime were charged with seven-year imprisonments.[101]

Managers channelled embezzled capital into two forms of expenditure.[102] First, managers embezzled to fund election campaigns. Elected administrators of cooperative banks were also candidates for elections in local governments. According to one administrator's address at a Co-operative Conference in 1935,

office bearers of co-operative societies have been found in several places to have used co-operative money obtained by means of *benami* (embezzling by lending to kin or third party) or direct loans for the purposes of their elections in Local Bodies or Legislatures. It is a tragedy; the result is that they find difficulty in repaying the same.[103]

Managers provided loans to supporters of some political groups but not others. According to a legislator in 1935, 'faction, favouritism and nepotism' was a frequent feature in the administration of primary banks.[104] Cooperatives became a platform to launch political ambitions from the early twentieth century. According to Robert, members of the Justice Party and the Indian National Congress in the 1920s and 1930s had strong links to the cooperative movement.[105] Lending for political gain persisted throughout the period. An official report in 1956 commented, 'local rivalries and factions tend to assume disproportionate importance and affect adversely the working of societies.'[106]

Bank managers embezzled to lend at high interest rates in the informal credit market. Members of the managing committee were either 'trader, moneylender or shopkeeper' in seven out of nineteen surveyed primary banks in the Coimbatore district in 1957.[107] Similarly, members of the management board were moneylenders in eight out of nineteen surveyed banks in the West Godavari district. The Rural Credit Survey reported that the vested interests of administrators cum moneylenders 'worked against the interests of the society' they were managing.[108] From the

---

Kilacheri Agricultural Co-operative Bank accepted deposits on behalf of the bank. The secretary subsequently embezzled these funds.

[101] Re: Patri Venkata Hanumantha v. Unknown.
[102] Managers who embezzled might have also channelled additional income into savings. However, this is not reported in the evidence.
[103] *Madras Journal of Co-operation* (1936), 366.
[104] *Report on Agricultural Indebtedness*, 60.
[105] Bruce Robert, "Agricultural Credit Cooperatives in Madras, 1893–1937: Rural Development and Agrarian Politics in Pre-independence India." *The Indian Economic and Social History Review* 16, no. 2 (1979): 163–84.
[106] *Report of the Committee* (1956), 34.   [107] *Rural Credit Follow-up Survey*, 446.
[108] *Rural Credit Follow-up Survey*, 446.

Table 6.3 *Survey of primary banks in two districts, 1956–57*

District	Banks	Legible accounts	Erroneous accounts	Failed audit
Coimbatore	19	9	10	8
West Godavari	19	17	2	3

Source: *Rural Credit Follow-up Survey*, 687–96.
Notes: The 'Legible' result in this survey measures the number of banks with account books without any errors. The 'Erroneous' result measures the number of banks that had errors in their account books. 'Failed Audit' measures the number of banks with audit certificates of 'C' grade and below. Savings were either negligible or non-existent in all banks. The survey anonymised the names and management boards of all banks.

recorded banks in Table 6.3, the report on bank W3 in the West Godavari district stated that the 'President was very powerful and used to take *benami* loans – traders and landlords were on the managing committee'.[109] The bank reported a 100 per cent ratio of overdue repayment to outstanding loans. The government disbarred the bank from lending in 1954. Similarly, the Rural Credit Survey also reported the following on a primary bank in the Coimbatore district,

Society C5, organised in 1919, was dominated by landowners. The ex-president misappropriated funds by making unreceipted collections. Since then, the members lost confidence in the society which gradually stopped functioning. Improper management, lack of proper supervision and timely help from the central bank and Co-operation Department resulted in misappropriation and consequent deterioration in the financial position of the society.[110]

Audits failed to restrict embezzlement for two reasons. First, siphoned money was left undetected as managers falsified accounts. Audits of primary banks commonly yielded inaccurate reports.[111] As one official report in 1956 suggested, 'as a result of its inability to employ paid staff, account-keeping leaves much to be desired and naturally demands more of the time of the supervisory and audit staff.'[112] This feature of primary banks persisted throughout the period. Approximately 92 per cent of audited banks in 1934 were reported to have defects in their account books.[113] Similarly, as shown in Table 6.3, ten out of nineteen surveyed

---

[109] *Rural Credit Follow-up Survey*, 731.   [110] *Rural Credit Follow-up Survey*, 363.
[111] C. F. Strickland, "Cooperation and the Rural Problem of India." *The Quarterly Journal of Economics* 43, no. 3 (1929): 500–31.
[112] *Provincial Banking Enquiry*, 151.
[113] *Annual Report* (1934), 16. Auditors reported that 12,550 out of 13,552 banks had defects in their account books.

primary banks in the Coimbatore district in 1957 were reported to have errors in accounting. Managers recorded defaults as extensions rather than overdue repayments in the balance sheet of primary banks. This lack of accounting transparency was a barrier to efficient regulation.

Second, the provincial government did not supplement audits with effective enforcement. Scholarship on cooperatives in Germany demonstrates that the publication of management dishonesty to various stakeholders ensured that managers did not resort to fraud.[114] Some government officials in 1930s Madras also recognised the importance of this form of social enforcement. One report in 1935 suggested, 'the maximum of publicity is required. This was Raiffeisen's (in the German context) great maxim.' The report proceeded to comment, 'Audit reports are not even opened and read for years together, meetings are not held to consider such reports and members are not kept informed of their financial position.'[115] Managers were unafraid of failed audits. According to one report, 'if *panchayats* who know their duties and responsibilities deliberately abuse their position, it cannot be effectively prevented. You may close the society for this reason but the mischief is already done. Therefore, supervision alone may not bring about the reform necessary in societies.'[116] Proposals were considered to increase the frequency of audits. The government attempted to solve the problem by increasing the number of audits to bi-annually. However, this policy change had an insignificant impact when enforcement remained weak. As an official report commented in 1935, 'audit is done only once in six months. In six months much can happen.'[117]

The chapter has so far shown that primary banks reported persistent losses due to low savings and weak regulation. However, the expansion of the cooperative sector in the 1940s and 1950s presents a paradox. A new level of state intervention explains this puzzle.

State Intervention: Prolonging Banking Failure

The provincial government did not lend to cooperatives and restricted its participation to conducting annual audits in the colonial period. District and municipal government departments saved unspent revenue in district banks. However, the value of government deposits was lower than the savings of members and non-members in the district banks.[118] The post-colonial government adopted a more interventionist stance in the

---

[114] Guinnane, "A 'Friend and Advisor'."   [115] *Report on Agricultural Indebtedness*, 63.
[116] *Madras Journal of Co-operation* (1936), 511.
[117] *Report on Agricultural Indebtedness*, 60.   [118] *Report of the Committee* (1928), 18–22.

late 1940s. While state officials did identify a problem in the failure of cooperative banks to be both equitable and profitable, the newly formed government believed that capital injections into the cooperative sector was the solution.

The risk of participation in a fragile banking sector motivated the colonial government's passive stance. Loans from government accounted for a negligible share of the working capital of primary banks in the 1930s. The ratio of government loans to the total working capital of primary banks fluctuated between 0.7 and 1.7 per cent between 1928 and 1939.[119] Government loans were not provided to either district banks or the provincial bank in the same period. The Indian central bank, Reserve Bank of India (RBI), in particular, played a limited role in the cooperative movement during the colonial period. Deposits from commercial banks formed the majority of the reserves held by the RBI. Rather than lend the savings of large commercial banks to risky rural cooperatives, the RBI adopted a non-interventionist approach to the cooperative movement. Justifying this non-interventionist stance in the Bombay Co-operative Quarterly in 1938, the RBI stated,

The sum and substance of the lengthy memorandum is that while the Reserve Bank is willing to offer advice and even to direct and control co-operative finance it is not willing at present, for various reasons, to deal with provincial co-operative banks – in the case of some because they are not creditworthy, in the case of others because they have established their credit and possess resources themselves.[120]

The end of colonial rule marked a turning point in the role of the RBI in the cooperative movement. The government's First (1951) and Second (1956) Five Year Plans focused on increasing intervention in rural credit through greater participation in cooperatives. The government attributed the limited success of cooperatives to displace informal sources of credit before 1947 to liquidity constraints in primary banks. Accordingly, the First Five Year Plan proposed large capital injections into the cooperative machinery to drive out moneylenders from rural credit markets. This increase in state participation did not translate to a direct interaction with primary banks.

The RBI extended large volumes of credit to district banks from the late 1940s. The first disbursement of loans to district banks was in 1947. Between 1947 and 1951, the value of state financing to district banks increased by over five times.[121] The capital injection into district banks

---

[119] *Annual Report* (1928–39).
[120] *History of the Reserve Bank of India* (Bombay, 1970), 207.
[121] *History of the Reserve Bank of India*, 782.

did translate into an increase in the loans provided by primary banks. Indeed, there was a significant rise in membership and working capital in primary banks from the late 1940s.[122]

Government officials perceived the growth in membership and lending as a success. It was a sign that cooperatives were able to capture a greater share of the credit market from village moneylenders. Accordingly, government reports in the early 1950s sustained the position that under-capitalisation was a primary driver of cooperatives' failure in the pre-1947 period.[123] The desire for increased capitalisation led to a further enhancement in state financing to district banks in the late 1950s. The government established various initiatives, involving the allocation of public funds to rural cooperatives to achieve two aims. First, as mentioned, to enhance the capitalisation of rural cooperatives in general.[124] State governments significantly increased their subscription of share capital in district banks during this period. Second, the government allotted public funds to some cooperatives in crisis years, particularly the banks incurring losses because borrowers were impacted by environmental shocks and crop failure.[125]

However, the level of savings in primary banks did not increase at the same rate as the level of state financing. The rate of growth in central bank loans exceeded the growth rate in savings during the late 1940s. Between 1947 and 1952, the ratio of savings to working capital in primary banks declined from 7 per cent to 4 per cent.[126] In other words, the transition in 1947 did not change the legacy of low savings. The ratio between savings and external borrowings widened as primary banks were less self-funded than they were before receiving financial assistance from the RBI. According to data from the 1940s and 1950s, loans from district banks continued to finance the loans provided by primary banks. Data on the primary banks shows that the ratio of external borrowings accrued to loans issued varied between 90 and 130 per cent between 1947 and 1955.[127]

In short, problems in the cooperative sector in the colonial period were carried forward in the post-colonial period. Governments intervened in cooperatives through financial contributions with limited impact on capital structure and regulation. Low savings perpetuated the lack of

---

[122] *Report of the Committee* (1956), 425–28.   [123] *Report of the Committee* (1956), 8–10.

[124] The National Agricultural Credit Fund, managed by the RBI, provided loans to state governments. The governments used the loans to invest in district bank shares.

[125] The National and State Cooperative Development Funds, also managed by the RBI, extended credit to cooperatives that reported high default rates because of harvest failures.

[126] See Figure 5.3.   [127] *Report of the Committee* (1956), 425–30.

bottom-up supervision. Managers of primary banks continued to be held accountable by ineffective top-down regulation. To make matters worse, public revenue was being allocated to a failing banking sector in the post-colonial period. This added moral hazard to the list of problems in cooperative banking in post-colonial South India.

Conclusion

Policymakers in colonial India identified market failure in rural credit as the driver of persistent rural impoverishment. They believed that cooperative banking would solve the problem by both expanding the supply of credit and restricting the monopoly power of the moneylender. Tested success of Raiffeisen banks in Europe inspired the government to create a structure of self-help banking in India in the early twentieth century. This intervention, however, failed to deliver the desired outcome. Cooperative banks rationed credit for many poor borrowers; despite expansion in size, cooperatives captured a small share of the business; and they were unprofitable throughout. The chapter investigates the reasons behind the persistence of these problems by showing where the Indian model departed from the stylised Raiffeisen one in the province where the experiment began.

One part of the explanation consists of showing how low savings reduced the role for self-supervision. The government created a three-tier banking structure, including primary banks, district banks and a provincial cooperative bank. In the primary banks, depositor and shareholder members were few while borrower members were many. Richer peasants crowded the top-end of the cooperative hierarchy as depositors while poorer peasants crowded the bottom-end as borrowers. Deposits in district banks had a stronger government guarantee than deposits in primary banks. This design flaw allowed the rich to refuse to cooperate with the poor. There was limited mutual supervision as managers were not held accountable by members.

External regulation could potentially solve the problem. The government established Supervising Unions and a top-down regulatory structure, including annual audits and a defined process for the liquidation of insolvent banks. However, embezzlement and insider lending persisted as the interests of the supervisors, auditors and managers conflicted. Although the sources used do not deal with the details of the problem, these suggest that the flaws lay in its design. The laws governing regulation were designed not by the banking regulator but by the provincial government. Enforcement was compromised, especially where bank managers carried social and political influence.

Though dysfunctional, the cooperative structure survived. The state allocated public revenue to cooperative banks. Local government departments deposited unspent revenue in district banks during the 1920s and 1930s. The state expanded its financial participation in the cooperative sector in the 1940s. Large capital injections were made into primary banks in the 1940s and 1950s. State intervention altered the capital structure of the cooperative sector. Whereas primary banks were debt dependent on apex banks in the 1930s and 1940s, the 1950s introduced the government as the source of lending in the rural credit market. Financial contributions from the state entrenched the problem of moral hazard into cooperative banking in post-colonial India. The problems of dependence on external funds, regulatory failure, and losses, therefore, persisted.

The chapter offers broader lessons on the challenges of top-down cooperative banking promotion in poor agrarian societies. One lesson is that economic inequality and unequal socio-political influence among rich and poor peasants prevented cooperation in Indian villages. The chapter goes further, analyses institutional and policy regimes, to suggest that thanks to a lack of management accountability, a small section of the rural population benefited from loss-making cooperative banks. Cooperative transplants required a regulatory structure that supported efficient banking. Additional capital injections into a fragile transplant extended rather than solved structural failures. For the governments in colonial and post-colonial India, providing easy access to credit was the central objective. The cooperative organisation was a casualty of this policy.

Further research could expand on the impact of banking regulation by the executive, rather than independent regulators, on the performance of cooperatives. In group lending arrangements, the expectation is that local and insider supervision would ensure efficient management. This case study of Madras suggests that internal supervision was not a sufficient condition, especially when savings rates were low. External regulation was needed. Cooperative banks in India continued to report losses after 1960, suggesting that the lessons drawn from early twentieth-century Madras are indeed robust.

7   Credit after 1960

After 1960, India experienced a Green Revolution, a transformation in production processes across the agrarian economy. Output and productivity levels grew in the agricultural sector following the planting of new seed types, spread in the use of fertilizers, public investment into large irrigation infrastructure and private investment in small irrigation projects. Expectedly some groups of farmers grew richer. Millions of Indians, however, continued to live in extreme poverty. Why, despite technological advancements, were poverty levels persistently high in rural India?

Credit access changed for some groups of borrowers and not others. A two-step process unshackled investment constraints for rich farmers after 1960. In the first step, expansion in credit supply enabled large landholders to invest in new, capital-intensive technologies. In the second step, new technologies reduced default risk, further increasing credit access and investment for the rich. We see little change, however, for low-income groups. Access to credit continued to be selective, and the application of new production inputs stayed unattainable for smallholders. The cycle of high risk and low investment became a problem of the past for the wealthy, yet, remained a reality for the poor throughout the twentieth and into the twenty-first centuries.

Examining credit markets in the South Indian states, this chapter briefly comments on changes and continuities in lending patterns after 1960.

Green Revolution, Government Action and Credit Supply

In 1947, the Indian government declared itself formally independent from colonial rule. Discussions within policy circles sought to establish goals for development of the economy. Socialist movements in late-colonial India penetrated the design of governance in post-colonial decades. The Indian National Congress controlled India's first legislature and established modernisation goals, seeking to achieve these goals through state control and planning. In 1951, the cabinet, led by Nehru as

India's first Prime Minister, passed a resolution to add a planning design and implementation body to the central executive branch of government. The Planning Commission included groups of economists and politicians as policy advisors, and was chaired by the Prime Minister. Agricultural development was a central focus point of the planning commission, which was logical considering three-quarters of the population worked in the sector. The commission crafted a series of Five Year Plans over the following decades, each of which included policy proposals to improve livelihoods and the wellbeing of rural households. Each quinquennial plan provided a description of ongoing progress and outlined goals for investment in key areas of the agricultural sector. The central government set targets for growth in agricultural output and productivity, and officials expected these targets to be met by improving the inputs into agricultural production. Each Five Year Plan set a target for expansion in irrigation infrastructure, increase in the use of fertilizers and the substitution of old seed types for new, high-yield varieties.

Public investment into major irrigation works increased several-fold after 1951. The government focused on heavy engineering, directly investing in building large irrigation projects. The government constructed dams as well as channels and canals across all states. Dam construction, in particular, was seen as a major break from colonial rule. The Indian executive believed that extending water access through large reservoirs and artificial spillways provided a tool to improve water access and control water allocation in drought- and flood-risk areas.

Dams were constructed across South India from the early 1950s onwards. Projects were large in size and cost. Take the Bhavanisagar Dam and the Nagarjuna Sagar Dam, for instance. The government constructed the Bhavanisagar Dam on the Bhavani River between 1948 and 1955, feeding water into canals and seeking to improve water access in districts located in current-day Tamil Nadu, south-central Madras in colonial times. The project is estimated to have cost public coffers approximately 200 million rupees.[1] The Nagarjuna Sagar Dam, one of the world's largest masonry dams, was built on the Krishna River, filling waterways and increasing water access in dry parts of north-eastern Madras (present-day Andhra Pradesh). Construction began in 1955 and took 12 years to complete with the help of over 50,000 construction workers. Some estimates suggest the dam irrigated 2.3 million acres of land, costing the public purse a far heavier sum than the building costs of

---

[1] "Bhavanisagar Project: Governor's Visit," *The Times of India*, 2 September 1956.

many other dams in peninsular India.[2] By 2000, dams were a major source of irrigation in the agricultural sector.[3] The government directly invested relatively smaller amounts of public money into other types of agricultural inputs. The construction of wells and tanks as well as purchase of electrically powered irrigation systems, artificial fertilizers and new seed varieties were only indirectly financed by the state. Farmers purchased new seed varieties and artificial fertilizers on the market. The government hoped to supplement direct investments in large irrigation engineering with greater private investment in new Green Revolution technologies.[4] Because savings rates were generally low across the region, the only way to achieve this goal of rising private investment was through expansion in credit supply.

The government championed two strategies to increase the supply of credit. One was through cooperatives. As discussed in previous chapters, the funnelling of tax-payer money into the cooperative banking structure started to increase in the 1950s. This approach continued in the 1960s and 1970s. Central and state governments as well as the Indian central bank provided large, long-term loans to both primary and central cooperative banks. The other government strategy was to extend access to loans from commercial banks in rural areas. Agriculture was labelled a priority sector and pubic banks were given priority sector lending targets from the mid-1960s. the government aimed to mobilise savings deposits from the farmers with disposable income and channel lending to farmers across income groups.[5] Additional liquidity in rural credit markets did lead to higher private investment levels. There was a noticeable increase in the uptake of new seeds and artificial fertilizers as well as expansion in the construction of tube wells between 1960 and 1990.[6]

Output and productivity numbers in the decades after 1960 indicated success from the growth in investment levels. Crop output in tons and land productivity in tons per acre saw steady increases of between 1 and 3 per cent annually across the different South Indian states. Dry parts of the region, districts in central and eastern Andhra Pradesh, for example, saw lower levels of productivity growth but positive annual growth

[2] "The Dam That Changed Lives of Millions," *The Times of India*, 11 December 2005.
[3] Esther Duflo and Rohini Pande, "Dams." *The Quarterly Journal of Economics* 122, no. 2 (2007): 601–46.
[4] *5 Year Plans*, Government of India (1951–2012), https://niti.gov.in/planningcommission .gov.in/docs/plans/planrel/fiveyr/index5.html.
[5] Tirthankar Roy and Anand Swamy, *Law and the Economy in a Young Democracy* (Chicago: The University of Chicago Press, 2022).
[6] Kapil Subramanian, "Revisiting the Green Revolution: Irrigation and Food Production in Twentieth-century India," PhD thesis, King's College (2015).

nonetheless. Rice and wheat saw the highest output growth levels, with cash crops such as cotton and sugarcane seeing some growth and cereals seeing the lowest growth rates.[7] Rice yields in the North Arcot district, for instance, grew at an average rate of 3 per cent annually between 1960 and 1985.[8] Income growth followed suit. Between 1975 and 2005, income and consumption patterns in surveys of South Indian villages suggest persistent levels of absolute growth.[9] The story, as it stands, seems mostly positive. Levels of growth suggest that expansion in public investment and credit supply led to the agriculture sector breaking subsistence constraints. The beneficiaries of this growth, however, were not widespread. Inequality in the rural economy rose. Tenants and smallholders, particularly in the arid regions, remained vulnerable to drought, supplementing volatile income from land with earnings as temporary labourers.[10] Large groups remained trapped in a cycle of low-yield agriculture and credit exclusion due to direct effects from public investments and indirect effects from credit policies.

The government's focus on major irrigation projects had inequitable effects on economic development. Dam construction eroded village settlements and displaced large groups of farmers. Research on dam construction shows that the majority of people displaced belonged to low-income groups. In other words, congregations of smallholder farms were more likely to see displacement during dam construction than larger estates. As a result of widespread displacement, the construction of dams also widened regional inequality. Construction of the Bhavanisagar Dam, for example, displaced approximately 5,000 households in 44 villages.[11] The ongoing construction of the Polavaram Dam shows that displacement remains a persistent problem from the government's focus on major irrigation projects. The dam is located along the Godavari River. Construction of the dam began in 2005 and is estimated to displace 42,701 households in 277 villages. Approximately 94 per cent

---

[7] 5 Year Plans, Government of India.
[8] Peter Hazell, C. Ramsamy, and P. K. Aiyasamy, *The Green Revolution Reconsidered: The Impact of High-Yielding Rice Varieties in South India* (Baltimore: Johns Hopkins University Press 1991), 14.
[9] Stefan Dercon, Pramila Krishnan, and Sofya Krutikova, "Changing Living Standards in Southern Indian Villages 1975–2006: Revisiting the ICRISAT Village Level Studies." *The Journal of Development Studies* 49, no. 12 (2013): 1676–93.
[10] Rajshri Jayaraman and Peter Lanjouw, "The Evolution of Poverty and Inequality in Indian Villages." *The World Bank Research Observer* 14, no. 1 (1999): 1–30; Barbara Harriss-White, "From Analysing 'Filières Vivrières' to Understanding Capital and Petty Production in Rural South India." *Journal of Agrarian Change* 16, no. 3 (2016): 478–500.
[11] "A Project That Changed Lakhs of Lives," *The Hindu*, 31 May 2016.

of displaced households live below the poverty line.[12] Owing to displacements, data shows that growth and living standards stagnated in catchment areas and in areas partially downstream from major dams. Areas further downstream from the catchment site may have benefitted more from irrigation works. However, recent research shows that seepage from waterways connected to dams has led to waterlogging and salinity, affecting aquifers and increasing flood risk in downstream areas, dampening potential economic benefits from major dam construction.[13] The direct effect of investment in public irrigation works, in other words, seems to have been a worsening of living conditions for large groups of the rural poor.

Government-backed initiatives to increase market competition among suppliers of credit did increase the volume of loans though made insignificant changes to loan allocation. From the 1960s, membership of cooperatives continued to see a steady increase. The RBI established initiatives, across Indian states, to increase membership of credit cooperatives. In the 1970s, the RBI established the Small Farmers Development Agency and the Marginal Farmers Development Agency groups. Each group acted on a mandate to increase membership in cooperatives, and access to credit from cooperatives, among smallholder farmers. Membership did rise. Farmers across income categories became members of local credit cooperatives. Absolute levels of lending also rose in the 1960s and 1970s. Deposits did increase, though not at the same rate as membership. More importantly, the number of borrowers, as a ratio of members, did not change much. By the end of the 1970s, only about one-quarter to one-third of members accessed loans from cooperatives across Tamil Nadu and Andhra Pradesh. Fewer than a third of total borrowers owned less than 2 acres of land.[14] Two acres is about an average, or marginally below average, plot size in rural India.[15] Despite selective lending to a small group of total membership, overdue loans remained a high percentage of total lending across primary cooperatives. In 1974, 5,184 credit cooperatives operated in rural Tamil Nadu.

---

[12] Chiara Mariotti, "Resettlement and Risk of Adverse Incorporation: The Case of the Polavaram Dam." *Development in Practice* 25, no. 5 (2015): 628–42.

[13] Duflo and Pande, "Dams."

[14] *Report of the Committee to Review Arrangements for Institutional Credit for Agriculture and Rural Development* (Bombay, 1981).

[15] Average landholding sizes declined steadily in the post-colonial decades. By 2015 the average size of agricultural holding was approximately 2.5 acres across rural India. "Average Farm Landholding Size Shrinks to 1.1 ha," *The Hindu*, 17 August 2018.

Together, primary cooperatives reported ratio of overdue loans to total borrowings of 34 per cent.[16]

Cooperative banks continued to be mismanaged after 1960. Political elites joined management ranks in cooperatives and the cooperative banking sector continued to be regulated by government, entrenching moral hazard in the system. A study of credit cooperatives in a district located in the southern part of Tamil Nadu reported that members of political parties managed the majority of cooperatives in the mid-1980s. Default rates reported by cooperatives in the study were between 30 and 40 per cent of total lending.[17] Interests of the managers of cooperatives did not match the goals of the cooperative movement.

When cooperatives were well run, low savings-to-loan ratios did not allow primary banks to take risks. Without substantial changes in the inputs to farming, default risk remained high for smallholder and tenant farmers, especially those in dry areas. High default rates, in turn, threatened the deposits of cooperative members and challenged the ability of primary banks to repay their outstanding bills to central banks. The absolute volume of credit supplied increased, though continued to be allocated either discriminately, according to political preference, or to low-risk borrowers. Farmers with large landholdings and political elites accessed credit easily. Smallholders and tenants were excluded from accessing loans. The government, recognising the inability for cooperatives to match the requirement for inclusive lending in the agricultural sector, looked to commercial banks as a vehicle to change credit allocation from the early 1970s.

In December 1967, the Indian government created the National Credit Council, a body of advisors with a mandate to assist the RBI in improving credit supply across agricultural India. The Council reported in 1968 that 'extending credit to agriculture (including commercially-viable projects of rural electrification and minor irrigation) ... would not only be of considerable help to agriculture but would also result in efficient use of commercial bank resources for agriculture'.[18] In the following year, the Indian government nationalised fourteen commercial banks, a culmination of a banking nationalisation process that began with the nationalisation of the Imperial Bank of India (later named State Bank of India) in 1955. The RBI, starting in 1971, set banks' mandatory

---

[16] *Report of the Committee on Integration of Co-operative Credit Institutions* (Bombay, 1976), 206.

[17] Steve Wiggins and Ben Rogaly, "Providing Rural Credit in Southern India: A Comparison of Commercial Banks and Cooperatives." *Public Administration and Development* 9, no. 2 (1989): 215–32.

[18] *Report of the Study Group on Area / Project Approach in Implementing Schemes for Extending Commercial Bank Credit to Agriculture* (Bombay, 1969), 1.

targets of lending to 'priority sectors'. Agriculture was, and continues to be, one of the priority sectors. By 1987, commercial banks operationalised over 3,000 branches in rural districts across Andhra Pradesh and Tamil Nadu.[19] Banks undoubtedly injected liquidity into rural credit markets. However, as we have seen, volume of lending does not tell us much about allocation. Who borrowed from banks?

Priority sector lending targets for commercial banks failed to make headway into more inclusive credit allocation. One reason is that banks could not manage default risk easily. Default rates were high for commercial banks lending in high-risk areas. Banks in Andhra Pradesh and Tamil Nadu, for example, recovered approximately 50–60 per cent of their loan advances to farmers in the early 1980s.[20] Lending to smallholder and tenant farmers puts the bank's recovery rates in precarious positions as long as farming remained exposed to climatic risk. Banks responded by trying to manage risk through selective lending, refusing to lend to groups of borrowers with a high risk of debt defaults. Indeed, the poor found it increasingly difficult to borrow from banks in the 1980s and 1990s. According to one study of a South Indian village, banking credit to landless labourers, tenants and smallholders of less than 2 acres accounted for less than 10 per cent of total debts accrued by these groups in the 1990s.[21] Interest rate regulation made lending to farmers more difficult. State governments in Andhra Pradesh and Tamil Nadu regulated interest rates charged by banks in accordance with the debt relief laws.[22] Not only did banks need to find innovative ways of managing high default rates, regulations prevented them from using credit pricing as a viable management tool.

The Reserve Bank of India attempted to resolve unequal credit allocation through further categorisations in lending targets. From the mid-1970s, the government implemented lending targets for banks that included the supply of credit to smallholder farmers. The goal, according to reports compiled by the RBI, was to allow smallholders to purchase and maintain agricultural land.[23] Indeed, land reforms in the 1950s accentuated the need for lending to low-income groups. Reforms gave tenants and smallholders ownership over cultivable land without sufficient access to

---

[19] *Report of the Committee to Examine Certain Operational Aspects of Rural Lending* (Bombay, 1988), Annexure I.

[20] *High Level Standing Committee to Review the Flow of Institutional Credit for Rural Sector and Other Related Matters* (Bombay, 1986), Annexure I.

[21] V. K. Ramachandran and Madhura Swaminathan, "Rural Banking and Landless Labour Households: Institutional Reform and Rural Credit Markets in India." *Journal of Agrarian Change* 2, no. 4 (2002): 502–44.

[22] *Report of the Study Group.*   [23] *Report of the Study Group*, 5–16.

working capital. Newly minted landowners needed capital to maintain land and purchase farming inputs. Land reforms in the 1950s enforced stringent regulation on the transfer of land between farmers that unintentionally discouraged banks from lending in the agricultural sector. State governments sought to regulate land transfers to prevent wealthy farmers from consolidating small plots of land and to protect the interests of tenants. Titles to land, as a result, were not easily tradable and contesting titles in courts was expensive. Banks incurred costs in time and money to collateralise land and obtain land from defaulters.[24] Collateral requirements, therefore, were not always an easy method to manage risk. Banks, since the 1970s, have not matched the demand for small- and medium-sized loans from the poor. The government's strategy of credit supply expansion through commercial banks cemented inequities in access, segmenting the market and leading to disparate economic outcomes for the rich and poor. Studies of rural banking in the 1990s and 2000s have shown that banks, much like cooperatives, exacerbated inequities further by socially discriminating borrowing groups. Banks, according to studies of South Indian villages, not only failed to supply low-income groups with credit but also discriminated borrowers by caste and gender.[25]

While farmers struggled to access credit from cooperatives and banks, microfinance institutions (MFIs) seemed to solve the allocation problem from the 1980s. Credit from MFIs increased both market competition and the supply of loans, potentially breaking investment constraints for the rural poor. MFIs did not ask for land titles or other types of physical collateral, typically providing small loans and relying on social capital to recover unpaid dues. The supply of loans from MFIs to the agricultural sector saw particular expansion in the early- to mid-1990s. There was initial euphoria among credit commentators on the benefits of the lending model adopted by microfinance groups. One key benefit was that MFIs were lending to the poor, to groups of borrowers otherwise excluded from accessing banking credit.[26] Looking at lending patterns of MFIs, they seemed better equipped to manage default risk, certainly more equipped than other regulated suppliers. MFIs provided loans

---

[24] *A Review of the Agricultural Credit System in India* (Bombay, 1989), 585.

[25] Isabella Guérin, Bert D'Espallier, and Govindan Venkatasubramanian, "Debt in Rural South India: Fragmentation, Social Regulation and Discrimination." *The Journal of Development Studies* 49, no. 9 (2013): 1155–71.

[26] Marguerite S. Robinson, *Microfinance Revolution: Sustainable Finance for the Poor*. 1st ed. (Washington, DC: World Bank Publications, 2001); Priya Basu, *Improving Access to Finance for India's Rural Poor* (Washington, DC: World Bank Publications, 2006); Shahidur R. Khandker, "Microfinance and Poverty." *The World Bank Economic Review* 19, no. 2 (2005): 263–86.

across ecological zones and income groups in South India. More surprisingly, loan recovery rates were higher than the formal sector despite high-risk lending. Euphoria translated to capital expansion. Development organisations, commercial banks and equity investors provided substantial capital injections in MFIs from the late 1990s.[27] MFIs, in other words, functioned as a financial intermediary, between the 'formal' credit sector and the poor farmer.

However, the prices and conditions attached to MFI loans were similar, if not worse, than those attached to loans provided by moneylenders in the colonial period. Loans were short-term and seasonal, and interest rates were higher on loans from MFIs than on loans from cooperatives or the formal banking sector. Though MFIs declared charging rates of between 24 and 28 per cent, studies suggest that rates fluctuated between 28 and 60 per cent (annualised) in the early 2000s.[28] Recent research also shows that MFIs imposed harsh enforcement conditions on loans. MFIs imposed inflexible contracts on poor borrowers. MFIs enforced weekly repayment schedules, without room for moratoriums or flexibility in recovery.[29] Lending organisations avoided courts, recovering loans through other forms of social punishment instead. Borrowers that failed to repay were excluded from accessing credit in the future, a substantial threat to the livelihoods of poor farmers that rely on working capital loans to run small farming businesses. MFIs supplemented economic punishment with social forms of harassment and by employing loan officers and residents in the defaulter's village to coerce the borrower into repaying loans.[30] Typically, loan officers in MFIs insisted on several co-applicants and guarantors on loans, coercing borrowers through friends and family – a low-cost, informal and inflexible method to recover

[27] James Copestake, "Microfinance and Development Finance in India: Research Implications," CEB Working Paper no. 10/028 (2010), Université Libre de Bruxelles; Marcus Taylor, "'Freedom from Poverty Is Not for Free': Rural Development and the Microfinance Crisis in Andhra Pradesh, India." *Journal of Agrarian Change* 11, no. 4 (2011): 484–504.

[28] Philip Mader, "Rise and Fall of Microfinance in India: The Andhra Pradesh Crisis in Perspective." *Strategic Change* 22, nos. 1–2 (2013): 47–66.

[29] Erica Field and Rohini Pande, "Repayment Frequency and Default in Microfinance: Evidence from India." *Journal of the European Economic Association* 6, nos. 2–3 (2008): 501–9; Giorgia Barboni and Parul Agarwal, "Knowing What's Good for You: Can a Repayment Flexibility Option in Microfinance Contracts Improve Repayment Rates and Business Outcomes?," IGC Working Paper, Ref.: F-89219-INC-1.

[30] "Impoverished Indian Families Caught in Deadly Spiral of Microfinance Debt," *The Guardian*, 31 January 2011; Isabelle Guérin and Santosh Kumar, "Market, Freedom and the Illusions of Microcredit: Patronage, Caste, Class and Patriarchy in Rural South India." *The Journal of Development Studies* 53, no. 5 (2017): 741–54.

unpaid dues. MFIs managed to lend to high-risk borrowers and maintain profitable loan recovery rates because prices were high and enforcement methods unforgiving.[31]

Problems with the microfinance setup became especially apparent during the Andhra Pradesh microfinance crisis in 2010. Groups of MFIs established large lending operations across dry areas of Andhra Pradesh, including in districts studied earlier in this book, from the mid-1990s. A string of droughts and bad harvests led to waves of defaults between 2008 and 2010. Borrowers, facing substantial reductions in earnings from land, were unable to meet the inflexible repayment requirements set by MFIs. Loans were not carried over and harsh enforcement conditions were imposed to recover defaulted loans. The outcome of the crisis was catastrophic for rural livelihoods. Large numbers of debtors, unable to meet the inflexible terms imposed by MFIs, took their own lives between 2010 and 2012.[32]

SKS Microfinance was one organisation at the centre of the crisis. The organisation, established in 1997, saw enormous growth in lending operations in the early 2000s, eventually encouraging the business to list equity shares on the Bombay Stock Exchange in 2010. The business model of the firm was small, non-collateralised loans to the poor. The firm reported charging interest rates of between 25 and 35 per cent (annualised).[33] SKS set up branches across water-scarce districts in Andhra Pradesh, the Kurnool district being a good example. Drought years severely affected the repayment capacity of SKS borrowers. Large waves of defaults and the harsh conditions imposed to recover loans brought media attention to the lives and livelihoods of affected farmers in SKS-operated regions in 2010.

The central government and state government in Andhra Pradesh intervened to protect borrowers during and after the crisis. The state government initiated formal enquiries into the methods of debt recovery in large MFIs. The central government responded with legislation to regulate microfinance organisations in rural India. Regulations imposed interest rate ceilings and instructed MFIs to charge lower annualised interest rates through limits on the size of repayments relative to the original principal, returning to a version of *damdupat*.[34] A familiar response to a persistent problem.

---

[31] *Report of the Sub-Committee of the Central Board of Directors of Reserve Bank of India to Study Issues and Concerns in the MFI Sector* (Bombay, 2011).
[32] "Small Loans Add up to Lethal Debts," *The Hindu*, 25 February 2012.
[33] Mader, "Rise and Fall of Microfinance in India."
[34] Mader, "Rise and Fall of Microfinance in India"; P. Satish, "Excluding the Poor from Credit: Lessons from Andhra Pradesh and Telangana." *Economic and Political Weekly*, 28 July 2018.

What role did moneylenders play in the credit market after 1960? Farmers with disposable income and private traders continued to lend in the agricultural sector. However, transaction costs for private moneylending was high. Government regulations persisted during and after the Green Revolution. State governments imposed interest rate ceilings, compulsory registration of lending businesses and mandatory compliance through government audits of moneylender account books.[35] Regulations aimed to discipline moneylenders. Laws branded typical loan prices and conditions from the colonial period illegal. Rules, as a result, pushed moneylenders underground, discouraged legitimate credit businesses and incentivised lenders to corner a segment of the market where prices and conditions were high and harsh.[36] Without sufficient access to credit from cooperatives and banks, low-income borrowers continued to rely on moneylenders for credit.[37] Repayment schedules and prices, however, were more stringent following regulations. Lenders provided small loans with daily repayment schedules and high prices. A recent study of credit in the South Indian state of Telangana from early 2001–2016 shows that moneylenders provided small loans at rates of about 40 per cent and enforced repayments through coercive measures.[38]

The expansion in credit supply from MFIs did little to solve the problem. Farmers who defaulted on loans to MFIs borrowed from moneylenders to meet consumption needs and compounding credit bills. Indeed, the 2010 crisis dried up credit from MFIs, forcing poor farmers to borrow from moneylenders at high prices to meet consumption and production costs.[39] The government later investigated moneylenders for illicit methods used to recover loans. In 2015, coinciding with legislation to regulate MFIs, the state government in Andhra Pradesh introduced compulsory auditing of moneylender account books and harsher punishments for lenders that charge higher rates of interest than legally permitted.[40]

In short, two sets of stories emerge from the Green Revolution and serial government intervention in South Indian credit markets. One story

---

[35] *Report of the Technical Group Set up to Review Legislations on Money Lending* (Bombay, 2007).
[36] Roy and Swamy, *Law and the Economy in a Young Democracy.*
[37] Narayan Chandra Pradhan, "Persistence of Informal Credit in Rural India: Evidence from 'All-India Debt and Investment Survey' and Beyond," RBI Working Paper Series, WPS (DEPR), 5/2013.
[38] Vaishnavi Surendra, "Are Moneylenders Financial Intermediaries," *Ideas for India*, 24 March 2021.
[39] "Loan Sharks Are Circling for Poor Indian Debtors Failed by Microfinance," *The Guardian*, 29 October 2018.
[40] "AP Enacts Law; No Money Lending without License Now," *The Economic Times*, 21 December 2015.

Figure 7.1 Cycle of risk, credit access and investment

is of transition, that richer farmers broke investment constraints. Access to affordable credit from cooperatives and banks allowed farmers to invest in new seed types, artificial fertilizers and groundwater extraction. The other story is one of persistence, that poorer farmers remained excluded from accessing credit, could not invest in productivity-enhancing inputs and continued to be vulnerable to rainfall volatility.

The cycle depicted in Figure 7.1 explains persistent credit and investment constraints for smallholder and tenant farmers. Borrowers with unpredictable default risk were excluded from accessing affordable credit, forced to borrow small and expensive loans from moneylenders and MFIs instead. Low investment rates perpetuated, leaving borrowers equally susceptible to risk and credit constraints in the following year. The process from colonial times repeated itself. Scale, in other words, continued to be the only form of risk management in the credit market. Safer borrowers – primarily large landholders – had preferential access to expanded credit in the decades after 1960.

The government's focus on disciplining some types of creditors and incentivising expansion in others continued to restrict credit access for the poor. The narrative of exploitative moneylenders and poor borrowers with limited bargaining power informs credit policies today. Regulating certain groups of lenders and increasing market competition has been the typical policy response. History tells us that regulating power balance is a superficial response to the problem and is unlikely to have the desired effect. The repayment capacity of borrowers in an economic sector vulnerable to output uncertainty needs to be addressed for supply-shifts in credit to have positive impact on investment and growth.

Climate change and the land-destructive effects of farming techniques during the Green Revolution tell us that a new model for investment and land improvement needs to be adopted by South Indian farmers, this time with a focus on designing sustainable livelihoods for low-income groups. The Green Revolution has deteriorated India's natural landscape. Overcultivation and excessive use of artificial fertilizers have eroded soil quality while groundwater extraction has depleted aquifers. Water-intensive crops, such as rice farming in fertile areas, and widespread construction of wells in arid areas over the last four decades have depleted groundwater reserves. Crop output is becoming increasingly vulnerable to changes in climate patterns.[41] The livelihoods of poor farmers are more affected than the rich. The growing unpredictability of rainfall patterns has a significant effect on farmers that own small holdings or low-quality land. India is in need of a new agrarian transformation, one that relies on more sustainable land use. We are yet to see widespread shifts in cropping and investment preferences to suit the growing need for transition in agricultural production. Poor peasants need regular access to affordable capital to make targeted investment decisions that account for region-specific conditions, however, investment potential for large groups of farmers in the twentieth and twenty-first centuries continues to be shackled.

Credit needs policy attention, though disciplining lenders is not a sustainable solution to the problem of selective allocation and high prices. Creditors need to have enforcement and pricing flexibility to manage default risk and lend to poor farmers. Moneylenders in the unregulated market possessed this flexibility, as the study of credit markets in the pre-1960 period shows. To secure investment-led, inclusive growth in agricultural India, the government needs to either focus on improving the repayment capacity of borrowers or design a system that transfers credit non-selectively and without concern for risk or profitability.

---

[41] Marcus Taylor, "Liquid Debts: Credit, Groundwater and the Social Ecology of Agrarian Distress in Andhra Pradesh, India." *Third World Quarterly* 34, no. 4 (2013): 691–709.

8   Conclusion

This book studies rural credit markets in South India during the early to mid-twentieth century. The period was one of weak economic development. Landholding was small and unequal, while production processes did not change much during the period. Most rural households relied on old seed varieties and natural fertilizers, with a comparatively small number of cultivators owning carts and ploughs. Growth in output required increases in inputs because of the lack of improvements in production processes. Yields were sensitive to seasonal rainfall patterns. Volatile climates, predictably, led to volatile output and income. In this context, there were several opportunities for private investment. Investments in land improvement could have seen high returns. But money was supply-constrained and expensive in rural areas.

Commercial banks did not lend in rural India until the 1960s. Private moneylenders controlled the supply of credit in the colonial and early post-colonial period. Urban traders and indigenous bankers were major players in some parts of Bombay and Punjab. *Marwari* traders, for example, were bankers by profession. They ran large and diverse lending portfolios, which included lending to cotton farmers in parts of nineteenth-century Bombay. Urban bankers did not lend to farmers in Madras. In the absence of professional moneylenders in the agricultural sector, money was circulated among cultivators. Farmers with disposable income provided credit to other farmers. This feature placed constraints on the money market though provided creditors flexibility in enforcing repayments.

Rural credit markets were fragmented within the province. Creditors were lending to borrowers in the same village. Moneylenders with disposable income in wet villages did not typically lend to borrowers in dry villages. As a result, credit supply in most villages was directly linked to the profitability of cultivation. When cultivation was profitable, savings increased and more cultivators could disburse loans in villages. When cultivation was unprofitable, savings decreased, as did the number of cultivators with the ability to provide credit. Short-term fluctuations in agricultural output and income made this structure particularly fragile.

The volume of credit supplied depended on the value and volume of crop output. The majority of land in rural Madras was unirrigated. The government constructed large irrigation projects along already naturally irrigated river deltas. Infrastructure to support groundwater extraction was limited in the hinterland. The entire province was vulnerable to fluctuations in rainfall. Low rainfall caused droughts and famines in the hinterland. The wet districts were better off but not entirely shielded from climate fluctuations as high rainfall caused waterlogging near the deltas. Crop output was impacted in the hinterland and the deltas, affecting the profitability of cultivation in the province. Environmental factors and crop failure continually impacted household revenue and determined accessibility to credit.

Climatic risks affected credit allocation in Madras. This study of credit points to complications when the suppliers and consumers of credit belonged to the same industry. When cultivation revenue fell, credit supply decreased and default rates increased. In bad years, creditors faced a dual problem as the revenue from their primary business fell and borrowers defaulted on loans, which also diminished their secondary income stream. Indeed, as crop failure was common, default rates were high. This had two implications for rural credit markets. First, markets were regularly illiquid. Creditors commonly provided small and seasonal working capital loans. Credit supply was not large enough to expand private investment in land improvement. Second, poor peasants were most impacted by these credit constraints. Lenders managed risk by lending to richer clients in dry districts and to a wider spectrum of borrowers in lower-risk regions. Poor peasants, especially in the dry districts, either could not access credit or borrowed money with harsh terms attached. When peasants could borrow, poor households were regularly over-leveraged as revenue from farming was low and uncertain.

Despite these constraints, evidence shows that creditors continued lending to over-leveraged households. From surveys of credit in rural Madras, one major purpose of borrowing was the repayment of prior loans. For the creditors, belonging to the same industry and locality as the borrowers offered information and enforcement advantages. Creditors knew the profile of the borrowers they were lending to. The cost of monitoring the borrowers was low. As such, borrowers could not, and did not, wilfully default on loans. When borrowers did default, moneylenders had flexible options to enforce repayment. Informally, creditors could impose inflexible methods of recovering loans, including coercing the borrower to part with jewellery and furniture, or acquiring the entirety of the borrower's harvest to satisfy the principal and interest on loans. Formally, lenders could attach contracts and enforce these in courts to recover defaulted loans. Moneylenders could choose between informal, formal or both types of enforcement structure depending on which offered the most cost-effective approach.

The accent on enforcement is a particular contribution of the book. When borrowers defaulted on loans and informal arbitration did not provide creditors with full repayment, courts were the final destination for lenders to enforce contracts. However, courts were inefficient as disputes lasted between three and ten times longer than seasonal loan agreements. The costs of approaching courts, in turn, significantly exceeded the average size of loans. In the unregulated market, nineteenth-century contract laws provided creditors with the flexibility to transmit enforcement costs to the price of credit. Creditors who initiated legal proceedings against defaulters charged borrowers for the additional enforcement expenses.

Creditors only approached courts when the size of the repayment included the costs of enforcement. When borrowers defaulted, lenders attached contracts that either inflated loan principals or increased interest rates to account for these costs. Creditors adopted a three-tiered loan structure, and charged flexible interest rates, to compensate for expensive contract enforcement. In the first stage, loans were unsecured. In the second stage, promissory notes were attached to loans and the price of these loans increased. In the third stage, mortgages were attached to loans and the price of these loans increased further.

Credit pricing has a large scholarship in development economics but less so in economic history. Scholars tend to revert to traditional market structure theories to analyse credit prices in colonial India. The expectation is that monopolistic structures explain high rates, suggesting that more competitive markets would bring prices down. The book challenges this approach and suggests that the rationale of lenders was more influenced by the design and functionality of legal institutional structures. Markets were not always monopolistic. Indeed, in good years, lenders were numerous within villages. Expensive enforcement explains the pricing strategies of lenders and the range of credit prices charged in the rural credit market. Loan structures were complex and multi-tiered. Prices fluctuated between the tiers to compensate for the costs of lending.

The provincial government in Madras acted on a belief that credit prices were high because moneylenders were not regulated strongly enough. The government commissioned reports and surveys from the late 1920s that attempted to estimate the size of the rural credit market. The larger the credit market, in the government's view, meant that the 'disease' of indebtedness was more widespread. The Legislative Assembly in Madras enforced laws from the mid-1930s that attempted to reduce the level of expensive borrowing. A series of policies ultimately culminated in the 1938 Madras Agriculturists Relief Act, a law which the government enforced until the mid-1970s. The MARA declared an interest rate ceiling of 6.25 per cent per annum on all rural loans. The judiciary administered the law. When creditors initiated legal proceedings against defaulters, judges voided contracts and imposed the new interest rate ceiling. Post-intervention, borrowers repaid loans at half or a quarter of the interest rates they incurred before 1938.

Credit intervention failed to achieve its desired goals and had other unintended negative effects. The credit market contracted and did not operate more equitably after the MARA. Lending in accordance with the regulations was unprofitable and, in the short term, the supply of mortgage and unsecured credit declined. The already illiquid money market was more constrained after intervention. Government reports and contemporary studies in the 1940s suggest that the creditors that continued to lend did so in a black market, outside the regulatory scope of the judiciary. Following intervention, creditors could not transmit the high costs of enforcement to the price of credit. Lenders avoided courts and relied on informal enforcement arrangements instead.

This finding has lessons for the role of property rights, courts and rural finance. The government strengthened property rights partially with the introduction of occupancy rights in the early twentieth century and more thoroughly with the abolition of the *zamindari* landlord system in 1948. The subsequent strengthening of property titles had limited impact when courts remained inefficient. Property rights alone is not enough protection or incentive to encourage expansion in lending. Private creditors required judicial protection from courts to incentivise lending. In the absence of this, creditors relied on informal arbitration methods, including acquiring the borrower's crop. Fortunately for the creditors in Madras, this institutional shift coincided with rising commodity prices. Crop-sharing arrangements became especially lucrative in the 1940s.

This finding has implications for studies of credit in other Indian provinces.[1] In a recent study of rural credit in colonial Punjab, Chaudhary and Swamy find that professional moneylenders captured a smaller share of the credit market following the implementation of laws that restricted land transfers in 1900.[2] The authors suggest that farmers

---

[1] The Epilogue provides an outline of credit supply, and the impact of regulation on credit supply, across Bengal, Bombay and Punjab during colonial rule.

[2] Latika Chaudhary and Anand V. Swamy, "A Policy of Credit Disruption: The Punjab Land Alienation Act of 1900." *Economic History Review* 73, no. 1 (2020): 134–58.

became the dominant creditors following intervention. Enforcement costs, and the convenience of informal arbitration, explains this shift. Agriculturist moneylenders had more enforcement flexibility than professional lenders. The book offers a cost-analysis framework to explain this institutional fluidity.

The winners were few, but the losers were many from credit regulations. Creditors lending in the black market won because they remained untouched by regulation. They could price loans higher than before and captured a larger share of the credit market. The impact of intervention on the government is hard to determine. The government might have won in the short term because it delivered on its promise to enact policies with the sole aim of protecting borrowers. The *1946 Report of the Economist for Enquiry into Rural Indebtedness* praised the MARA for reducing the volume of indebtedness in the province. The government did believe that the policy was a success at the time. Not long after this intervention, key policymakers in the Congress-led provincial government earned influential positions in the federal government of independent India. C. Rajagopalachariar and P. J. Thomas, for example, held influential positions in the Congress Party and federal government in the late 1940s and early 1950s.

Most importantly, and contrary to the government's expectations, the borrowers lost. The amount of credit available in the market declined. The remaining credit was not accessible at lower interest rates than before. Working capital loans were more difficult to obtain, especially at a time when prices were increasing and the agrarian economy offered more profitable opportunities. Moneylenders lending in accordance with the law also lost. Moneylending provided cultivators with an additional source of income, especially when they were protected by contract laws and could transmit the high costs of lending to the borrowers. The interest rate ceiling barred this practice, constraining lending as an additional income stream for cultivators with disposable income. This outcome highlights a broader contradiction in the government's approach to market failure. The definition between formal and informal credit was not entirely clear in the unregulated market. Creditors were unregulated but contracts and administrative procedures played a role in the market, blurring the boundary between formal and informal. Whereas the success of intervention hinged on the market operating within the scope of formal procedure, it ultimately had the opposite effect. The market operated more informally as lenders opted to avoid administrative procedures altogether. The emergence of the black market demonstrates that regulations themselves were a significant part of the market failure problem.

Perhaps it was the design of the MARA that explains its failure. If artificial price ceilings did not work, did increasing market competition with cooperatives solve problems in rural credit markets? The government launched credit cooperatives in rural Madras from 1904. The establishment of these cooperatives had more potential for success than the price ceilings. If designed well, cooperatives could solve the liquidity problem by expanding the credit supply and successfully lending to poor peasants at lower interest rates than in the informal market. Members absorbed the risk of lending in cooperatives that were self-funded and well-managed. This allowed cooperatives to lend to poor peasants and remain insured against bad years. Under the right conditions, cooperatives did not need to access courts. If deposits were high, then members enforced other members to repay loans, and imposed punishments on the defaulters. Social capital substituted courts as a method of enforcement.

The intervention to establish cooperatives did not achieve the desired outcome. The book demonstrates that the government designed a cooperative model that was poorly regulated and failed to nurture cooperation between the rich and poor in villages. The government's main objective was to increase the supply of low-cost credit. It designed two features of the cooperative model to allow for this increase in supply. First, the government established a multi-layered cooperative banking structure to compensate for low savings in villages. Second, the postcolonial Indian government injected public money to the cooperative structure to increase the volume of lending. The book shows that credit supply increased but cooperatives failed to capture a sizable share of the market. A small sub-section benefitted from loss-making cooperative banks throughout the early- to mid-twentieth century.

Incurring losses is in itself not a measure of failure. Cooperatives were potentially a profit satisficing rather than profit-maximising banking initiative. Indeed, cooperatives could have claimed success if they were incurring losses but lending to the poor and increasing private investment in the countryside. Given the volatile nature of the agrarian economy in South India, it is feasible that cooperatives were loss-making because they were lending to the poor. However, the cooperatives in South India were neither profit satisficing nor profit maximising. The poor did not have access to credit, and repayment rates remained low despite selective lending to the rich.

Weak regulation and the resulting mismanagement of cooperatives explain this outcome. The government designed a regulatory system that resulted in conflicts of interest between auditors, supervisors and managers of cooperative banks. External bodies did not regulate the cooperative sector. Managers supervised themselves while government audited the banks. Laws did not specify a regulatory structure for cooperatives until the mid-1960s, and even then, the law delegated regulation to the executive. In these circumstances, it was common for the economically and politically influential to manage and embezzle from local cooperatives.

The focus on credit expansion, at the expense of strong institutional development, reflects an ideological failure in the design of credit intervention. Governments in late-colonial and post-colonial India prioritised equity over efficiency in their policy approach. Artificially constructing credit markets with expanded supply that were fair to the poor, in the government's view, would reduce inequality and improve living standards. Illiquid and expensive credit markets were symptoms, rather than causes of the problem. The government acted on an assumption that peasants remained poor because of failures in market allocation. However, intervention further restricted investment potential of the rural poor.

The government failed to acknowledge the real problem. The credit market was allocatively efficient before intervention. However, the market was not productively efficient. Production costs, or the costs of lending, and transaction costs were high. This had a detrimental effect on prices, which in turn affected the poor consumers more than the rich. In this context, altering the price of credit was a largely superficial response. The market became less transparent, more allocatively inefficient and similarly productively inefficient. In other words, the government's misdiagnosis encouraged policy strategies that made the problem worse. Markets operated less efficiently and as inequitably after intervention.

Policy lessons from the book demonstrate that cosmetic changes to credit markets have negligible effects when underlying public institutions are either missing or callously designed. As long as credit constraints shackled private investment levels, expansion in ecologically sensitive irrigation infrastructure needed prudent public investment. The colonial government collected a tax in the form of an 'Irrigation Cess' from the mid-nineteenth century. This failed to translate to the size and type of investments needed to make crop production less unpredictable and more profitable. Though the size of investments increased after 1960, large groups of poor farmers remained vulnerable to ecological risk in post-colonial decades. The Green Revolution saw rising public investment in large-scale irrigation engineering, new seed varieties and artificial fertilizers, though these strategies eroded soils, displaced communities and only benefitted richer landowners. Legal institutions, concurrently, functioned unproductively throughout the late twentieth century. The design of contract laws was not entirely the problem.

Courts themselves remained expensive and unproductive into modern times.[3] The government continued to intervene in the informal credit market, however, restrictions on interest rates, loan waivers and similarly cosmetic interventions were unlikely to have any positive effects while risk and enforcement problems persisted.

The study of cooperatives in Madras has further implications on the development of financial markets in poor agrarian economies. One lesson is that poverty was a constraint on the development of rural finance. The poor rely on informal sources of finance because the risk of lending is too high for banks to enter the market. From the 1970s, state and private sector initiatives offered new avenues of lending in rural India. Cooperatives continued to expand their market presence while government-owned banks and microfinance organisations began lending in the countryside. Microfinance organisations, in particular, offered a potential solution to credit expansion in risky markets. Self-help and group banking arrangements, analogous to the credit cooperatives model, had the potential to overcome risk barriers and expand lending to the poor. However, a Reserve Bank of India report in 2013 finds that poor households continued to rely on fringe lenders for credit in the latter half of the twentieth century. According to the report, 43 per cent of rural households borrowed from 'non-institutional' agencies, including private moneylenders, traders, landlords and friends.[4] The problem was worse in dry, rainfed districts. For example, 73 per cent of rural households in Andhra Pradesh, a mostly dry region located in the north-eastern part of the Madras province in colonial times, relied on non-institutional agencies for credit in 2002.[5] The report shows that banking initiatives did not expand credit access for the 'small and marginal farmers' in rural India.[6] Similar to the performance of credit cooperatives in early twentieth-century Madras, the supply of credit increased but

---

[3] Further research could consider the sources of unproductivity in the functioning of civil courts. One problem could be the number and quality of judges. Another could be the design of laws themselves. The duration of civil disputes increased exponentially in the post-colonial period. The number of credit disputes in courts declined in the same period. This presents a puzzle in which the volume of cases was not necessarily causing delays in judgements. This outcome could be explained by arising complications due to the creation of a new constitution or the challenges in hiring enough judges with the establishment of new legal systems after independence.

[4] Narayan Chandra Pradhan, "Persistence of Informal Credit in Rural India: Evidence from 'All-India Debt and Investment Survey' and Beyond," RBI Working Paper Series, WPS (DEPR), 5/2013, 6.

[5] Pradhan, "Persistence of Informal Credit in Rural India," 10.

[6] Pradhan, "Persistence of Informal Credit in Rural India," 11.

organisations continued to exclude the poor from accessing this expansion in the late twentieth century.

The RBI study goes further to suggest that policy and institutional persistence restricted the impact of rural banking initiatives. Moneylenders continued to benefit from enforcement flexibilities. Formal creditors relied on legal procedures which accentuated the risk of lending to poor households. Group lending initiatives avoided formal enforcement, but they required the cooperation of rich and poor households. It was unfeasible for poor households to raise enough capital to circulate among themselves. The rich needed to participate in order to generate enough money to expand credit and investment. In this context, policies, such as external banking regulations, were required to ensure that the participation of the rich did not translate to exclusion of the poor. Indeed, recent studies find that caste and class played a significant role in early twenty-first-century rural banking.[7] Scholars show that the wealthy managed cooperatives and microfinance organisations. The managers selected borrowers by caste and income class in rural India. These findings suggest that the hypotheses in this book are robust and applicable in different temporal settings. Environmental, institutional and policy drivers of problems in rural credit markets are not just significant in historical contexts but also in the rural economies of modern India.

Through an analysis of a diverse range of historical sources, this book provides reliable lessons for readers of economic history and comparative development. Findings in this study tackle problems of risk in poor agrarian economies, and the methods adopted to mitigate these risks in the past. In doing so, the individual chapters integrate theories relevant to climate, institutional and policy discourses to understand why in a period where some parts of the global economy might have flourished, the rural economy in South India did not see the required expansion in capital markets. Apart from contributing to the historiography of a region in an under-researched time, these theories can be tested against preceding and succeeding periods, as well as positioned in comparative global context, substantiating the importance of the book's findings.

---

[7] Isabelle Guérin, Bert D'Espallier, and Govindan Venkatasubramanian, "Debt in Rural South India: Fragmentation, Social Regulation and Discrimination." *The Journal of Development Studies* 49, no. 9 (2013): 1155–71; Sunil Mitra Kumar, "Does Access to Formal Agricultural Credit Depend on Caste?." *World Development* 43, no. C (2013): 315–28; Isabelle Guérin and Santosh Kumar, "Market, Freedom and the Illusions of Microcredit: Patronage, Caste, Class and Patriarchy in Rural South India." *The Journal of Development Studies* 53, no. 5 (2017): 741–54.

Epilogue
Risk and Regulation across Colonial India

Farmers in north Indian provinces faced similar challenges as farmers in Madras did during colonial rule. Rainfall levels were low in arid parts and higher though volatile in the river deltas. Public investment in large irrigation works was regionally concentrated. The majority of farmers relied on rainfed land and their livelihood remained sensitive to seasonal shocks. Poor farmers, those in drought-prone regions in particular, needed affordable credit but few were willing to lend to them.

As discussed earlier, strategies to regulate credit markets were implemented by the individual provinces during colonial rule, and regulations in some of the northern provinces came earlier than they did in Madras. The design of these regulations varied; however, the general goal of diminishing the market power of moneylenders transcended provincial boundaries. Regulations were typically triggered by crop failure. In bad years, borrowers could not repay loans and lenders petitioned courts for the transfer of the borrowers' assets, informally coerced the borrower to repay loans and excluded peasants from accessing credit in subsequent seasons. The government, fearful of organised protests by groups of borrowers, attempted to regulate moneylenders. The design of credit regulation rarely treated the source of the problem, often implementing a superficial form of borrower protection. The outcome from each type of regulation was similar to what we have seen in Madras. Contracts became more difficult to enforce and credit supply shrank, becoming harder to access for poor peasants.

Superficial attempts to deal with the problem slowed courts. Sudden changes to the law increased the volume of disputes and confused judges. Courts, according to contemporary reports and historians, were expensive forums for the enforcement of contracts across the major provinces, a problem made worse by credit intervention. Targeted regulation was not the only source of legal constraints to credit expansion. Opaque land titles and tenure regimes that disadvantaged tenants were barriers to inclusive lending in some regions, colonial Bengal being a key example.

In the following pages, I provide a brief reflection on credit supply across three major Indian provinces during colonial rule.

Credit Markets in Bengal, Bombay and Punjab, 1850–1950

The quality of land across India followed similarly distinctive patterns as it did in Madras. Naturally irrigated areas received plentiful rainfall, though faced the prospect of floods due to poor soil drainage. The Ganges delta in the east and submontane tracts fed by snowmelt rivers in the west were suitable for water-intensive cropping. Farmers commonly grew rice and jute along the Bengal delta in the east, and wheat in the colder winters across Punjab in the west. Just north of the Deccan Plateau, the Bombay Presidency in colonial times, black soils encouraged farmers to grow cotton. Cash cropping, the cropping of cotton in particular, increased across Bombay from the 1850s. Substantial parts of these major provinces were dry and rainfed. Amidst water scarcity in the nineteenth century, farmers had few options to protect against drought, relying on low-yield millet crops to subsist in an average year and facing the threat of starvation in bad years.

The strategy to engineer water access in nineteenth- and early twentieth-century India was selective and favoured some regions and communities over others. One of the most ambitious projects to irrigate rural areas at the time, the British government designed a plan to construct a series of canals to carry water from rivers to marginal lands in Punjab. South-west of the five perennial rivers in Punjab was several million acres of parched land occupied by indigenous communities. Land in these regions received little annual rainfall and was designated by the colonial regime as wasteland before the construction of canals. The colonial government constructed canals in four phases. The first set of canals was constructed in the 1880s, the second in the late 1890s, the third set in the 1910s and construction of the fourth major set took place from the mid-1920s to the 1940s.[1] The government displaced indigenous communities during the construction phase and, following the construction of each stage, the government cut out land plots, allocating some land plots to military officers and others to farmers from central Punjab.[2] Government officials defended their decision to award grants of

---

[1] Canal construction continued until the 1940s, though the major phases of construction during colonial rule were complete by the late 1920s. See Imran Ali, *The Punjab under Imperialism, 1885–1947* (Princeton, NJ: Princeton University Press, 1988), 9–13.

[2] David Gilmartin, "Migration and Modernity: The State, the Punjabi Village, and the Settling of the Canal Colonies." In *People on the Move: Punjabi Colonial and Post-colonial Migration*, edited by Ian Talbot and Shinder Thandi, 3–20 (Karachi: Oxford University

newly irrigated land selectively by claiming that fertile areas in central Punjab had become overpopulated and farmers with experience in growing marketed crops in central regions would be more likely to bring newly irrigated lands to productive use.[3] One of the motivations for the government's strategic investment in irrigation works was securing additional revenue from taxing marginal lands.[4] The government determined the return on public investment in irrigation by the marginal increase in tax revenue earned from each rupee invested. Writing in the 1920s, Malcolm Darling praised the investments made in Punjab for bringing profits to the public purse equivalent to 27 per cent above capital expenditure. Darling made this calculation by estimating the additional lands cropped from public investments, and the tax revenue generated from additional cropping, relative to the investment amount.[5] The strategy to extend the frontier in order to increase tax collections from land was also a key factor in the conversion of forests to agricultural land in nineteenth-century Bengal. The colonial government reclaimed forest wetland in the east, portioned reclaimed fields into estates, as well as assessed and granted these estates to new holders.[6] Each holder incurred an annual tax bill. How did credit systems function across these diverse landscapes? Owing to distinctive land tenure institutions, I explore this question by looking at credit supply first in Bombay and Punjab and then in Bengal.

Moneylenders controlled the supply of rural credit across Bombay and Punjab in the mid-nineteenth century.[7] In several villages, lending was localised. Smallholders and tenants, especially in villages that specialised in millet or rice farming, accessed credit from neighbours, richer farmers and local shopkeepers. Land was transferrable in both provinces. The *ryotwari* system was common across Bombay. Officially, the government officially assigned taxes to villages and tax obligations within villages were distributed in agreement between households. Individual land holdings,

---

Press, 2004); Zahid Ali Khalid, "State, Society and Environment in the Ex-state of Bahawalpur: A Case Study of the Sutlej Valley Project, 1921–1947," PhD thesis, University of Sussex (2018).

[3] Hubert Calvert, *Wealth and Welfare of the Punjab* (Lahore: Civil and Military Gazette Press 1922), 9; Malcolm Darling, *Punjab Peasant in Prosperity and Debt*. 4th ed. (Bombay: Oxford University Press, 1947), 133.

[4] Ali, *The Punjab under Imperialism*.

[5] Darling, *Punjab Peasant in Prosperity and Debt*, 131–32.

[6] Iftekhar Iqbal, *The Bengal Delta: Ecology, State and Social Change, 1840–1943* (London: Springer, 2010).

[7] Neil Charlesworth, *Peasants and Imperial Rule: Agriculture and Agrarian Society in the Bombay Presidency, 1850–1935* (Cambridge: Cambridge University Press, 1985), 70–95; Mridula Mukherjee, *Colonizing Agriculture: The Myth of Punjab Exceptionalism*, Vol. 9 (New Delhi: Sage, 2005), 31–53.

however, were titled in late nineteenth and early twentieth-century Punjab. Land was a viable form of collateral for farmers. The sources of credit changed in some districts and for a distinct period from 1860. The emergence of courts and integration with global markets between 1850 and 1860 attracted urban credit businesses to select rural areas. When the colonial government replaced company courts with appellate district and provincial courts in the early 1860s, the instruction given to judges was to protect creditors' rights. Courts issued punishments to defaulters, including ordering the transfer of crop and cattle to the lender or, in extreme cases, imprisoning the defaulter. The judicial process in the 1860s Bombay was quick. It was common for judges to issue *ex-parte* decisions against borrowers.[8] Protection of the lender's interests brought capital from the cities to areas that saw cash crop production. *Marwari* and *Gujarati* bankers provided loans to cotton farmers in Bombay, and *banias* or traders cum moneylenders provided loans to cotton and wheat farmers in Punjab.[9] Information on borrowers was key. *Marwari* lenders from urban Bombay extended credit solely to cotton farmers or to large landholders in districts where they could appoint agents with knowledge of local clients.[10] These urban bankers or 'professional moneylenders', as colonial officials called them, typically extended loans against crop as collateral. Their business model was not far different from the combined credit services provided by agriculturist lenders in Madras during the 1940s and 1950s. Lenders extended loans for working capital expenses at the start of the season, obtained a set volume of crop at the harvest determined by adjusting for potential price shocks, and traded this crop by transporting the product from rural farms to either their own export houses or third-party exporters in port cities.[11] The dominance of professional moneylenders in these regions was short-lived and declined after provincial governments enforced laws to protect borrowers.[12]

---

[8] Rachel E. Kranton and Anand V. Swamy, "The Hazards of Piecemeal Reform: British Civil Courts and the Credit Market in Colonial India." *Journal of Development Economics* 58, no. 1 (1999): 1–24.

[9] Sumit Guha, "Commodity and Credit in Upland Maharashtra, 1800–1950." *Economic and Political Weekly* 22, no. 52 (1987): A126–40; Muhammad Ali Jan, "The Complexity of Exchange: Wheat Markets, Petty-Commodity Producers and the Emergence of Commercial Capital in Colonial Punjab." *Journal of Agrarian Change* 19, no. 2 (2019): 225–48.

[10] Tirthankar Roy, "The Monsoon and the Market for Money in Late-colonial India." *Enterprise & Society* 17, no. 2 (2016): 324–57, 344.

[11] Neeladri Bhattacharya, "Lenders and Debtors: Punjab Countryside, 1880–1940." *Studies in History* 1, no. 2 (August 1985): 305–42; Guha, "Commodity and Credit," A130.

[12] Afghan moneylenders or *Kabuliwalas* started lending in rural India from the late nineteenth century. *Kabuliwalas* provided small loans and typically operated in few select parts of rural North India. See H. William Warner, "The Kabuliwalas: Afghan

The problem with strong lender protection was that it assumed borrowers strategically defaulted on loans. In other words, the colonial administration imposed harsh punishments on borrowers to ensure that peasants did not have the flexibility to borrow large sums and take flight, a feasible problem when lenders could not monitor the borrower's actions easily. In practice, borrowers often defaulted on loans due to reasons out of their control, drought and crop failure being important ones. Fixing liability on borrowers to repay loans when their income was threatened by external factors created friction between borrowers and lenders. Unsurprisingly, peasants started to protest.

The Deccan Riots sent shockwaves through the colonial regime and sparked change in the government's approach to credit. Following a bad harvest and widespread credit defaults in 1874, moneylenders in rural Bombay adopted coercive measures to recover unpaid loans and restricted credit access, especially for poor peasants. Farmers in Ahmednagar, Poona, Satara and Sholapur districts, arid areas in eastern Bombay, vandalised the houses and offices of moneylenders in 1875. Unable to both repay loans and obtain extensions on overdue bills during a period of drought, defaulters shredded contracts held in moneylenders' offices.[13] The government responded with the Deccan Agriculturists Relief Act (DARA) a few years later. Among other forms of regulation, the DARA regulated land alienation, restricting the transfer of land from farmer to professional moneylender, and instructed judges to impose fairer terms for borrowers in credit disputes. The DARA initially applied to the four districts that saw protest and was extended across Bombay in the early 1900s.[14] Though the law was province-specific, courts across colonial India applied the change in tune from creditor-friendly dispute resolution to borrower protection. Judges across provincial courts started to question the terms of credit arrangements.

Historians have been puzzled by the design of the DARA on two counts. One is that the districts that saw protests were also severely affected by drought. Borrowers did not earn enough to repay their loans, and moneylenders were reluctant to lend when the risk of default was high. And yet, this underlying problem of fragility in the agricultural sector seemed to have received little policy attention in colonial

Moneylending and the Credit Cosmopolis of British India, c. 1880–1947." *The Indian Economic & Social History Review* 57, no. 2 (2020): 171–98.

[13] Charlesworth, *Peasants and Imperial Rule*, 95–115.

[14] Latika Chaudhary and Anand V. Swamy, "Protecting the Borrower: An Experiment in Colonial India." *Explorations in Economic History* 65, no. C (2017): 36–54.

Bombay.[15] The other is that the government seemed to overstate the volume of land transfers from farmers to urban bankers. Government officials themselves reported in the early twentieth century that the actual volume of land transfers from farmers to professional moneylenders was lower than nineteenth-century officials claimed.[16]

Herein lies some difference in official thinking between the provinces. Whereas the moneylender was strongly regulated early in Bombay, officials in Madras were not citing the lack of regulation as a concern, partly because land transfers between farmers and urban bankers occurred at an even smaller scale in Madras. The Chettiars, the major indigenous banking community in nineteenth-century South India, extended credit to the cloth and sugar industry in the early nineteenth century though were driven out of this business due to competition from British firms.[17] They did not return to finance the expansion of cash crop cultivation in Madras, as the Marwaris did in Bombay, seeking alternative investment opportunities in Southeast Asia instead. Despite the lack of targeted credit regulation, the courts in Madras followed the government's instruction to review the borrower's condition from the 1870s. Reviewing disputes on a case-by-case basis, combined with an already poorly funded and slow-moving judiciary, led to severe delays in procedure. Credit disputes, according to S. S. Raghavaiyangar a senior colonial official, had started to take years to settle and lenders, as a result, incurred high costs to recover loans through the Madras courts by the early 1880s.[18] Courts seemed to have been more efficient in some provinces than others. Though even in provinces with relatively more timely proceedings, the general trend of legal delays meant that enforcement costs were high across India in the late nineteenth century.[19] Following the shift to greater judicial scrutiny, the number of professional moneylenders lending in rural Punjab declined between 1880 and 1895, a period preceding targeted credit regulation in the province.[20]

[15] Neil Charlesworth, "The Myth of the Deccan Riots of 1875." *Modern Asian Studies* 6, no. 4 (1972): 401–21.

[16] I. J. Catanach, *Rural Credit in Western India, 1875–1930: Rural Credit and the Co-operative Movement in the Bombay Presidency* (Berkeley: University of California Press, 1970), 10–30.

[17] David West Rudner, *Caste and Capitalism in Colonial India: The Nattukottai Chettiars* (Berkeley: University of California Press, 1994), 60–70.

[18] *Memorandum on the Progress of the Madras Presidency during the Last Forty Years of British Administration* (Madras, 1893), 309.

[19] See Tirthankar Roy and Anand V. Swamy, *Law and the Economy in Colonial India* (Chicago: The University of Chicago Press, 2017), 54–79, for a comparison of the time taken to settle disputes across the major provinces during colonial rule.

[20] Darling, *Punjab Peasant in Prosperity and Debt*, 207; Bhattacharya, "Lenders and Debtors," 315.

Regulatory responses to credit defaults, ones that continued to solely address the relationship between lender and borrower and overlook structural issues in the agricultural sector, were not unique to Bombay. Two decades after the DARA, officials in colonial Punjab conducted several rounds of discussion on regulating land alienation. They were concerned about the rate at which land was passing from farmer to *bania*. Drought and famine in 1896 accelerated these discussions. Two successive dry seasons, droughts in the winter season of 1895 and the autumn season of 1896, affected farmers across India. According to one government report on the 1896–97 famine, peasants in Punjab were severely affected. Farmers in naturally irrigated districts lost 30 per cent of their expected crop in 1896, the expected volume arrived at by calculating a ten-year average of crop output in each season across each district. Dry districts fared much worse. The Hissar district in dry south-east Punjab, for instance, lost 75 per cent of its expected crop in the autumn and winter seasons of 1896.[21] Unsurprisingly, drought shocked the credit market. Borrowers defaulted on loans across the province.

By the time the 1896 famine hit, the provincial government had started to design regulation restricting land alienation in Punjab. The government asked the committee compiling the famine report mentioned earlier to comment on whether land transfers from farmer to professional moneylender increased during the famine. The committee responded strongly, claiming that land alienation was not a problem in Punjab. The report suggested that the rapid increase in the value of land during the late nineteenth century, brought about by both population growth and the extension of canal irrigation, led to a more active credit market. Urban moneylenders did not lend in several high-risk districts and their business was limited in the canal colonies. Farmers with disposable income were the primary source of lending in each case. Indeed, wealthier farmers typically received land grants and relocated to the canal colonies upon completion of canal projects, and often brought capital with them.[22] The report also suggested that peasants were able to rely on credit to tide over the bad harvest. Had credit borrowed against land and from professional moneylenders not been available, the report proclaims, 'large numbers of persons would have starved', and, 'relief works would have been swamped'.[23] And yet, two years after the Famine report, the provincial

---

[21] *Report of the Famine in Punjab in 1896–97* (Punjab, 1898), 5–7.
[22] Darling, *Punjab Peasant in Prosperity and Debt*; Ali, *The Punjab under Imperialism*; Mukherjee, *Colonizing Agriculture*.
[23] *Report of the Famine in Punjab*, 77–78.

government passed the Punjab Land Alienation Act, restricting the ability for professional moneylenders to permanently possess agricultural land.

How did credit markets in Bombay and Punjab respond after land alienation laws? Studies have shown that credit supply contracted in the short term.[24] Professional lenders shut shop in areas they were previously lending in.[25] Contracts were costly to enforce, court judges difficult to convince and disputes hard to settle. By the early twentieth century, agriculturist lenders remained unregulated by land alienation laws, and became the dominant credit providers to farmers in their village.[26] The dual risk of lending, that is the risk of borrowers defaulting and losing income from lending business coinciding with the risk of losing earnings from the farming business, in bad years affected the supply of credit from farmers cum moneylenders. Lending risk was especially high in dry areas and disparity in credit access between wet and dry regions widened. According to one study, 'increasing insecurity and the fear of deliberate default' prompted moneylenders to charge high rates and ration credit in dry parts of Punjab. The value of debts accrued in central fertile part of the province was double the same value in the dry south-east in the 1920s.[27] In 1920s Hissar, according to the Punjab edition of the Provincial Banking Enquiry Committee Report, loans were small while each lender was careful to, 'know his debtors very well', choosing borrowers by their capacity to repay.[28] By the late colonial period, in other words, the presence of the urban banker had substantially declined and farmers themselves controlled credit, restricting access for risky borrowers. Amidst stringent laws and expensive court proceedings, mortgages were used infrequently, despite transferrable property titles.

How accessible was credit, and how was regulation designed, in provinces where land was not easily transferrable? The Permanent Settlement agreement between East India Company officials and the *zamindars* of Bengal remained intact throughout colonial rule, albeit with gradual adjustments in the rights of tenants in the nineteenth and early twentieth centuries. To recap, the Permanent Settlement agreement cemented proprietary rights held by pre-colonial elites over vast estates. Wealthy

---

[24] Chaudhary and Swamy, "Protecting the Borrower"; Latika Chaudhary and Anand V. Swamy, "A Policy of Credit Disruption: The Punjab Land Alienation Act of 1900." *Economic History Review* 73, no. 1 (2020): 134–58.

[25] Vinay Kumar Chopra, "Debt Legislation in the Punjab," A Paper Presented to the 22nd Session of the All-India Economic Conference, held in December 1938 at Nagpur (Lahore, 1938); Bhattacharya, "Lenders and Debtors"; Chaudhary and Swamy, "Protecting the Borrower," "A Policy of Credit Disruption."

[26] Darling, *Punjab Peasant in Prosperity and Debt*, 227–28.

[27] Bhattacharya, "Lenders and Debtors," 338–40.

[28] *Punjab Provincial Banking Enquiry Committee Report*, Vol. I (Lahore, 1930), 248.

zamindars portioned estates into smaller plots and leased these to tenants, the actual cultivators. The contract was designed by East India Company officials to maintain a steady rate of tax revenue by fixing assessments while also delegating administrative duties to local landlords, thereby keeping Company costs low. The agreement, however, was vague in its instruction on the transferability of land and, in turn, the rights of tenants. Over the course of the nineteenth century, incomplete property rights severely affected factor markets in Bengal. In some cases, *zamindars* appointed intermediaries to set and collect rents from tenant cultivators. In others, tenants sub-leased plots, transferring rent obligations and creating further discrepancies in the rights of the cultivator.[29] The *zamindar* invested little in land improvement, restricting their responsibilities to maintaining their tax obligation to the Company and later crown. Could leased plots be collateralised in return for credit? Who, among landlords, rent-collectors, tenants and sub-tenants, held the rights to transfer land? These questions were repeatedly brought to the courts in the mid-nineteenth century, and judges tended to lean towards protecting the rights of the non-cultivating landlord.[30] Land, as a result, did not play a role in obtaining credit during this period. Landlords and intermediaries were typically the major suppliers of credit, and sharecropping, the interlinking of rent, wages and credit, was the typical contract type between lender and borrower. Before 1860, credit transfers were commonly in kind. Growth in cash cropping and integration with local and global markets monetised credit transactions in some parts during the late nineteenth century.[31]

Tenancy laws in 1885 and again in 1928 century strengthened the rights of tenants. Having cultivated fields for a defined period of years, tenants could claim occupancy rights over plots. *Zamindars* initially petitioned the courts to disallow the transfers of occupancy rights. When courts started to permit the exchange of occupancy rights, *zamindars* sought alternative ways of stopping tenants from buying and selling land.[32] The outcome of this was that land and credit markets were more active in some districts than others. In areas where *zamindars* had stronger control over tenants, including in districts where they were the dominant moneylender, land was not easily transferrable and loans more difficult to obtain. The dry plateau in western Bengal, for instance, saw

---

[29] Sugata Bose, *Peasant Labour and Colonial Capital: Rural Bengal since 1770* (Cambridge: Cambridge University Press, 1993), 114–22.
[30] Roy and Swamy, *Law and the Economy*, 30–41.
[31] Biplab Dasgupta, "Sharecropping in West Bengal during the Colonial Period." *Economic and Political Weekly* 19, no. 13 (1984): A2–A8.
[32] Roy and Swamy, *Law and the Economy*, 41–45.

significant power exercised by *zamindars*. Courts were rarely approached in these areas. When they were approached, landlord cum lender combined credit with rent disputes.[33] In other areas, the fertile estates in the converted parts of the Ganges delta, for example, occupiers wielded greater bargaining power. Rich peasants as well as town and city dwellers with capital settled on fertile plots near the delta.[34] By the early twentieth century, occupancy rights were more commonly collateralised for credit in these regions than they were in estates under stringent control of local *zamindars*. Influx of occupiers with disposable income changed the landscape of credit in fertile regions. Multiple types of lenders, from landlords to occupiers to shopkeepers extended loans. By the late 1920s, the number of moneylenders per 100,000 residents was much higher in the 'richer districts of Eastern Bengal', than in the west.[35]

Either because land was not appropriately titled and land alienation not a concern or because of strong opposition from *zamindars*, the provincial government did not enforce targeted credit regulations in Bengal until the 1930s. The Great Depression ignited a series of credit regulations in Bengal, as it did in the other provinces. The provincial government set up Debt Conciliation Boards in 1936 dedicated to resolving the rising number of credit disputes, while ensuring fairness to the borrower. In 1940, the provincial government enforced an interest rate ceiling on rural loans. The market tightened. Credit transfers slowed. Several lenders exited the market and the ones that remained tended to be large landowners in the east accepting repayment in kind, seeking to benefit from rising commodity prices in the early 1940s.[36] Whereas rising prices facilitated some additional lending in rural Madras, the disastrous famine in 1943 constrained credit markets in Bengal during the mid- to late-1940s.[37]

Amidst regulations that restricted the volume of lending from moneylenders, provincial governments across India set up credit cooperatives with the aim of expanding the supply of affordable credit. Between 1904 and 1905, most provincial governments had a Department of Cooperatives, and a Registrar in charge of each department. In the early

[33] The number of rent suits increased significantly in the 1920s. See Bose, *Peasant Labour and Colonial Capital*, 128.
[34] Iftekhar Iqbal, "Return of the Bhadralok: Ecology and Agrarian Relations in Eastern Bengal, c. 1905–19471." *Modern Asian Studies* 43, no. 6 (2009): 1325–53.
[35] *Report of the Bengal Provincial Banking Enquiry Committee*, Vol. I (Calcutta, 1930), 194–95.
[36] Bose, *Peasant Labour and Colonial Capital*, 128–29.
[37] Nariaki Nakazato, "Regional Pattern of Land Transfer in Late Colonial Bengal." In *Local Agrarian Societies in Colonial India: Japanese Perspectives*, edited by Peter Robb, Kaoru Sugihara, and Haruka Yanagisawa (Surrey: Routledge, 1996), 260–61.

years, Registrars set different rules on where to install cooperatives.[38] Some departments were more selective than others. The Registrar in Punjab, for instance, set up cooperatives in the richer villages, in the hope that if loan recoveries were high and cooperatives functioned well, the movement would spread and peasants would be more willing to invest in it.[39] This strategy did change in the early 1910s as governments believed that the spread of cooperatives was crucial to welfare improvements in rural areas. Ultimately, cooperatives did not capture sizeable market share in any of the provinces, and reports of corruption and discriminatory lending were widespread.[40]

A common belief within policy circles was that the state was central to the spread of cooperative enterprises.[41] The number of members increased in the 1910s, the value of savings and share capital per member, however, stayed small. From the 1920s, governments across the provinces invested public money in district banks, indirectly aiding the expansion of credit cooperatives in villages. The ratio of private savings and investment to total lending was low in the early 1900s and declined further in subsequent decades.[42] The price shock from the Great Depression hit cooperatives as they struggled to recover loans and several went into liquidation.[43] When prices returned to pre-Depression levels, provincial governments and the Reserve Bank of India initiated plans to invest large sums in village cooperatives, public investments that increased several-fold in the 1960s and 1970s. The ratio of savings to loans remained small, reliance on public money increased over time, and the cooperative sector became a breeding ground for political careers.[44] The story of political intervention, mismanagement and discrimination in rural cooperatives was common across the

---

[38] The expansion of cooperatives and the strategies adopted by Registrars in Bombay is well documented in Catanach, *Rural Credit in Western India*.

[39] *Annual Report on the Working of Co-operative Credit Societies in the Punjab* (Lahore, 1905), 1.

[40] Anwar Iqbal Qureshi, *The Future of the Cooperative Movement in India* (Madras: Oxford University Press, 1947), 1–31.

[41] Iqbal provides a convincing account of how political elites, 'dominated the cooperative movement', erecting barriers to bottom-up participation and inclusive access. See Iftekhar Iqbal, "Cooperative Credit in Colonial Bengal: An Exploration in Development and Decline, 1905–1947." *The Indian Economic and Social History Review* 54, no. 2 (2017): 221–37.

[42] Eleanor Margaret Hough, *The Co-operative Movement in India: Its Relation to a Sound National Economy* (London: P. S. King & Son, 1932), 65–70.

[43] Catanach, *Rural Credit in Western India*, 218–19.

[44] Subrata Ghatak, "Rural Money Markets in India," PhD thesis, University of London, School of Oriental and African Studies (1972), 170–90.

different provinces and persisted well into the latter decades of the twentieth century.[45]

Conclusion

Investigating the lender's position, and how lending impacted rural development, in three major Indian provinces substantiates the original position of this book. Region-specific ecology, the design and persistence of colonial institutions and ineffectual market regulation worked in tandem to constrain capital markets across colonial India.

Climatic risk was a persistent barrier to credit expansion in the nineteenth century. Drought-prone regions saw frequent crop failures and famine. Savings rates were low, and credit was controlled by moneylenders and in short supply. When droughts did hit, lenders coerced borrowers to repay loans, often by obtaining crops or by petitioning the courts to transfer the borrower's land. Unclear property rights and laws that disadvantaged permanent occupiers of land accentuated the problem in Bengal. As tenant protection laws strengthened from the late nineteenth century, peasants in fertile parts of Bengal had better borrowing conditions than peasants in the dry plateau.

Seeking to remedy high interest rates and harsh repayment conditions, provincial governments regulated credit suppliers from the 1870s. The general approach was similar across provinces. Governments regulated moneylenders through the courts. Though regulations were designed differently and instituted at different times depending on the province, the outcome from each type of regulation was similar. Credit supply tightened. Groups of moneylenders exited the market, others remained though found ways of lending outside the scope of administrative procedure. Lenders acted strategically, rationing credit in high-risk zones. Poor peasants in dry areas struggled to obtain credit. Provincial governments counted on credit cooperatives to meet the high demand for credit, though cooperatives were mismanaged and captured a small share of the market across colonial India. Misplaced design of the cooperative transplant embedded excessive state interference and moral hazard in the cooperatives sector.

Private investment levels remained persistently low, stunting economic growth in agricultural India during colonial rule. Capital shortage perpetuated underdevelopment, and attempts to deal with the problem ignored the underlying source and had unintended effects.

---

[45] A. Vaidyanathan, "Future of Cooperatives in India." *Economic and Political Weekly* 48 no. 18 (2013): 30–34.

Bibliography

Government Publications

Memorandum on the Progress of the Madras Presidency during the Last Forty Years of British Administration. Madras, 1893.

Report Regarding the Possibility of Introducing Land and Agricultural Banks into the Madras Presidency. Madras, 1897.

Report of the Famine in Punjab in 1896–97. Lahore, 1898.

A Soil Survey of the Tanjore Delta. Vol. III. Madras, 1921.

Report of the Committee on Co-operation in Madras. Madras, 1928.

Madras Provincial Banking Enquiry Committee Report. Vols. I–V. Madras, 1930.

Punjab Provincial Banking Enquiry Committee Report. Vol. I. Lahore, 1930.

Report of the Bengal Provincial Banking Enquiry Committee. Vol. I. Calcutta, 1930.

Sathyanathan, W. R. S. *Report on Agricultural Indebtedness*. Madras, 1935.

Madras Chamber of Commerce Centenary Handbook 1836–1936. Madras, 1936.

Foulkes, G. F. F. *Local Autonomy*. Madras, 1937.

Madras Estates Land Act Committee Report. Part I. Madras, 1939.

Bahadur, Rao and B. V. Narayanaswamy Naidu. *Report of the Economist for Enquiry into Rural Indebtedness*. Madras, 1945.

Famine Commission Inquiry. Madras, 1945.

Krishnaswamy, S. Y. *Rural Problems in Madras: Monograph*. Madras, 1947.

Madras State Administration Report. Madras, 1947.

A Scheme of Crop Insurance for the Province of Madras. Madras, 1949.

Report of the Rural Banking Enquiry Committee. Delhi, 1950.

5 Year Plans, Government of India, 1951–2012. https://niti.gov.in/planning commission.gov.in/docs/plans/planrel/fiveyr/index5.html.

1951 Census of India Volume III: Madras and Coorg. Part I. Madras, 1951.

Agricultural Statistics of India. Delhi, 1951.

Agriculture and Fisheries in the Madras State. Madras, 1954.

India Crop Calendar. New Delhi, 1954.

Report of the Committee on Co-operation in Madras. Madras, 1956.

All-India Rural Credit Survey. Vols. I–IV. Bombay, 1957.

Rural Credit Survey District Monograph: Coimbatore. Bombay, 1957.

Rural Credit Follow-up Survey. Bombay, 1960.

Techno-Economic Survey of Madras: Economic Report. Madras, 1961.

Report of the Study Group on Area / Project Approach in Implementing Schemes for Extending Commercial Bank Credit to Agriculture. Bombay, 1969.

History of the Reserve Bank of India. Bombay, 1970.

Report of the Committee on Integration of Co-operative Credit Institutions. Bombay, 1976.

Report of the Committee to Review Arrangements for Institutional Credit for Agriculture and Rural Development. Bombay, 1981.

High Level Standing Committee to Review the Flow of Institutional Credit for Rural Sector and Other Related Matters. Bombay, 1986.

Report of the Committee to Examine Certain Operational Aspects of Rural Lending." Bombay, 1988.

A Review of the Agricultural Credit System in India. Bombay, 1989.

India Administrative Atlas, 1872–2001: A Historical Perspective of Evolution of Districts and States in India. Delhi, 2004.

Report of the Cauvery Water Disputes Tribunal Volume II: Agreements of 1892 and 1924. New Delhi, 2007.

Report of the Technical Group Set up to Review Legislations on Money Lending. Bombay, 2007.

Report of the Sub-Committee of the Central Board of Directors of Reserve Bank of India to Study Issues and Concerns in the MFI Sector. Bombay, 2011.

Government Annuals

Annual Report on the Working of Co-operative Credit Societies in the Punjab. Lahore, 1905.

Proceedings of the Council of the Governor of Fort St. George. Madras, 1905.

Report on the Administration of the Registration Department. Madras, 1905–47.

Season and Crop Report of the Madras Presidency. Madras, 1907–30.

Statistics of Civil Courts in the Madras Presidency." Madras, 1920–60.

Annual Report on the Working of the Co-operative Credit Societies Act. Madras, 1922–39.

Madras Legislative Assembly Debates. Vol. I. Madras, 1937.

Gazetteers, Manuals and Pamphlets

Statistical Abstract Relating to British India. London, 1870–1905.

Imperial Gazetteer of India. Oxford, 1909.

Madras District Gazetteers: Bellary. Part I. Madras, 1915.

Madras District Gazetteers: Godavari. Part I. Madras, 1915.

Madras District Gazetteers: Tanjore. Part I. Madras, 1915.

A Short Introduction to Cooperation in the Madras Presidency. Madras, 1920.

The Madras Co-operative Manual. Madras, 1921.

A Statistical Atlas of the Madras Presidency. Madras, 1936.

Report of the Madras Famine Code Revision Committee. Vols. I–II. Madras, 1938.

Strickland, C. F. *The Relief of Agricultural Debt.* London, 1939.

Government Journals and Speeches

Presidential Address by K. Venkata Reddy Naidu at the Second Malabar
Tenant's Conference 1924.
Madras Journal of Co-operation. Madras, 1930–37.

Laws

India Contract Act 1872.
Negotiable Instruments Act 1881.
The Cooperative Societies Act 1904.
Madras Estates Land Act 1908.
The Cooperative Societies Act 1912.
Madras Cooperative Societies Act 1932.
Government of India Act 1935.
Madras Agriculturists Relief Act 1938.
Madras Estates (Abolition and Conversion to Ryotwari) Act 1948.
Tamil Nadu Debt Relief Act 1976.

Case Judgements

Re: Patri Venkata Hanumantha v. Unknown (1934 66 MLJ 193, Madras,
6 October 1933).
Most Revd. Dr. L. Mathias, SC, the Archbishop of Madras and the President of
the Catholic Indian Association and anr. v. Kilacheri Agricultural Co-
operative Bank (1938 1 MLJ 241, Madras, 5 October 1937).
P. R. Govindaswami Naicker v. C. Javanmull Sowcar and anr. (1938 2 MLJ 918,
Madras, 21 May 1938).
Mada Nagaratnam v. Puvvada Seshayya and anr. (1939 I MLJ 272, Madras,
7 February 1939).
V. Sreenivasachariar and anr. v. Krishniah Chetty and ors. (1939 1 MLJ 860,
Madras, 4 September 1939).
Kruttiventi Mallikharjuna Rao and ors. v. Vemuri Pardhasaradhirao and anr.
(1943 2 MLJ 584, Madras, 12 October 1943).
B. K. Narayanaswami Chettiar v. Gurukkar Rudrappa and anr. (1943 AIR
1944 Mad 314, Madras, 26 November 1943).
A. L. Vr. St. Veerappa v. Chinnasamy Alias Samba Goundan and ORS. (AIR
1951 Mad 263, 2 MLJ 328, 20 March 1951).
Garimella Mallikharjuna Rao v. Mangipudi Tripura Sundari. (AIR 1953 Mad
975, 2 MLJ 313, 27 March 1953).
N. S. Sreenivisa Rao v. G. M. Abdul Rahim Sahib (AIR 1956 Mad 618, 2 MLJ,
20 March 1956).

Newspapers

"India's 'Dumb Millions'." *The Times of India*, 23 January 1893.

"Moneylending in the East." *The Spectator*, 15 February 1896.

"Big Irrigation Job under way in India." *The New York Times*, 30 June 1930.

"The Indebtedness of the Indian Peasant: A Report from the Reserve Bank." *The Manchester Guardian*, 5 March 1937.

"Federal Court." *The Times of India*, 7 December 1940.

"Bhavanisagar Project: Governor's Visit." *The Times of India*, 2 September 1956.

"The Dam That Changed Lives of Millions." *The Times of India*, 11 December 2005.

"Impoverished Indian Families Caught in Deadly Spiral of Microfinance Debt." *The Guardian*, 31 January 2011.

"Small Loans Add up to Lethal Debts." *The Hindu*, 25 February 2012.

"AP Enacts Law; No Money Lending without License Now." *The Economic Times*, 21 December 2015.

"A Project That Changed Lakhs of Lives." *The Hindu*, 31 May 2016.

"Average Farm Landholding Size Shrinks to 1.1 ha." *The Hindu*, 17 August 2018.

"Loan Sharks Are Circling for Poor Indian Debtors Failed by Microfinance." *The Guardian*, 29 October 2018.

Articles and Book Chapters

Abraham, Santhosh. "Colonial Law in Early British Malabar: Transparent Colonial State and Formality of Practices." *South Asia Research* 31, no. 3 (2011): 249–64.

Acemoglu, Daron, Simon Johnson, and James A. Robinson. "Chapter 6: Institutions as a Fundamental Cause of Long-Run Growth." In *Handbook of Economic Growth*, edited by Philippe Aghion and Steven N. Durlauf, 385–472, Vol. 1. North Holland: Elsevier B.V., 2005.

Agnihotri, Indu. "Ecology, Land Use and Colonisation: The Canal Colonies of Punjab." *The Indian Economic & Social History Review* 33, no. 1 (March 1996): 37–58.

Ahuja, Ravi. "Labour Relations in an Early Colonial Context: Madras, c. 1750–1800." *Modern Asian Studies* 36, no. 4 (2002): 793–826.

Aleem, Irfan. "Imperfect Information, Screening, and the Costs of Informal Lending: A Study of a Rural Credit Market in Pakistan." *The World Bank Economic Review* 4, no. 3 (1990): 329–49.

Amrith, Sunil. "Risk and the South Asian Monsoon." *Climatic Change* 151, no. 1 (2018): 17–28.

Anonymous. "Obituary: Professor M.L. Dantwala." *Indian Journal of Agricultural Economics* 53, no. 4 (1998): 567.

Appadurai, Arjun. "Kings, Sects and Temples in South India, 1350–1700 A.D." *The Indian Economic and Social History Review* 14, no. 1 (1977): 47–73.

Arnold, David. "Looting, Grain Riots and Government Policy in South India 1918." *Past & Present*, no. 84 (1979): 111–45.

Arnott, Richard, Bruce Greenwald, and Joseph E. Stiglitz. "Information and Economic Efficiency." *Information Economics and Policy* 6, no. 1 (1994): 77–82.

Austin, Gareth. "The 'Reversal of Fortune' Thesis and the Compression of History: Perspectives from African and Comparative Economic History." *Journal of International Development* 20, no. 8 (2008): 996–1027.

"Factor Markets in Nieboer Conditions: Pre-colonial West Africa, c.1500–c.1900." *Continuity and Change* 24, no. 1 (2009): 23–53.

Austin, Gareth, and Kaoru Sugihara, "Local Suppliers of Credit in the Third World, 1750–1960: Introduction." In *Local Suppliers of Credit in the Third World, 1750–1960*, edited by Gareth Austin and Kaoru Sugihara, 1–25. London: Macmillan Press, 1993.

Bagchi, Amiya Kumar. "Land Tax, Property Rights and Peasant Insecurity in Colonial India." *The Journal of Peasant Studies* 20, no. 1 (1992): 1–49.

Baker, Christopher John. "The Congress at the 1937 Elections in Madras." *Modern Asian Studies* 10, no. 4 (1976): 557–89.

"Colonial Rule and the Internal Economy in Twentieth-century Madras." *Modern Asian Studies* 15, no. 3 (1981): 575–602.

Banerjee, Abhijit, Timothy Besley, and Timothy Guinnane. "Thy Neighbor's Keeper: The Design of a Credit Cooperative with Theory and a Test." *The Quarterly Journal of Economics* 109, no. 2 (1994): 491–515.

Banerjee, Abhijit, and Lakshmi Iyer. "History, Institutions, and Economic Performance: The Legacy of Colonial Land Tenure Systems in India." *American Economic Review* 95, no. 4 (2005): 1190–213.

Barboni, Giorgia, and Parul Agarwal. "Knowing What's Good for You: Can a Repayment Flexibility Option in Microfinance Contracts Improve Repayment Rates and Business Outcomes?," IGC Working Paper, Ref.: F-89219-INC-1.

Bardhan, Pranab K. "Interlocking Factor Markets and Agrarian Development: A Review of Issues." *Oxford Economic Papers* 32, no. 1 (1980): 82–98.

"Institutions Matter, but Which Ones?." *Economics of Transition* 13, no. 3 (2005): 499–532.

Bardhan, Pranab K., and Ashok Rudra. "Terms and Conditions of Sharecropping Contracts: An Analysis of Village Survey Data in India." *The Journal of Development Studies* 16, no. 3 (1980): 287–302.

Basu, Kaushik. "Exploitation and Efficiency." *Economic and Political Weekly* 24, no. 28 (1989): 1554.

Bates, Robert H. "Social Dilemmas and Rational Individuals: An Assessment of the New Institutionalism." In *The New Institutional Economics and Third World Development*, edited by John Harriss, Janet Hunter, and Colin M. Lewis, 27–49. London: Routledge, 1997.

Bell, Clive. "Chapter 16: Credit Markets and Interlinked Transactions." In *Handbook of Development Economics*, edited by T. Paul Schultz and John Strauss, 763–830, Vol. 1. Amsterdam: Elsevier B.V., 1988.

Bentham, Jeremy. "ART. VII.-USURY LAWS." *Calcutta Review* 101, no. 201 (1895): 150–67.

Besley, Timothy. "How Do Market Failures Justify Interventions in Rural Credit Markets?." *The World Bank Research Observer* 9, no. 1 (1994): 27–47.

Besley, Timothy, and Stephen Coate. "Group Lending, Repayment Incentives and Social Collateral." *Journal of Development Economics* 46, no. 1 (1995): 1–18.

Bhaduri, Amit. "A Study in Agricultural Backwardness under Semi-Feudalism." *The Economic Journal* 83, no. 329 (1973): 120–37.
    "On the Formation of Usurious Interest Rates in Backward Agriculture." *Cambridge Journal of Economics* 1, no. 4 (1977): 341–52.

Bhattacharya, Neeladri. "Lenders and Debtors: Punjab Countryside, 1880–1940." *Studies in History* 1, no. 2 (August 1985): 305–42.

Bogart, Dan, and Latika Chaudhary. "Engines of Growth: The Productivity Advance of Indian Railways, 1874–1912." *The Journal of Economic History* 73, no. 2 (2013): 339–70.

Bottomley, Anthony. "The Premium for Risk as a Determinant of Interest Rates in Underdeveloped Rural Areas." *The Quarterly Journal of Economics* 77, no. 4 (1963): 637–47.
    "Interest Rate Determination in Underdeveloped Rural Areas." *American Journal of Agricultural Economics* 57, no. 2 (1975): 279–91.

Bowman, Andrew. "Mass Production or Production by the Masses? Tractors, Cooperatives, and the Politics of Rural Development in Post-independence Zambia." *The Journal of African History* 52, no. 2 (2011): 201–21.

Braverman, Avishay, and Joseph E. Stiglitz. "Sharecropping and the Interlinking of Agrarian Markets." *The American Economic Review* 72, no. 4 (1982): 695–715.

Brennan, Lance, John McDonald, and Ralph Shlomowitz. "Trends in the Economic Well-Being of South Indians under British Rule: The Anthropometric Evidence." *Explorations in Economic History* 31, no. 2 (1994): 225–60.

Broadberry, Stephen, Johann Custodis, and Bishnupriya Gupta. "India and the Great Divergence: An Anglo-Indian Comparison of GDP per Capita, 1600–1871." *Explorations in Economic History* 55, no. 1 (2015): 58–75.

Broadberry, Stephen, and Bishnupriya Gupta. "The Historical Roots of India's Service-led Development: A Sectoral Analysis of Anglo-Indian Productivity Differences, 1870–2000." *Explorations in Economic History* 47, no. 3 (2010): 264–78.

Brown, Rajeswary. "Chettiar Capital and Southeast Asian Credit Networks in the Interwar Period." In *Local Suppliers of Credit in the Third World, 1750–1960,* edited by Gareth Austin and Kaoru Sugihara, 254–87. London: Macmillan Press, 1993.

Chang, Ha-Joon. "Institutions and Economic Development: Theory, Policy and History." *Journal of Institutional Economics* 7, no. 4 (2011): 473–98.

Charlesworth, Neil. "The Myth of the Deccan Riots of 1875." *Modern Asian Studies* 6, no. 4 (1972): 401–21.

Chattopadhyay, Suhas. "On the Class Nature of Land Reforms in India since Independence." *Social Scientist* 2, no. 4 (1973): 3–24.

Chaudhary, Latika, and Anand V. Swamy. "Protecting the Borrower: An Experiment in Colonial India." *Explorations in Economic History* 65, no. C (2017): 36–54.

"A Policy of Credit Disruption: The Punjab Land Alienation Act of 1900." *Economic History Review* 73, no. 1 (2020): 134–58.

Cheesman, David. "'The Omnipresent Bania:' Rural Moneylenders in Nineteenth-Century Sind." *Modern Asian Studies* 16, no. 3 (1982): 445–62.

Chopra, Vinay Kumar. "Debt Legislation in the Punjab," A Paper Presented to the 22nd Session of the All-India Economic Conference, Held in December 1938 at Nagpur (Lahore, 1938).

Colvin, Christopher L. "Banking on a Religious Divide: Accounting for the Success of the Netherlands' Raiffeisen Cooperatives in the Crisis of the 1920s." *The Journal of Economic History* 77, no. 3 (2017): 866–919.

Colvin, Christopher L., and Eoin McLaughlin. "Raiffeisenism Abroad: Why Did German Cooperative Banking Fail in Ireland but Prosper in the Netherlands?." *Economic History Review* 67, no. 2 (2014): 492–516.

Copestake, James. "Microfinance and Development Finance in India: Research Implications," CEB Working Paper no. 10/028 (2010), Université Libre de Bruxelles.

Dandekar, V. M. "Crop Insurance in India." *Economic and Political Weekly* 11, no. 26 (1976): A61–80.

Dantwala, M. L. "Agricultural Credit in India – The Missing Link." *Pacific Affairs* 25, no. 4 (1952): 349–59.

Dasgupta, Biplab. "Sharecropping in West Bengal during the Colonial Period." *Economic and Political Weekly* 19, no. 13 (1984): A2–A8.

De Mesquita, Ethan Bueno, and Matthew Stephenson. "Legal Institutions and Informal Networks." *Journal of Theoretical Politics* 18, no. 1 (2006): 40–67.

Demont, Timothée. "Microfinance Spillovers: A Model of Competition in Informal Credit Markets with an Application to Indian Villages." *European Economic Review* 89 (2016): 21–41.

DeQuidt, Jonathan, Thiemo Fetzer, and Maitreesh Ghatak, "Group Lending without Joint Liability." *Journal of Development Economics* 121 (2016): 217–36.

Dercon, Stefan, Pramila Krishnan, and Sofya Krutikova. "Changing Living Standards in Southern Indian Villages 1975–2006: Revisiting the ICRISAT Village Level Studies." *The Journal of Development Studies* 49, no. 12 (2013): 1676–93.

Djankov, Simeon, Rafael La Porta, Florencio Lopez-De-Silanes, and Andrei Shleifer. "Courts." *The Quarterly Journal of Economics* 118, no. 2 (2003): 453–517.

Donaldson, Dave. "Railroads of the Raj: Estimating the Impact of Transportation Infrastructure." *American Economic Review* 108, nos. 4–5 (2018): 899–934.

Duflo, Esther, and Rohini Pande. "Dams." *The Quarterly Journal of Economics* 122, no. 2 (2007): 601–46.

Field, Erica, and Rohini Pande. "Repayment Frequency and Default in Microfinance: Evidence from India." *Journal of the European Economic Association* 6, nos. 2–3 (2008): 501–9.

Galanter, Marc. "The Aborted Restoration of 'Indigenous' Law in India." *Comparative Studies in Society and History* 14, no. 1 (1972): 53–70.

Gelderblom, Oscar, Joost Jonker, and Clemens Kool. "Direct Finance in the Dutch Golden Age." *The Economic History Review* 69, no. 4 (2016): 1178–98.

Ghatak, Maitreesh. "Screening by the Company You Keep: Joint Liability Lending and the Peer Selection Effect." *Economic Journal* 110, no. 465 (2000): 601–31.

Ghatak, Maitreesh, and Timothy W. Guinnane. "The Economics of Lending with Joint Liability: Theory and Practice." *Journal of Development Economics* 60, no. 1 (1999): 195–228.

Ghatak, Subrata. "Rural Money Markets in India," PhD thesis University of London, School of Oriental and African Studies (1972), 170–90.

"Rural Interest Rates in the Indian Economy." *The Journal of Development Studies* 11, no. 3 (1975): 190–201.

Ghosh, Parikshit, and Debraj Ray. "Information and Enforcement in Informal Credit Markets." *Economica* 83, no. 329 (2016): 59–90.

Gilmartin, David. "Migration and Modernity: The State, the Punjabi Village, and the Settling of the Canal Colonies." In *People on the Move: Punjabi Colonial and Post-colonial Migration*, edited by Ian Talbot and Thandi Shinder, 3–20. Karachi: Oxford University Press, 2004.

Gough, E. Kathleen. "Brahman Kinship in a Tamil Village 1." *American Anthropologist* 58, no. 5 (1956): 826–53.

Greif, Avner. "Contract Enforceability and Economic Institutions in Early Trade: The Maghribi Traders' Coalition." *The American Economic Review* 83, no. 3 (1993): 525–48.

Guérin, Isabelle, Bert D'Espallier, and Govindan Venkatasubramanian. "Debt in Rural South India: Fragmentation, Social Regulation and Discrimination." *The Journal of Development Studies* 49, no. 9 (2013): 1155–71.

Guérin, Isabelle, and Santosh Kumar. "Market, Freedom and the Illusions of Microcredit: Patronage, Caste, Class and Patriarchy in Rural South India." *The Journal of Development Studies* 53, no. 5 (2017): 741–54.

Guha, Sumit. "Commodity and Credit in Upland Maharashtra, 1800–1950." *Economic and Political Weekly* 22, no. 52 (1987): A126–40.

Guinnane, Timothy W. "A Failed Institutional Transplant: Raiffeisen's Credit Cooperatives in Ireland, 1894–1914." *Explorations in Economic History* 31, no. 1 (1994): 38–61.

"Cooperatives as Information Machines: German Rural Credit Cooperatives, 1883–1914." *The Journal of Economic History* 61, no. 2 (2001): 366–89.

"A 'Friend and Advisor': External Auditing and Confidence in Germany's Credit Cooperatives, 1889–1914." *Business History Review* 77, no. 2 (2003): 235–64.

Gupta, Bishnupriya. "Discrimination or Social Networks? Industrial Investment in Colonial India." *The Journal of Economic History* 74, no. 1 (2014): 141–68.

"Falling behind and Catching Up: India's Transition from a Colonial Economy." *The Economic History Review* 72, no. 3 (2019): 803–27.

Gupta, Bishnupriya, Dilip Mookherjee, Kaivan Munshi, and Mario Sanclemente. "Community Origins of Industrial Entrepreneurship in Pre-Independence India." CAGE Working Paper Series, no. 402 (2019).

Haines, Daniel. "Disputed Rivers: Sovereignty, Territory and State-Making in South Asia, 1948–1951." *Geopolitics* 19, no. 3 (2014): 632–55.

Hall, Kenneth R. "Coinage, Trade and Economy in Early South India and Its Southeast Asian Neighbours." *The Indian Economic and Social History Review* 36, no. 4 (1999): 431–59.

Harriss-White, Barbara. "From Analysing 'Filières Vivrieres' to Understanding Capital and Petty Production in Rural South India." *Journal of Agrarian Change* 16, no. 3 (2016): 478–500.

Hazareesingh, Sandip. "Cotton, Climate and Colonialism in Dharwar, Western India, 1840–1880." *Journal of Historical Geography* 38, no. 1 (2012): 1–17.

Heston, A. "National Income." In *The Cambridge Economic History of India*, edited by Dharma Kumar and Meghnad Desai, 2: 376–462. Cambridge: Cambridge University Press, 1983.

Hurd, John. "Railways and the Expansion of Markets in India, 1861–1921." *Explorations in Economic History* 12, no. 3 (1975): 263–88.

"Railways." In *The Cambridge Economic History of India*, edited by Dharma Kumar and Meghnad Desai, 2: 878–904. Cambridge: Cambridge University Press, 1983.

Iqbal, Iftekhar. "Return of the Bhadralok: Ecology and Agrarian Relations in Eastern Bengal, c. 1905–19471." *Modern Asian Studies* 43, no. 6 (2009): 1325–53.

"Cooperative Credit in Colonial Bengal: An Exploration in Development and Decline, 1905–1947." *The Indian Economic and Social History Review* 54, no. 2 (2017): 221–37.

Islam, M. Mufakharul. "The Punjab Land Alienation Act and the Professional Moneylenders." *Modern Asian Studies* 29, no. 2 (1995): 271–91.

Iyer, Lakshmi. "Direct versus Indirect Colonial Rule in India: Long-Term Consequences." *The Review of Economics and Statistics* 92, no. 4 (2010): 693–713.

Jan, Muhammad Ali. "The Complexity of Exchange: Wheat Markets, Petty-Commodity Producers and the Emergence of Commercial Capital in Colonial Punjab." *Journal of Agrarian Change* 19, no. 2 (2019): 225–48.

Jayaraman, Rajshri, and Peter Lanjouw. "The Evolution of Poverty and Inequality in Indian Villages." *The World Bank Research Observer* 14, no. 1 (1999): 1–30.

Kaiwar, Vasant. "Nature, Property and Polity in Colonial Bombay." *The Journal of Peasant Studies* 27, no. 2 (2000): 1–49.

Kamenov, Nikolay. "The Place of the 'Cooperative' in the Agrarian History of India, c. 1900–1970." *The Journal of Asian Studies* 79, no. 1 (2020): 103–28.

Karashima, N., and Y. Subbarayalu. "The Emergence of the Periyandu Assembly in South India during the Chola and Pandyan Periods." *International Journal of Asian Studies* 1, no. 1 (2004): 87–103.

Khalid, Zahid Ali. "State, Society and Environment in the Ex-state of Bahawalpur: A Case Study of the Sutlej Valley Project, 1921–1947," PhD thesis, University of Sussex (2018).

Khandker, Shahidur R. "Microfinance and Poverty." *The World Bank Economic Review* 19, no. 2 (2005): 263–86.

Khusro, A. M. "Land Reforms since Independence." In *Economic History of India, 1857–1956*, edited by V. B. Singh, 180–200. Bombay: Allied Publishers, 1965.

Kingwell-Banham, Eleanor. "Dry, Rainfed or Irrigated? Reevaluating the Role and Development of Rice Agriculture in Iron Age-Early Historic South India Using Archaeobotanical Approaches." *Archaeological and Anthropological Sciences* 11, no. 12 (2019): 6485–500.

Koul, Autar Krishen, and Mihir Chatterjee. "International Financial Institutions and Indian Banking: A Legal Profile." In *India and International Law*, edited by Bimal N. Patel, 207–30, Vol. 2. Leiden: Brill, 2008.

Kranton, Rachel E., and Anand V. Swamy. "The Hazards of Piecemeal Reform: British Civil Courts and the Credit Market in Colonial India." *Journal of Development Economics* 58, no. 1 (1999): 1–24.

Kumar, Dharma. "Landownership and Inequality in Madras Presidency: 1853–54 to 1946–47." *The Indian Economic & Social History Review* 12, no. 3 (January 1975): 229–61.

"Private Property in Asia? The Case of Medieval South India." *Comparative Studies in Society and History* 27, no. 2 (1985): 340–66.

Kumar, Sunil Mitra. "Does Access to Formal Agricultural Credit Depend on Caste?." *World Development* 43, no. C (2013): 315–28.

La Porta, Rafael, Florencio Lopez-de-Silanes, and Andrei Shleifer. "The Economic Consequences of Legal Origins." *Journal of Economic Literature* 46, no. 2 (2008): 285–332.

Ludden, David. "Patronage and Irrigation in Tamil Nadu: A Long-Term View." *The Indian Economic & Social History Review* 16, no. 3 (July 1979): 347–65.

"Spectres of Agrarian Territory in Southern India." *The Indian Economic and Social History Review* 39, nos. 2–3 (2002): 233–57.

Mader, Philip. "Rise and Fall of Microfinance in India: The Andhra Pradesh Crisis in Perspective." *Strategic Change* 22, nos. 1–2 (2013): 47–66.

Madestam, Andreas. "Informal Finance: A Theory of Moneylenders." *Journal of Development Economics* 107 (2014): 157–74.

Mariotti, Chiara. "Resettlement and Risk of Adverse Incorporation: The Case of the Polavaram Dam." *Development in Practice* 25, no. 5 (2015): 628–42.

Martin, Marina. "Project Codification: Legal Legacies of the British Raj on the Indian Mercantile Credit Institution Hundi." *Contemporary South Asia* 23, no. 1 (2015): 67–84.

Mayer, P. B. "The Penetration of Capitalism in a South Indian District." *South Asia* 3, no. 2 (1980): 1–24.

"Trends of Real Income in Tiruchirapalli and the Upper Kaveri Delta, 1819–1980." *The Indian Economic and Social History Review* 43, no. 3 (2006): 349–64.

McAlpin, Michelle. "Railroads, Prices, and Peasant Rationality: India 1860–1900." *The Journal of Economic History* 34, no. 3 (1974): 662–84.

"Railroads, Cultivation Patterns, and Foodgrain Availability: India 1860–1900." *The Indian Economic and Social History Review* 12, no. 1 (1975): 43–60.

"Price Movements and Fluctuations in Economic Activity (1860–1947)." In *The Cambridge Economic History of India*, edited by Dharma Kumar and Meghnad Desai, 2: 878–904. Cambridge: Cambridge University Press, 1983.

Mishra, Saurabh. "Cattle, Dearth, and the Colonial State: Famines and Livestock in Colonial India, 1896–1900." *Journal of Social History* 46, no. 4 (2013): 989–1012.

Mizushima, Tsukasa. "From Mirasidar to Pattadar: South India in the Late Nineteenth Century." *The Indian Economic and Social History Review* 39, nos. 2–3 (2002): 259–84.

Moore, Frank J. "Money-Lenders and Co-Operators in India." *Economic Development and Cultural Change* 2, no. 2 (1954): 139–59.

Moosvi, Shireen. "The Rural Moneylender, 1888: The Dufferin Report for West UP." *Studies in People's History* 6, no. 2 (2019): 170–75.

Moro, Andrea, Daniela Maresch, and Annalisa Ferrando. "Creditor Protection, Judicial Enforcement and Credit Access." *The European Journal of Finance* 24, no. 3 (2018): 250–81.

Mosse, David. "Colonial and Contemporary Ideologies of 'Community Management': The Case of Tank Irrigation Development in South India." *Modern Asian Studies* 33 (1999): 303–38.

Musgrave, P. J. "Rural Credit and Rural Society in the United Provinces 1860–1920." In *The Imperial Impact*, edited by Clive Dewey and A. G. Hopkins, 216–33. London: The Athlone Press, 1978.

Naidu, Narayanaswami B. V. "The Co-operative Movement in the Madras Presidency." *Indian Journal of Economics* 14 (1934): 426.

Nair, K. C., and A. C. Dhas. "Agricultural Change in Tamil Nadu: 1918–1955." In *The South Indian Economy: Agrarian Change, Industrial Structure and State Policy c. 1914–1947*, edited by Sabyasachi Bhattacharya, Sumit Guha, Raman Mahadevan, Sakti Padhi, D. Rajasekhar, and G. N. Rao, 120–58. Delhi: Oxford University Press, 1991.

Nair, Reshmy. "Crop Insurance in India: Changes and Challenges." *Economic and Political Weekly* 45, no. 6 (2010): 19–22.

Nakazato, Nariaki. "Regional Pattern of Land Transfer in Late Colonial Bengal." In *Local Agrarian Societies in Colonial India: Japanese Perspectives*, edited by Peter Robb, Kaoru Sugihara, and Haruka Yanagisawa, 250–80. Surrey: Routledge, 1996.

Nath, Maanik. "Do Institutional Transplants Succeed? Regulating Raiffeisen Cooperatives in South India, 1930–1960." *Business History Review* 95, no. 1 (2021): 59–85.

"Credit Risk in Colonial India." *The Economic History Review* 75 (2022): 396–420.

Mandar, Oak, and Anand V. Swamy. "Only Twice as Much: A Rule for Regulating Lenders." *Economic Development and Cultural Change* 58, no. 4 (2010): 775–803.

Parthasarathi, Prasannan. "Rethinking Wages and Competitiveness in the Eighteenth Century: Britain and South India." *Past & Present* 1998, no. 158 (1998): 79–109.

"Water and Agriculture in Nineteenth-Century Tamilnad." *Modern Asian Studies* 51, no. 2 (March 2017): 485–510.

Patnaik, Utsa. "The Agrarian Question and Development of Capitalism in India." *Economic and Political Weekly* 21, no. 18 (1986): 781–93.

Porta, Rafael La, Florencio Lopez-De-Silanes, Andrei Shleifer, and Robert W. Vishny. "Law and Finance." *Journal of Political Economy* 106, no. 6 (1998): 1113–55.

Pradhan, Narayan Chandra. "Persistence of Informal Credit in Rural India: Evidence from 'All-India Debt and Investment Survey' and Beyond," RBI Working Paper Series, WPS (DEPR), 5/2013.

Price, Pamela G. "Ideology and Ethnicity under British Imperial Rule: 'Brahmans', Lawyers and Kin-Caste Rules in Madras Presidency." *Modern Asian Studies* 23, no. 1 (1989): 151–77.

Rajasekhar, D. "Commercialisation of Agriculture and Changes in Distribution of Land Ownership in Kurnool District of Andhra (c.1900–50)." In *The South Indian Economy: Agrarian Change, Industrial Structure and State Policy c. 1914–1947*, edited by Sabyasachi Bhattacharya, Sumit Guha, Raman Mahadevan, Sakti Padhi, D. Rajasekhar, and G. N. Rao, 78–119. Delhi: Oxford University Press, 1991.

Ramachandran, V. K. and Madhura Swaminathan. "Rural Banking and Landless Labour Households: Institutional Reform and Rural Credit Markets in India." *Journal of Agrarian Change* 2, no. 4 (2002): 502–44.

Ramesh, Aditya. "Custom as Natural: Land, Water and Law in Colonial Madras." *Studies in History* 34, no. 1 (February 2018): 29–47.

"The Value of Tanks: Maintenance, Ecology and the Colonial Economy in Nineteenth-century South India." *Water History* 10, no. 4 (2018): 267–89.

"Indian Rivers, 'Productive Works', and the Emergence of Large Dams in Nineteenth-Century Madras." *The Historical Journal* 64, no. 2 (2020): 1–29.

Rao, G. N., and D. Rajasekhar. "Commodity Production and the Changing Agrarian Scenario in Andhra: A Study in Interregional Variations, c.1910 –c.1947." In *The South Indian Economy: Agrarian Change, Industrial Structure and State Policy c. 1914–1947*, edited by Sabyasachi Bhattacharya, Sumit Guha, Raman Mahadevan, Sakti Padhi, D. Rajasekhar, and G. N. Rao, 1–49. Delhi: Oxford University Press, 1991.

Rich, Paul B. "Bernard Huss and the Experiment in African Cooperatives in South Africa, 1926–1948." *The International Journal of African Historical Studies* 26, no. 2 (1993): 297–317.

Robert, Bruce. "Agricultural Credit Cooperatives in Madras, 1893–1937: Rural Development and Agrarian Politics in Pre-independence India." *The Indian Economic and Social History Review* 16, no. 2 (1979): 163–84.

"Economic Change and Agrarian Organization in 'Dry' South India 1890–1940: A Reinterpretation." *Modern Asian Studies* 17, no. 1 (1983): 59–78.

Roy, Tirthankar. "Factor Markets and the Narrative of Economic Change in India, 1750–1950." *Continuity and Change* 24, no. 1 (2009): 137–67.

"Geography or Politics? Regional Inequality in Colonial India." *European Review of Economic History* 18, no. 3 (2014): 324–48.

"The Monsoon and the Market for Money in Late-colonial India." *Enterprise & Society* 17, no. 2 (2016): 324–57.

"Climate and the Economy in India." CAGE Working Paper Series, no. 445 (2019).

Saikia, Arupjyoti. "The Moneylenders and Indebtedness: Understanding the Peasant Economy of Colonial Assam, 1900–1950." *Indian Historical Review* 37, no. 1 (2010): 63–88.

Salman, Salman M. A. "Inter-states Water Disputes in India: An Analysis of the Settlement Process." *Water Policy* 4, no. 3 (2002): 223–37.

Sami, Leela. "Starvation, Disease and Death: Explaining Famine Mortality in Madras 1876–1878." *Social History of Medicine : The Journal of the Society for the Social History of Medicine* 24, no. 3 (2011): 700–19.

Saravanan, Velayutham. "Technological Transformation and Water Conflicts in the Bhavani River Basin of Tamil Nadu, 1930–1970." *Environment and History* 7, no. 3 (2001): 289–334.

Satish, P. "Excluding the Poor from Credit: Lessons from Andhra Pradesh and Telangana." *Economic and Political Weekly* (28 July 2018).

Satyanarayana, A. "Commercialisation, Money Capital and the Peasantry in Colonial Andhra, 1900–1940." In *The South Indian Economy: Agrarian Change, Industrial Structure and State Policy c. 1914–1947*, edited by Sabyasachi Bhattacharya, Sumit Guha, Raman Mahadevan, Sakti Padhi, D. Rajasekhar, and G. N. Rao, 51–77. Delhi: Oxford University Press, 1991.

Schwecke, Sebastian. "A Tangled Jungle of Disorderly Transactions? The Production of a Monetary outside in a North Indian Town." *Modern Asian Studies* 52, no. 4 (2018): 1375–419.

Sen, Srabani. "Scientific Enquiry in Agriculture in Colonial India: A Historical Perspective." *Indian Journal of History of Science* 45, no. 2 (2010): 199–239.

Sharma, G. D. "Urban Credit and the Market Economy in Western India, c.1750–1850." In *Local Suppliers of Credit in the Third World, 1750–1960*, edited by Gareth Austin and Kaoru Sugihara, 36–54. London: Macmillan Press, 1993.

Southall, Aidan. "The Segmentary State in Africa and Asia." *Comparative Studies in Society and History* 30, no. 1 (1988): 52–82.

Stiglitz, Joseph E. "Chapter 5: Economic Organization, Information, and Development." In *Handbook of Development Economics*, edited by T. Paul Schultz and John Strauss, 93–160, Vol. 1. Amsterdam: Elsevier B.V., 1988.

"Peer Monitoring and Credit Markets." *The World Bank Economic Review* 4, no. 3 (1990): 351–66.

Stiglitz, Joseph E., and Andrew Weiss. "Credit Rationing in Markets with Imperfect Information." *The American Economic Review* 71, no. 3 (1981): 393–410.

Strickland, C. F. "Cooperation and the Rural Problem of India." *The Quarterly Journal of Economics* 43, no. 3 (1929): 503–31.

Suesse, Marvin, and Nikolaus Wolf. "Rural Transformation, Inequality, and the Origins of Microfinance." *Journal of Development Economics* 143 (2020): 102429.

Sultan, Atiyab, and David Washbrook. "Introduction: Institutions and Economic Development in South Asia." *Modern Asian Studies* 51, no. 6 (2017): 1657–67.

Syvitski, James P. M., Albert J. Kettner, Irina Overeem, Eric W. H. Hutton, Mark T. Hannon, G. Robert Brakenridge, John Day, Charles Vörösmarty, Yoshiki Saito, Liviu Giosan, and Robert J. Nicholls. "Sinking Deltas due to Human Activities." *Nature Geoscience* 2, no. 10 (2009): 681–86.

Taylor, Marcus. "'Freedom from Poverty Is Not for Free': Rural Development and the Microfinance Crisis in Andhra Pradesh, India." *Journal of Agrarian Change* 11, no. 4 (2011): 484–504.

"Liquid Debts: Credit, Groundwater and the Social Ecology of Agrarian Distress in Andhra Pradesh, India." *Third World Quarterly* 34, no. 4 (2013): 691–709.

Thorner, Alice. "Semi-Feudalism or Capitalism? Contemporary Debate on Classes and Modes of Production in India." *Economic and Political Weekly* 17, no. 50 (1982): 1993–99.

Timberg, Thomas A., and C. V. Aiyar. "Informal Credit Markets in India." *Economic Development and Cultural Change* 33, no. 1 (1984): 43–59.

Vaidyanathan, A. "Future of Cooperatives in India." *Economic and Political Weekly* 48, no. 18 (2013): 30–34.

Vaishnavi, Surendra. "Are Moneylenders Financial Intermediaries." *Ideas for India*, 24 March 2021.

Van Bochove, Christiaan, Heidi Deneweth, and Jaco Zuijderduijn, "Real Estate and Mortgage Finance in England and the Low Countries, 1300–1800." *Continuity and Change* 30, no. 1 (2015): 9–38.

Vedula, S. "Optimal Irrigation Planning in River Basin Development: The Case of the Upper Cauvery River Basin." *Sadhana* 8, no. 2 (1985): 223–52.

Visaria, Leela, and Pravin Visaria. "Population (1757–1947)." In *The Cambridge Economic History of India*, edited by Dharma Kumar and Meghnad Desai, 2: 878–904. Cambridge: Cambridge University Press, 1983.

Warner, H. William. "The Kabuliwalas: Afghan Moneylending and the Credit Cosmopolis of British India, c. 1880–1947." *The Indian Economic & Social History Review* 57, no. 2 (2020): 171–98.

Washbrook, David A. "Country Politics: Madras 1880 to 1930." *Modern Asian Studies* 7, no. 3 (1973): 475–531.

"Law, State and Agrarian Society in Colonial India." *Modern Asian Studies* 15, no. 3 (1981): 649–721.

"The Commercialization of Agriculture in Colonial India: Production, Subsistence and Reproduction in the 'Dry South', c. 1870–1930." *Modern Asian Studies* 28, no. 1 (1994): 129–64.

"Colonialism, Globalization and the Economy of South-East India, c.1700–1900," Working Papers of the Global Economic History Network, no. 24/06 (2006).

"Merchants, Markets, and Commerce in Early Modern South India." *Journal of the Economic and Social History of the Orient* 53, nos. 1–2 (2010): 266–89.

"Forms of Citizenship in Pre-modern South India." *Citizenship Studies* 23, no. 3 (2019): 224–39.

Wiggins, Steve, and Ben Rogaly. "Providing Rural Credit in Southern India: A Comparison of Commercial Banks and Cooperatives." *Public Administration and Development* 9, no. 2 (1989): 215–32.

Yanagisawa, Haruka. "Elements of Upward Mobility for Agricultural Labourers in Tamil Districts, 1865–1925." In *Local Agrarian Societies in Colonial India: Japanese Perspectives*, edited by Kaoru Sugihara, Haruka Yanagisawa, and Peter Robb, 199–238. Surrey: Curzon Press, 1996.

Zegarra, Luis Felipe. "Information Asymmetries and Agricultural Credit: Evidence from the Pre-banking Era in Lima, 1825–1865." *Agricultural Finance Review* 79, no. 2 (2019): 217–33.

Zwart, De Pim, and Lucassen, Jan. "Poverty or Prosperity in Northern India? New Evidence on Real Wages, 1590s–1870s." *The Economic History Review* 73, no. 3 (2020): 644–67.

Books

Acemoglu, Daron, and James A. Robinson. *Why Nations Fail: The Origins of Power, Prosperity, and Poverty*. London: Profile, 2012.

Adams, Dale W., and Delbert A. Fitchett. *Informal Finance in Low-income Countries*. New York: Taylor & Francis Group, 1992.

Adeyeye, Samuel Oladele. *The Co-operative Movement in Nigeria Yesterday, Today and Tomorrow*. Göttingen: Vandenhoeck Und Ruprecht, 1978.

Agarwal, G. D., *Reorganisation of Agricultural Credit*. Kanpur: Industrial Art Printery, 1952.

Ali, Imran. *The Punjab under Imperialism, 1885–1947*. Princeton, NJ: Princeton University Press, 1988.

Ali, S., and K. K. Singh. *Role of Pancbayati Raj Institutions for Rural Development*. New Delhi: Sarup & Sons, 2001.

Amin, Shahid. *Sugarcane and Sugar in Gorakhpur: An Inquiry into Peasant Production for Capitalist Enterprise in Colonial India*. Delhi: Oxford University Press, 1984.

Amrith, Sunil. *Unruly Waters: How Rains, Rivers, Coasts and Seas Have Shaped Asia's History*. New York: Basic Books, 2018.

Arbuthnot, Alexander J., *Major-General Sir Thomas Munro, Governor of Madras: A Memoir*. London: Kegen Paul, Trench, 1889.

Bagchi, Amiya Kumar. *The Political Economy of Underdevelopment*. Cambridge: Cambridge University Press, 1982.

Colonialism and Indian Economy. New Delhi: Oxford University Press, 2010.

Baker, Christopher John. *The Politics of South India 1920–1937*. Cambridge: Cambridge University Press, 1976.

An Indian Rural Economy 1880–1955: The Tamilnad Countryside. Oxford: Oxford University Press, 1984.

Bardhan, Pranab K. *The Economic Theory of Agrarian Institutions*. Oxford: Clarendon, 1989.

Basu, Priya. *Improving Access to Finance for India's Rural Poor*. Washington, DC: World Bank Publications, 2006.

Birla, Ritu. *Stages of Capital: Law, Culture, and Market Governance in Late Colonial India*. Durham, NC: Duke University Press, 2009.

Bose, Sugata. *Peasant Labour and Colonial Capital: Rural Bengal since 1770*. Cambridge: Cambridge University Press, 1993.

Credit, Markets, and the Agrarian Economy of Colonial India. New York: Oxford University Press, 1994.

Calvert, Hubert. *Wealth and Welfare of the Punjab*. Lahore: Civil and Military Gazette Press, 1922.

Catanach, I. J. *Rural Credit in Western India, 1875–1930: Rural Credit and the Co-operative Movement in the Bombay Presidency*. Berkeley: University of California Press, 1970.

Champakalakshmi, R. *Trade, Ideology, and Urbanization: South India 300 BC to AD 1300*. Delhi and New York: Oxford University Press, 1996.

Charlesworth, Neil. *Peasants and Imperial Rule: Agriculture and Agrarian Society in the Bombay Presidency, 1850–1935*. Cambridge: Cambridge University Press, 1985.

Chaudhary, Latika, Bishnupriya Gupta, Tirthankar Roy, and Anand V. Swamy. *A New Economic History of Colonial India*. 1st ed. London: Routledge, 2016.

Darling, Malcolm. *Some Aspects of Co-operation in Germany, Italy and Ireland*. Lahore: Government Printing, 1922.

The Punjab Peasant in Prosperity and Debt. 4th ed. Bombay: Oxford University Press, 1947.

Dutt, Romesh Chunder. *Indian Famines: Their Causes and Prevention*. London: P. S. King & Son, 1901.

Floro, Sagrario L., and Pan A. Yotopoulos. *Informal Credit Markets and the New Institutional Economics: The Case of Philippine Agriculture*. Boulder: Westview Press, 1991.

Gokhale, Gopal Krishna. *Speeches of the Honourable Mr. G. K. Gokhale, C. I. E.* Madras: G. A. Natesan, 1908.

Goldsmith, Raymond W. *The Financial Development of India, 1860–1977*. New Haven, CT and London: Yale University Press, 1983.

Gough, Kathleen. *Rural Society in Southeast India*. Cambridge: Cambridge University Press, 1981.

Gupta, Akhil. *Red Tape: Bureaucracy, Structural Violence, and Poverty in India*. Durham, NC: Duke University Press, 2012.

Hall-Matthews, David. *Peasants, Famine and the State in Colonial Western India*. New York: Palgrave Macmillan, 2005.

Hardiman, David. *Feeding the Baniya: Peasants and Usurers in Western India*. Delhi: Oxford University Press, 1996.

Hazell, Peter, C. Ramsamy, and P. K. Aiyasamy, *The Green Revolution Reconsidered: The Impact of High-Yielding Rice Varieties in South India*. Baltimore: Johns Hopkins University Press, 1991, 14.

Henley, David, and P. Boomgaard. *Credit and Debt in Indonesia, 860–1930: From Peonage to Pawnshop, from Kongsi to Cooperative*. A Modern Economic History of Southeast Asia. Leiden: KITLV Press, 2009.

Hoffman, Philip T., Gilles Postel-Vinay, and Jean-Laurent Rosenthal. *Dark Matter Credit: The Development of Peer-to-Peer Lending and Banking in*

France. Princeton, NJ: Princeton Economic History of the Western World, 2019.

Hough, Eleanor Margaret. *The Co-operative Movement in India: Its Relation to a Sound National Economy*. London: P. S. King & Son, 1932.

Iqbal, Iftekhar. *The Bengal Delta: Ecology, State and Social Change, 1840–1943*. London: Springer, 2010.

Irschick, Eugene F. *Politics and Social Conflict in South India: The Non-Brahman Movement and Tamil Separatism, 1916–1929*. Berkeley: University of California Press, 1969.

Jain, L. C. *Indigenous Banking in India*. London: Macmillan, 1929.

Karashima, Noboru. *South Indian History and Society: Studies from Inscriptions A.D. 850–1800*. Delhi: Oxford University Press, 1984.

Kumar, Dharma. *Land and Caste in South India: Agricultural Labour in the Madras Presidency during the Nineteenth Century*. Cambridge: Cambridge University Press, 1965.

Kumar, Prakash. *Indigo Plantations and Science in Colonial India*. Cambridge: Cambridge University Press, 2012.

Levy, Juliette. *The Making of a Market: Credit, Henequen, and Notaries in Yucatán, 1850–1900*. University Park: Pennsylvania State University Press, 2012.

Ludden, David. *Peasant History in South India*. Princeton, NJ: Princeton University Press, 1985.

Mahalingam, T. V. *South Indian Polity*. 2nd ed. Madras: University of Madras, 1967.

Manikumar, K. A. *A Colonial Economy in the Great Depression, Madras (1929–1937)*. Chennai: Orient Longman, 2003.

Martin, Marina. "An Economic History of Hundi, 1858–1978," PhD thesis, London School of Economics and Political Science (2012).

Mencher, Joan P. *Agriculture and Social Structure in Tamil Nadu: Past Origins, Present Transformations and Future Prospects*. Durham, NC: Carolina Academic Press, 1978.

Mishra, Pramod Kumar. *Agricultural Risk, Insurance and Income: A Study of the Impact and Design of India's Comprehensive Crop Insurance Scheme*. Aldershot: Avebury, 1996.

Mootham, Orby. *The East India Company's Sadar Courts 1801–1834*. Bombay: N. M. Tripathi, 1983.

Mukherjee, Mridula. *Colonizing Agriculture: The Myth of Punjab Exceptionalism*. New Delhi: Sage, 2005.

Naidu, Bijayeti Venkata Narayanaswami, and P. Vaidyanathan, *The Madras Agriculturists' Relief Act: A Study*. Annamalainagar: Annamalai University, 1939.

Naoroji, Dadabhai. *Poverty and Un-British Rule in India*. London: S. Sonnenschein, 1901.

Neal, Larry, and Jeremy Atack. *The Origins and Development of Financial Markets and Institutions: From the Seventeenth Century to the Present*. Cambridge and New York: Cambridge University Press, 2009.

North, Douglass C. *Institutions, Institutional Change, and Economic Performance*. Cambridge: Cambridge University Press, 1990.

Okun, Arthur M. *Equality and Efficiency: The Big Tradeoff.* Washington, DC: Brookings Institution, 1975.

Panikar, P. G. K. *Rural Savings in India.* Bombay: Somaiya Publications, 1970.

Parthasarathi, Prasannan. *The Transition to a Colonial Economy in South India: Industry and Commerce in the Eighteenth Century.* New York: Cambridge University Press, 2001.

Qureshi, Anwar Iqbal. *The Future of the Cooperative Movement in India.* Madras: Oxford University Press, 1947.

Ranade, Mahadev Govind. *Essays on Indian Economics: A Collection of Essays and Speeches.* 2nd ed. Madras: G. A. Natesan & Co., 1906.

Rao, Narayana, Shulman Velcheru, David Dean, and Sanjay Subrahmanyam. *Symbols of Substance Court and State in Nāyaka Period Tamilnadu.* Delhi and New York: Oxford University Press, 1992.

Robb, Peter. *Rural India: Land, Power and Society under British Rule.* London: Curzon Press, 1983.

Peasants, Political Economy, and Law. New York: Oxford University Press, 2007.

Robinson, Marguerite S. *Microfinance Revolution: Sustainable Finance for the Poor.* 1st ed. Washington, DC: World Bank Publications, 2001.

Rothermund, Dietmar. *An Economic History of India: From Pre-colonial Times to 1991.* 2nd ed. London: Routledge, 1993.

Roy, Tirthankar. *The Economic History of India, 1857–1947.* Oxford: Oxford University Press, 2000.

How British Rule Changed India's Economy: The Paradox of the Raj. Palgrave Studies in Economic History. ebook, Palgrave Macmillan, 2019.

Roy, Tirthankar, and Anand V. Swamy. *Law and the Economy in Colonial India.* Chicago: The University of Chicago Press, 2017.

Law and the Economy in a Young Democracy. Chicago: The University of Chicago Press, 2022.

Rudner, David West. *Caste and Capitalism in Colonial India: The Nattukottai Chettiars.* Berkeley: University of California Press, 1994.

Saravanan, Velayutham. *Water and the Environmental History of Modern India.* London: Bloomsbury Academic, 2020.

Sharma, Krishna Kumar. *The Indian Money Market.* Bangalore City: Bangalore Print & Pub., 1934.

Sivasubramonian, S. *National Income of India in the Twentieth Century.* Oxford: Oxford University Press, 2000.

Sivaswamy, Kodaganallur Ganapattri. *Legislative Protection and Relief of Agriculturist Debtors in India.* Poona: Gokhale Institute of Politics and Economics, 1939.

Southall, Aidan. "The Segmentary State in Africa and Asia." *Comparative Studies in Society and History* 30, no. 1 (1988): 52–82.

Stein, Burton. *Peasant State and Society in Medieval South India.* Delhi and Oxford: Oxford University Press, 1980.

Vijayanagara. Cambridge and New York: Cambridge University Press, 1989.

Stokes, Eric. *The Peasant and the Raj: Studies in Agrarian Society and Peasant Rebellion in Colonial India.* Cambridge: Cambridge University Press, 1978.

Stone, Ian. *Canal Irrigation in British India: Perspectives on Technological Change in a Peasant Economy*. Cambridge: Cambridge University Press, 1984.

Subbarayalu, Y. *Political Geography of the Chola Country*. Madras: State Department of Archaeology, Government of Tamilnadu, 1973.

Subramanian, Kapil. "Revisiting the Green Revolution: Irrigation and Food Production in Twentieth-century India," PhD thesis, King's College (2015).

Subrahmanyam, Sanjay. *The Political Economy of Commerce: Southern India 1500–1650*. Cambridge: Cambridge University Press, 1989.

Talbot, Ian, and Shinder Thandi. *People on the Move: Punjabi Colonial and Post-colonial Migration*. Karachi: Oxford University Press, 2004.

Thirumalai, S. *Post-war Agricultural Problems and Policies in India*. Bombay: The Indian Society of Agricultural Economics, 1954.

Thomas, P. J. *The Problem of Rural Indebtedness*. Madras: Diocesan Press, 1934.

Thomas, P. J., and K. C. Ramakrishnan. *Some South Indian Villages: A Resurvey*. Madras: University of Madras, 1940.

Thomas, P. J., and Narasimhadevara Sundara Rama Sastry. *Commodity Prices in South India, 1918–1938*. Madras: University of Madras, 1940.

Thorburn, Septimus Smet. *Musalmans and Money-Lenders in the Punjab*. London: W. Blackwood, 1886.

Timberg, Thomas A. *The Marwaris: From Traders to Industrialists*. Delhi: Vikas, 1978.

Tomlinson, B. R. *The Economy of Modern India, 1860–1970*. Cambridge: Cambridge University Press, 1996.

Washbrook, David A. *The Emergence of Provincial Politics: The Madras Presidency, 1870–1920*. Cambridge: Cambridge University Press, 1976.

Whitcombe, Elizabeth. *Agrarian Conditions in Northern India*. Berkeley: University of California Press, 1972.

Zacharias, C. W. B. *Madras Agriculture*. Madras: University of Madras, 1950.

Index

Printed in the United States
by Baker & Taylor Publisher Services